Unsung Heroes
of the Dachau Trials

Unsung Heroes of the Dachau Trials

The Investigative Work of the U.S. Army 7708 War Crimes Group, 1945–1947

SECOND EDITION

JOHN J. DUNPHY

McFarland & Company, Inc., Publishers
Jefferson, North Carolina

LIBRARY OF CONGRESS CATALOGING-IN-PUBLICATION DATA

Names: Dunphy, John J. (John Joseph), author.
Title: Unsung heroes of the Dachau Trials : the investigative work
    of the U.S. Army 7708 War Crimes Group, 1945–1947 / John J. Dunphy.
Description: Second Edition. | Jefferson, North Carolina : McFarland & Company, Inc.,
    Publishers, 2024. | Includes bibliographical references and index.
Identifiers: LCCN 2024032916 | ISBN 9781476695402 (paperback : acid free paper) ∞
    ISBN 9781476653426 (ebook)
Subjects: LCSH: Dachau Trials, Dachau, Germany, 1945-1947. | War crimes
    investigation—Germany—History—20th century. | United States. Army.
    European Command. Deputy Judge Advocate for War Crimes.
Classification: LCC KZ1179.D33 D86 2024 | DDC 341.6/9—dc23
LC record available at https://lccn.loc.gov/2024032916

BRITISH LIBRARY CATALOGUING DATA ARE AVAILABLE

ISBN (print) 978-1-4766-9540-2
ISBN (ebook) 978-1-4766-5342-6

© 2024 John J. Dunphy. All rights reserved

*No part of this book may be reproduced or transmitted in any form
or by any means, electronic or mechanical, including photocopying
or recording, or by any information storage and retrieval system,
without permission in writing from the publisher.*

Front cover: A defendant testifies during the Dachau Military Tribunal
on December 7, 1946 (Department of Defense)

Printed in the United States of America

McFarland & Company, Inc., Publishers
 Box 611, Jefferson, North Carolina 28640
   www.mcfarlandpub.com

For the men and women who served
in the U.S. Army 7708 War Crimes Group

Table of Contents

Preface	1
Introduction	5
1. Of Lies and Truth	9
2. The Necessity of the War Crimes Trials	17
3. Report of the Deputy Judge Advocate for War Crimes	28
4. Bill Kasich: A Nineteen-Year-Old in Post-War Germany	53
5. Ralph Schulz: Seminarian Turned Record Keeper	65
6. The Malmédy Massacre	73
7. Otto Skorzeny: "The Most Dangerous Man in Europe"	90
8. Downed American Airmen: Descent into Hell	112
9. Project Paperclip: The Harvest of Nazi Technology	116
10. Barbie and Bormann: War Criminals	140
11. The Buchenwald Case	145
12. The Nazi Underground in Post-War Germany	156
13. Walter Kirkland: Family Man	171
14. Otto Ludwig Stein: Refugee and Interpreter	174
15. John Henry Pohlman: War Crimes Attorney from the Gateway City	180
16. The Struggle Continues	195
Epilogue	197
Bibliography	203
Index	209

Preface

THIS BOOK DEALS WITH the 7708 War Crimes Group of the U.S. Army, which rendered justice in the aftermath of World War II. These young Americans—many of them barely out of their teens—investigated war crimes perpetrated in Germany and Nazi-occupied Europe. They were responsible for gathering evidence, interviewing witnesses, apprehending suspects and securing convictions in trials conducted by the U.S. Army and held at Dachau. Some members of the group collected and maintained files, an assignment that some might regard as tedious. As one of the veterans I interviewed explained, however, these files were vitally important since they documented the group's work as well as the horrors that had transpired during the war years. Other members of the 7708 War Crimes Group worked in the field: locating and interviewing witnesses; tracking down suspects and taking them into custody.

Regardless of one's job, membership in the group could be hazardous. Despite the defeat of Germany's military forces and the nation's formal surrender, my interviews with veterans indicated that post-war Germany was a dangerous place. A Nazi underground existed and its agents preyed on Americans—especially those who investigated war crimes and helped to secure justice for the victims of those crimes.

Remarkably little about the 7708 War Crimes Group has been published that is readily available to the reading public. I wrote this book to help remedy that situation. I also wanted to preserve the testimony of those War Crimes Group members who agreed to be interviewed. Their accounts couldn't be found in any book—until now. The men I contacted were cooperative and eager to share their narratives with me. Only one veteran later changed his mind about letting me publish his recollections in this book. None of the men asked that I use a pseudonym to conceal his identity.

The desire to provide the global community with yet another refutation of Holocaust denial also figured in my decision to write this book. I felt particularly compelled to write the present work upon discovering that the Institute for Historical Review had published a book in 1993 about the Dachau trials. Ironically, the book is titled *Innocent at Dachau*. Those familiar with the Institute for Historical Review, which has been criticized by the Anti-Defamation League and the Southern Poverty Law Center for promoting Holocaust denial, needn't be told this book's ideological slant. The chapter "Of Lies and Truth" addresses some of the inaccuracies in *Innocent at Dachau*. My book contains no verbatim passages from that tome, however. I had no desire to contact the Institute for Historical review to ask permission to quote from *Innocent at Dachau*.

Readers who wanted to learn the truth about the Dachau trials surely welcomed the publication in 2004 of Joshua M. Greene's *Justice at Dachau: The Trials of an American Prosecutor*. The work provides an overview of the Dachau trials through the work of William Denson, who achieved a 100 percent conviction rate. Greene's book proved useful as I researched the War Crimes Group. Readers will note that I make extensive use of government and military documents in my research. Some were hard copies that Bill Kasich, a proud veteran of the group, passed along to me. Others were located online.

The web sites of the United States Holocaust Memorial Museum and the Jewish Virtual Library contain a plethora of documents related to the war crimes trials. The sources for the material utilized in this work are typically cited in the text itself. The bibliography lists all sources that I employed in writing this book.

I want to express my appreciation to Rachael Heriford of the State Historical Society of Missouri and Jason D. Stratman of the Missouri Historical Society Library for their generous research assistance regarding the career of John Henry Pohlman. I also want to thank Paul Dowd and Deborah Stein for providing me with information regarding Walter C. Kirkland and Otto Ludwig Stein, respectively. The four of you were instrumental in making the second edition a reality.

The author's late father was drafted into the U.S. Army during World War II. He rarely talked about his experiences at any length. His wife—my mother—as well as other family members assured me that his time in wartime Europe had left him a changed man. I recall my father watching the TV news one night when a particular story caught his attention: an aged Nazi war criminal had been located living incognito in the United States.

"Hang him. Hang the bastard. I saw what they did," he said to no one in particular. Dad's statement that he saw what the Nazis had done implied that he had seen at least one concentration camp. I knew better than to ask him precisely what he had seen at that camp, however. Researching and writing this work has allowed me to see "what they did" through my father's eyes. No wonder Dad didn't want to talk about it.

Introduction

THIS BOOK BEGAN WITH an article that appeared in my hometown newspaper, *The Telegraph* of Alton, Illinois. Its September 18, 2000, edition carried a feature story with the headline "War Crimes Vets Holding Reunion" and the subtitle "World War II group to meet in Alton." I wasn't surprised. I was astonished. Alton, a small city of less than 30,000 located on the Mississippi River in Madison County, seemed an unlikely place for a reunion of army veterans who had apprehended and prosecuted Nazi war criminals. Reading the article introduced me to Bill Kasich, a veteran of this group and identified as a native of Benld, a small coal-mining town in Macoupin County, which is just north of Madison County. Kasich had played a major role in organizing the reunion, and Alton's proximity to St. Louis, Missouri, offered the veterans opportunities for recreation. Kasich was quoted as telling the reporter, "We'll share memories of our service together 50 years ago and have some fun at a St. Louis Cardinals baseball game."

Kasich's quotations in the article introduced me to the work of the 7708 War Crimes Group of the U.S. Army. He was a 19-year-old corporal when his commanding officer told him, "Kasich, you're going on a special assignment to work for the prosecutor of Nazi war criminals in Germany." Kasich told the reporter that he and other American officers and enlisted men were chosen for the group because of their intelligence and special abilities. "I spoke Russian and a number of Slavic languages," Kasich said.

Bill Kasich was much more than a witness to history. He and the other members of the 7708 War Crimes Group made history. His first case involved gathering documents to facilitate the prosecution of those Nazi officers and enlisted men who were responsible for the Malmédy massacre, which involved the murder of American POWs during the Battle of the Bulge in 1944. The passing of decades hadn't lessened Kasich's anger at the atrocity. "The 18-and-19-year-old American POWs, who were unarmed and defenseless, were herded into a field like cattle and shot to death," he told the reporter.

"It was a horrible crime." Kasich was also involved in the prosecution of Hermann Göring, commander-in-chief of the Luftwaffe, who was appointed by Hitler to the position of Reichsmarschall. Göring was the second-highest ranking Nazi to be prosecuted at the Nuremberg trials. Kasich recalled sitting in that Nuremberg courtroom and, when Göring happened to look his way, "I looked into his eyes and whispered the curse words SOB to him."

The September 22 edition of *The Telegraph* carried a follow-up piece on the reunion of the War Crimes Group veterans that contained even more intriguing material. Ralph Schulz, another veteran of the group who grew up in Alton, was quoted as saying, "I'll never forget the horror at the atrocities of Dachau." Schulz noted that he "took photographs of a mass grave with the bodies of 135,000 murdered people."

Myron Smith, another veteran, told the reporter, "Our War Crimes Group was so unique in the U.S. Army that many people didn't even know we existed." Smith was later quoted as saying, "We've been forgotten by historians." Those two statements convinced me that I needed to write a book about the 7708 War Crimes Group. These veterans deserved recognition and appreciation for their work—and not just from their fellow Americans. Every member of the global community should be aware of the role they played in bringing Nazi war criminals to justice.

War Crimes Group veteran Bruce Abraham gave another reason that a book about their work was needed. The reporter wrote that Abraham "gets upset when he sees someone appear on national television to claim that the murder of Jews at Auschwitz and Dachau never happened." "I saw the evidence of the Holocaust," Abraham told the reporter. "We have photographs of innocent victims in the concentration camps." Schulz noted that the group had compiled ample evidence of Nazi war crimes. "Hundreds of stacks of files on the murder of American POWs and innocent Jews at Auschwitz and other death camps were kept in a vault at our headquarters," he stated. "We had about 3,000 personal affidavits from people who were witnesses to the terrible atrocities."

The final *Telegraph* article dealing with the veterans' reunion helped to convinced me that these men would work with me to produce a book about their years with the 7708 War Crimes Group. The veterans had allowed a local high school teacher to bring his students to the Holiday Inn, where the reunion was held, so that they could share their experiences with them. "We saw the bodies of innocent people who died in human ovens," Myron Smith was quoted as telling the students. "We saw their blood on the walls of the concentration camps."

Introduction 7

Schulz said that he was pleased that young people, such as these students, were learning about the Holocaust. "We hope they will remember and maybe they can help prevent it from ever happening again." The article's closing statement—another quote from Schulz—burned itself into my memory. "It's been 56 years but I still remember the smell of the remains of innocent people who were killed at Dachau," he said. "I can still see the scratches of fingernails on the walls of the gas chambers where people tried to claw up the walls to escape the gas."

Ralph Schulz and the other veterans of the War Crimes Group had performed an invaluable service by agreeing to address my region's high school students. Those memories they had shared needed to be recorded and published. And time was of the essence. Schulz himself said as much in another *Telegraph* quotation when he observed, "The veterans of our group are getting old and we won't be around for many years to tell the story of the Holocaust." A book of their accounts will allow them to tell of their work in the 7708 War Crimes Group long after the last of these veterans has passed away.

It was time to act. I called Ande Yakstis, the *Telegraph* reporter who had covered the reunion, for contact information regarding Bill Kasich, who had been quoted extensively in all the articles. Kasich and I talked on the phone and then he showed up at my book shop on October 13, 2000, although I hadn't yet scheduled an appointment for an interview. Fortunately, I had my cassette recorder at the shop, so I could record his words. The project was officially launched.

1

Of Lies and Truth

ANXIOUS TO LEARN MORE about the U.S. Army 7708 War Crimes Group and the Dachau trials, I conducted a Web search. The first item that came up was a book titled *Innocent at Dachau* by Joseph Halow, who had worked as a court reporter at some of the Dachau trials. The book had been published in 1993 by the Institute for Historical Review, which also placed lengthy selections from the book on its web site.

The Southern Poverty Law Center defines the Institute for Historical Review as "a pseudo-academic organization that claims to seek 'truth and accuracy in history,' but whose real purpose is to promote Holocaust denial and defend Nazism." The Anti-Defamation League states:

> The core of the IHR's mission [is] propagating the contention that the Holocaust, in which approximately six million European Jews were murdered, mainly by poison gas, by the Nazi regime during World War II, did not occur. IHR strenuously objects to the term "Holocaust denial," and its staff and contributors cast themselves as legitimate historians engaged in revising and reevaluating historical events. But the consistent thrust of its "research," its espousal of lies, half-truths and methodically flawed arguments demonstrate that, far from revisiting the historical evidence, it aims to deny that what has become known as the Holocaust ever occurred.

Founded in 1978, the Institute made headlines a year later when Lewis Brandon, its director, announced that the IHR would pay $50,000 to anyone who could prove that the Nazis had operated gas chambers for the purpose of killing Jews during World War II. According to Deborah Lipstadt's *Denying the Holocaust: The Growing Assault on Truth and Memory*, Brandon later admitted that this challenge had never been meant in earnest. It had been a stunt to generate some free publicity for the IHR. The offer also earned publicity for Brandon, whose real name was William David McCalden. He had been born in Northern Ireland and also employed at least four other pseudonyms including, oddly enough, Julius Finkelstein.

Mel Mermelstein, a Holocaust survivor, wrote a letter to the *Jerusalem Post* that was published in its August 17, 1980, international edition about the IHR challenge. Regarding Holocaust denial, which is often referred to "Holocaust revisionism" by its adherents, Mermelstein denounced those who "are teaching our new generation that the chimneys of Auschwitz were only those of bakeries. That there were no gas chambers at Auschwitz-Birkenau. That Dachau was a peaceful town within Nazi Germany and that the 'six million' European Jews fled Nazism and have been living peacefully in Israel ever since."

He had personally witnessed the horrors of the Holocaust. "As one who survived the infernos of Auschwitz-Birkenau and Buchenwald, my eyes are still blurring from the vision of that nightmare and my ears are still ringing with the agonizing sounds of men, women and little children who were lured and driven into the gas chambers disguised as shower rooms, solely and exclusively because they were Jewish."

Mermelstein was contacted by the IHR and challenged to "prove" that inmates had been gassed at Auschwitz. According to Lipstadt, various Jewish groups that Mermelstein consulted, including the Anti-Defamation League and the Simon Wiesenthal Center, advised him to ignore the IHR challenge because it would merely give the organization the publicity it craved. Nonetheless, Mermelstein decided to accept the challenge.

He submitted a notarized statement of his interment in Auschwitz— including his eyewitness account of Nazi guards taking inmates that included his mother and two sisters into a gas chamber. The IHR, however, refused to pay him the $50,000. Mermelstein sued the IHR in the Superior Court of Los Angeles County for breach of contract, anticipatory repudiation, libel, injurious denial of established fact, intentional infliction of emotional distress and declaratory relief. Judge Thomas T. Johnson, in a pre-trial determination, stated: "This court does take judicial notice of the fact that Jews were gassed to death at Auschwitz Concentration Camp in Poland during the summer of 1944. It is not reasonably subject to dispute. And it is capable of immediate and accurate determination by resort to sources of reasonably indisputable accuracy. It is simply a fact."

The court ordered the IHR to pay Mermelstein the sum of $90,000 and issue an apology to him and all other survivors of Auschwitz. And this is the organization that published *Innocent at Dachau*. Although the IHR still exists today, years of internal disputes have left it a shadow of its former self. McCalden left the IHR after a falling out with its other founding members but continued to engage in Holocaust denial until his death in 1990. The October 25, 1990, edition of the *Los Angeles Times* headlined his obituary "David McCalden; Failed to Disprove Holocaust."

Even a cursory reading of *Innocent at Dachau* reveals glaring historical inaccuracies designed to mislead readers. For example, the chapter titled "Ilse Koch" opens with an account of Karl Koch, the commandant of Buchenwald concentration camp. Halow wrote that Koch promised freedom to Buchenwald's Jewish inmates in exchange for their money and valuables, but then had them killed. When the German authorities learned of Koch's misdeeds, Halow stated, he was tried at Buchenwald by the SS. While Ilse was found innocent, Halow wrote, Karl was found guilty of at least three murders, sentenced to death and executed on April 5, 1945.

The truth is that Karl Koch was the most dangerous of human beings—a sadist with power—whose penchant for cruelty long predated his appointment as Buchenwald commandant. While stationed at a prison in Berlin, Koch had inmates locked in doghouses and chained by the neck. They were compelled to lap up their food and water from bowls as though they indeed were canines. Inmates who failed to bark when Koch walked by their cages received twenty-five blows from a cane. Koch ordered an inmate who had incurred his wrath to have his anus sealed with hot asphalt and then forced to drink castor oil.

Koch's sadism reached new depths when he became commandant of Buchenwald. When four thousand Polish prisoners arrived by train at Weimer and were being marched to the camp, Koch had his car driven through their lines. Those convicts who attempted to dodge the speeding vehicle were shot and the reason for their deaths given as "killed while trying to escape." When Koch contracted syphilis, he procured treatment from Dr. Walter Kramer, who worked as an orderly in the Buchenwald infirmary. To ensure that his indiscretion would remain a secret, Koch had Kramer and his medical assistant executed on trumped-up charges.

Karl and Ilse Koch enjoyed the good life. Karl funded frequent festivals for his staff that featured ample food and drink by forcing the entire camp to go without food. While even the SS was subject to tobacco and wine rationing, Ilse literally bathed in Madeira. Karl indulged his wife by forcing inmates to build her a villa as well as a riding hall. This hall, three hundred feet long and sixty feet wide, was lined with mirrors so that Ilse could observe and improve her equestrian skills. Its financial cost was 250,000 marks, while its human cost was the thirty inmates who died during its construction.

Josias, Prince zu Waldeck, whose name sometimes appears in print as Prince Josias von Waldeck-Pyrmont, served as Koch's superior. Josias secured a dubious place in history when, in 1929, he became the first member of a royal family to join the SS. Kramer had once treated Josias and he was surprised to find his name on the camp's list of deceased inmates. He discovered that Koch had ordered Kramer's execution on the patently false charge of discussing politics in the infirmary. He also uncovered evidence that the commandant had been subverting vast sums of money to finance his lavish lifestyle. Josias turned the matter over to Konrad Morgen, a judge who was also an SS officer, who conducted a formal investigation. Koch was relieved of his duties as Buchenwald commandant in 1941 and installed as commandant of the Majdanek concentration camp, only to be sacked when a number of Soviet POWs managed to escape. He was then given an administrative post in Berlin. Ilse remained at Buchenwald.

Morgen's investigation revealed the astonishing level of the Kochs' avarice. While giving testimony at the Buchenwald war crimes trial after Germany's defeat, Morgen stated that Koch had stolen millions of marks from the camp. Koch indeed had Jews murdered at Buchenwald for their money and valuables—but he was not executed by the SS for killing Jews, as Halow implied. If the SS had regarded the killing of Jews as a capital offense, it would have executed itself out of existence long before the war ended. In his book *Justice at Dachau*, Joshua Greene pointed out that Koch had committed a serious breach of SS protocol. Himmler had issued a clear directive that money taken from Jews was to go to the Reich, not into any officer's pocket.

Halow's suggestion that the SS meted out what passed for justice in Nazi Germany to Koch was voiced at the Nuremberg trials by Karl Kauffmann, legal counsel for Ernst Kaltenbrunner, second only to Himmler in the SS and chief of the Reich Central Security Office. Kauffmann had been enraged by the prosecution's presentation of evidence concerning the barbaric treatment of inmates at Buchenwald. He castigated the prosecution for failing to mention that an SS court had convicted Koch for his crimes at Buchenwald and condemned him to death. According to Joseph E. Persico, in *Nuremberg: Infamy on Trial*, the prosecution responded by introducing evidence that proved the SS had convicted Koch for embezzling funds meant for the Reich. As Persico succinctly noted, torturing and murdering the inmates of a concentration camp were not crimes in the canon of the SS.

Halow insinuated that accounts of the Holocaust have been exaggerated on pages 32–33 when he remarks on the large number of DPs (displaced persons) he saw in Germany after the war, many of whom appeared to be Polish or Jewish. He wrote that such a large number of Jews puzzled him, since Americans had been hearing reports that indicated that Germans had been systematically killing Jews.

An actual denial of the Holocaust doesn't appear in Halow's book until page 304. Most readers are likely to question the reliability and objectivity of Halow's source: Heinz Detmers, a former SS lieutenant, who was convicted of war crimes at *two* trials held at Dachau.

Detmers served as adjunct to Alex Piorkowski, the camp commander at Dachau. According to the official JAG review of the case, which is posted on the Jewish Virtual Library web site, Piorkowski and Detmers

> did ... willfully, deliberately and wrongfully encourage, aid, abet and participate in the subjection of members of the armed forces of nations then at war with the then German Reich, who were then and there surrendered and unarmed prisoners of war in the custody of the then German Reich, to cruelties and mistreatment, including killings, beatings, tortures, starvation, abuses and indignities, the exact names and number of such prisoners of war being unknown, but aggregating many hundreds.

The review further states that Detmers "was feared among the prisoners as much as the camp commander" and "was present at the rifle range during executions by shootings of Russian prisoners of war." Detmers was also "present during executions of prisoners in the bunkers which was called 'Headquarters arrest building.'"

A witness for the defense attempted to exonerate Detmers of wrongdoing by offering the opinion that he was "a very young man [who] had become the tool of a criminal system and its leaders." The JAG review states that while no "personal cruelties" were proved against Detmers, his position as adjunct to Piorkowski, who served as camp commander, gave him "knowledge of the administration and executions of Camp Dachau." Detmers "is guilty of participating in the common design," the JAG review concluded. Detmers' petition for clemency, submitted by his defense counsels on January 22, 1947, was denied.

Following his service at Dachau, Detmers had been transferred to the Dora concentration camp, part of the Nordhausen concentration camp complex, and also stood trial for his actions at that site. According to United States Army *Investigations and Trial Records of War Criminals: United States of America v. Kurt Andrae et al. (And Related Cases) April 27, 1945–June 11, 1958,* Heinz Georg Alfred Detmers was an SS lieutenant who served as adjunct and judge advocate at Dora from December 1943 to November

1944. The Deputy Judge Advocate examined Detmers' conviction in the *Andrae* case and published its conclusion in *Review and Recommendations of the Deputy Judge Advocate for War Crimes*, a report dated April 15, 1948. The reports include a summation of the prosecutor's case as well as Detmers' defense. Detmers maintained that he was merely a liaison officer for Berlin and had been assigned to investigate offenses of SS personnel. He insisted that his only duties at Dora had been consolidating punishment reports against the SS, interrogating SS men and forwarding copies of reports to higher authorities. Detmers insisted that he never interrogated inmates.

Detmers' claims were challenged by witnesses for the prosecution. An inmate testified that "the accused was known and feared as a beater." Another witness stated that "the interrogation of inmates by the accused were accompanied with beatings." The same witness testified Detmers had continued beatings "even after being requested by the camp physician to refrain." Detmers was also "present at all hangings, including the hangings in the main camp lumberyard." Detmers was sentenced to seven years' imprisonment for his crimes at Dora, and the review board allowed his sentence to stand. He had already drawn a fifteen-year imprisonment for his crimes at Dachau but the review board reduced that sentence to just five years, which Detmers served concurrently with his Dora sentence. His term in Landsberg Prison began on January 17, 1947.

Halow met Detmers, who was reasonably fluent in English, while serving as a court reporter during the Nordhausen trial. He gave a cigarette to Detmers and each of the Nordhausen defendants. He upped his generosity that Christmas by giving each Nordhausen defendant a pack of cigarettes in order to—paraphrasing his explanation in *Innocent at Dachau*—make their holidays somewhat less unpleasant.

Halow located Detmers in the 1980s and surprised him with a phone call. They became pen pals. Halow traveled to Germany in 1988 on a business trip and took the opportunity to look up Detmers, who lived in a village near Norden in what was then West Germany. Their conversation is fascinating to read.

Detmers—or "Heinz," as Halow referred to him—had built a good life for himself. He was the leader of the local Christian Democratic Union, a center-right political party founded in 1945. Halow also informed us that Detmers was one of only two accomplished bassists in a local choir and had taken up flower gardening. Indeed, Detmers was highly regarded in the village and so beloved by the local children that they called him "Uncle Heinz."

1. *Of Lies and Truth*

When their conversation turned to the Dachau trials, Detmers informed Halow that he harbored no ill will towards the Americans who had tried and imprisoned him for war crimes. He stated his belief, which was shared by Halow, that Piorkowski had been innocent of any wrongdoing. Halow, a veteran of the War Crimes Group and court reporter at the Dachau trials, asked Detmers, a former SS lieutenant and twice-convicted war criminal, whether the government of Nazi Germany had instituted a program to kill Jews. Detmers' answer, recorded on page 304, demonstrates why the Institute for Historical Review chose to publish this work. He replied that it might have been true, but he—a member of the SS who served at both Dachau and Dora—had never heard of such a policy. Detmers then destroys whatever credibility he might have had for historically literate readers by stating that such a policy, if indeed it had existed, would have applied only to the terminally ill. Therefore, it would have applied to all inmates, not just Jews. Halow didn't challenge Detmers' assertion.

The book's title blatantly suggests that the Dachau defendants were innocent of the crimes for which they were convicted. Halow's use of the term "innocent" is actually more inclusive, as he demonstrates on pages 309–310. He listed the admirable qualities that he sees in Detmers such as choir singer, family man and pet owner and then remarks that such traits are not to be found in a cruel person. Halow therefore concluded that he, the young court reporter, couldn't possibly have been the only "innocent" at Dachau all those years ago. He ended his book by insisting that the world has grown weary of hearing about the wartime atrocities, whether real or not real, attributed to Nazi Germany, and needs to hear about the atrocities that were inflicted on the German people. Halow vowed to try to contact others who, like his friend Detmers, were convicted at the Dachau trials.

Innocent at Dachau is currently (September 2023) in 87 libraries according to Worldcat, a web site that lists holdings at libraries the world over. While Halow's book is in few public libraries, it can be found in a surprisingly large number of college and university libraries that are hardly obscure degree mills. Harvard, Cornell, Duke, Princeton, Yale, Penn, Rutgers, UCLA, California-Davis, Stanford and the Air University at Maxwell Air Force Base in Alabama have copies. The U.S. Holocaust Museum Library in Washington, D.C., Holocaust Center of Northern California and Jewish Theological Seminary of America in New York City, all of which surely have no illusions about this book and its publisher, possess copies. A German-language edition of the book exists. Worldcat notes four German libraries, three of which are university libraries. *Innocent at Dachau* is also among the holdings of the Nelson Mandela Metropolitan University libraries in Port Elizabeth, South Africa. Kasich was familiar with the book and thoroughly despised it.

Students and others interested in learning the truth about the Dachau trials should read Joshua M. Greene's *Justice at Dachau; The Trials of an American Prosecutor*, published in 2004 and alluded to earlier. It provides an excellent introduction to the Dachau trials through the work of William Denson, a Harvard Law School graduate who taught law at West Point and was recommended by a fellow West Pointer to serve as a judge advocate general at Dachau. He prosecuted more Nazi war criminals than any other lawyer in the post-war era and achieved a one hundred percent conviction rate. Of the 177 guards and officers he prosecuted, ninety-seven were sentenced to death, fifty-four to life imprisonment and the rest to sentences of hard labor. Denson's widow allowed Greene access to her husband's personal archive of material relating to the Dachau war crimes trials: trial transcripts; letters from SS officers and their victims; miles of microfilm and much more. Greene utilized this plethora of information when writing *Justice at Dachau*. The book is especially valuable for its chapters dealing with the trials of defendants associated with the Dachau, Mauthausen and Buchenwald concentration camps. *Justice at Dachau* is a powerful scholarly antidote for anyone who finds it necessary to read *Innocent at Dachau*.

2

The Necessity of the War Crimes Trials

As Durwood "Derby" Reidel pointed out in his article "The U.S. War Crimes Tribunals at the Former Dachau Concentration Camp: Lessons for Today?," our government regarded the punishment of Nazi war criminals as absolutely vital for moral reasons. Washington also desired their punishment for the entirely pragmatic concern that Nazi leaders who escaped justice could instigate a revival of national socialism. Summary executions, Reidel noted, would have been a flagrant violation of the principles of justice that the Allied nations had claimed to embody throughout the war—and could possibly have transformed the war criminals into martyrs in the eyes of those Germans who still believed in the principles of the Third Reich.

In the spring of 1945, the U.S. Office of War Information, responding to an order from the Supreme Commander of the Allied Military Forces, published a brochure titled *Concentration Camp* (German title: *KZ: Bildbericht aus funf Konzentrationslager*), which contained 38 photographs taken in Buchenwald, Bergen-Belsen, Gardelegen, Nordhausen and Ohrdruf. Sybil Milton, in her review of the book *The Warsaw Ghetto in Photographs*, stated that the horrifying images from these liberated camps were meant to comprise an "instantaneous emotional indictment" of the Third Reich and "it was believed that the shock value of the photographs would prove salutatory for the denazification and re-education of the civilian populace."

While the publication of these horrifying photographs undoubtedly constituted an "emotional indictment" and played some role in the denazification of Germans who had idolized their Führer, the American government firmly believed that actual trials of those who had perpetrated the scenes depicted in those photos would prove much more persuasive. A prosecutor who presented tangible evidence that established what crimes had been committed as well as the identity of those who had perpetrated those crimes would provide a text as well as a context to the photographs contained in Concentration Camp. The convictions of those found guilty for these crimes, the American government reasoned, would forever convince Germans of the inherent evil of national socialism.

Brigadier General Telford Taylor (1908–1998) served as chief counsel at twelve of the Nuremberg Trials. In his book *Nuremberg and Vietnam: An American Tragedy*, he traced the genesis of the Nuremberg and Dachau trials to October 25, 1941, when FDR and Winston Churchill, in separate declarations, denounced Germany for its execution of hostages in occupied nations. Representatives from nine German-occupied nations—Belgium, France, Greece, Luxemburg, Poland, Norway, the Netherlands, Czechoslovakia and Yugoslavia—met in London the following year, to establish an Inter-Allied Conference on the Punishment of War Crimes. The United States, China, Soviet Union, British dominions and India were also present as observers. On January 13, 1942, this conference released the Declaration of St. James, which repudiated the idea that the perpetrators of wartime atrocities should be punished by acts of vengeance committed by civilians. The signatory nations demanded that the war aims of the Allied nations must include the punishment of those who had committed atrocities through organized channels of justice, Taylor noted.

He neglected to mention, however, that Franklin Roosevelt issued, on October 7, 1942, a landmark statement outlining the plan to try Nazi war criminals when the conflict was concluded. FDR's statement reads:

> On August twenty-first I said that this government was constantly receiving information concerning the barbaric crimes being committed by the enemy against civilian populations in occupied countries, particularly on the continent of Europe. I said it was the purpose of this Government, as I knew it to be the purpose of the other United Nations, to see that when victory is won the perpetrators of these crimes shall answer for them before courts of law.
>
> The commission of these crimes continues.
>
> I now declare it to be the intention of this Government that the successful close of the war shall include provision for the surrender to the United Nations of war criminals.
>
> With a view to establishing responsibility of the guilty individuals through the collection and assessment of all available evidence, this Government is prepared to cooperate with the British and other Governments in establishing a United Nations Commission for the Investigation of War Crimes.
>
> The number of persons eventually found guilty will undoubtedly be extremely small compared to the total enemy populations. It is not the intention of this

Government or of the Governments associated with us to resort to mass reprisals. It is our intention that just and sure punishment shall be meted out to the ringleaders responsible for the organized murder of thousands of innocent persons and the commission of atrocities which have violated every tenet of the Christian faith.

When he issued this declaration, Roosevelt had no way of knowing that Nazi victims numbered in the millions, not "thousands." He can justly be faulted, however, for implying that the "commission of atrocities" violated only the tenets of the Christian faith.

Taylor also excluded mention of the Moscow Declaration of October 30, 1943, which was an important precursor of the Nuremberg and Dachau trials. The three most powerful Allied nations—the United States, Britain and the USSR—issued a joint statement declaring that German war criminals should be punished and judged in the countries where their crimes had been committed. The declaration further stated "the major criminals, whose offenses had no particular geographic localization" would be punished "by the joint decision of the Governments of the Allies." This principle was embodied in Article 1 of the Agreement for the Prosecution and Punishment of the Major War Criminals of the European Axis, and Charter of the International Military Tribunal, which was adopted in London on August 8, 1945, and stated: "There shall be established after consultation with the Control Council for Germany an International Military Tribunal for the trial of war criminals whose offences have no particular geographic location whether they be accused individually or in their capacity as members of organizations or groups or in both capacities." Article 4 also emphasized the importance of the earlier Moscow Declaration by stating: "Nothing in this agreement shall prejudice the provisions established by the Moscow Declaration concerning the return of war criminals to the countries where they committed their crimes."

Taylor pointed out that while the best-known war criminals were tried at Nuremberg and Tokyo, those numbers were dwarfed by the war crimes defendants tried at Dachau. The Dachau trials are still the subject of no small amount of controversy. As Riedel noted, these trials have been criticized for allegedly denying the defendants due process and emphasizing haste rather than fairness. Trials conducted without juries and the alleged use of improper interrogation techniques by war crimes investigators, particularly in the Buchenwald and Malmédy cases, ensured an inherently flawed judicial system. Critics cite that fact that 426 of the 1,672 Dachau defendants were originally sentenced to death as proof that the trials were biased. Sentences in earlier cases were harsher than those in later cases. For instance, thirty-six of the forty defendants in the Dachau case, tried in late 1945, drew the death sentence, while only one defendant in the Nordhausen case, tried in late 1947, was sentenced to hang. Such a discrepancy, critics of the trials claim, indicates that justice at the Dachau trials was arbitrary and capricious.

Reidel noted that the U.S. Army specifically created clemency and review boards to address such issues.

The U.S. Army indeed wanted the accused war criminals to be brought to trial as soon as possible. A memo dated September 25, 1945, from the Deputy Theater Judge Advocate and sent to Col. Clio Straight reads in part:

> a. The Dachau case will be given first priority over all other activities with a view to trial of the accused in possession within one month's time.
>
> b. In furtherance of this program it is desired that the report of investigation in that case be brought to this office at the earliest possible date.... If you, Colonel Straight, are able to bring it up on your return tomorrow and thus hasten its arrival here, I should appreciate it.
>
> c. A team of the most competent personnel in sufficient numbers to develop the case in the shortest possible time will be placed on the Dachau case.
>
> d. Because Colonel Chavez investigated the case, arrangements will be made to bring him into the office with another investigator who was also involved if the second investigator would be of benefit to us. If necessary, temporary replacement from this office of Colonel Chavez and the other member of the team is authorized. I suggest that this matter be discussed with the Third Army War Crimes branch tomorrow.
>
> e. Returning to the Dachau case, at the earliest possible moment a list of principal accused and witnesses not known to be in custody will be prepared for submission to G-2. When it is prepared it will be delivered to General Betts who will hand process it to General Sibert. I told General Betts that we should have such a list ready within four or five days after receipt of the report of investigation.
>
> f. Prepare and dispatch to the War Crimes Office, Washington, D.C., a brief but informative cable as to the Hademar trial. Something along the lines of the report to the Group Control Council is suggested.

"Any other steps which would hasten the bringing to trial of the Dachau case which are deemed appropriate by either of you should be undertaken" the memo concluded.

The desire of the Deputy Theater Judge Advocate to have the Dachau defendants tried as soon should hardly be a cause for criticism. The right to a speedy trial is guaranteed to Americans by the Sixth Amendment to the U.S. Constitution. The decision by a victorious army to extend that right to the accused war criminals of a defeated enemy nation in which justice hadn't existed since the Nazis came to power was commendable—even magnanimous. A speedy trial in no way precluded a fair trial for the Dachau defendants—or, for that matter, any of the accused who were tried by the U.S. Army at the site of the Dachau concentration camp. Indeed, they embodied a degree of impartial justice not seen in Germany for two decades.

In *Justice at Dachau*, Joshua M. Greene stated that the Judge Advocate General had two reasons for choosing Dachau as the site for war crimes trials. Since it was the first concentration camp established by the Nazi government, trying the accused at Dachau would symbolize returning them to the scene of their crimes. The second reason was entirely utilitarian. Dachau contained large buildings that possessed functioning plumbing and heating. Following a bit of renovation, a U-shaped courthouse was created that featured a two-hundred-meter long main building as well as east and west wings that were each seventy meters long. Those accused of major war crimes were tried in Courtroom A, while smaller cases were held in Courtroom B.

Located on the grounds of an abandoned munitions factory, Dachau was established in 1933 by Heinrich Himmler in his capacity as police president of Munich. It was Nazi Germany's first concentration camp and served as a model for all later concentration camps throughout the Third Reich and occupied territory. Its facilities included a training school for SS guards About 4,800 inmates were incarcerated in Dachau during the first year of its existence, most of whom were political enemies of the Nazis such as members of the German Communist and Social Democratic parties. Later, the prisoners included Jehovah's Witnesses, Roma, homosexuals and others deemed enemies of the Reich.

Jehovah's Witnesses, a religious denomination founded in the United States, regard themselves as citizens of Jehovah's heavenly kingdom and refuse to swear allegiance to any earthly nation, including Nazi Germany. They had refused to fight in the German army during World War I, which stood in stark contrast to the Nazi glorification of militarism. The American origin of this denomination also made its adherents seem like unassailable aliens to Nazi ideologues.

So many members of the clergy were imprisoned in Dachau that a special building—the "priest block"—was designated for them. Over 2,500 were Roman Catholic priests and bishops, 1,780 of them Polish. Records indicate that over 1,000 clergymen did not survive Dachau. Incarcerated Protestants fared no better. Martin Niemöller was a Lutheran minister who co-founded the Confessional Church, a coalition of German Protestants who opposed the Nazi party's attempt to dominate and control the Protestant Church in Germany. The Confessional Church also protested the refusal of the Nazi government to recognize Jews who had converted to Christianity. Some radical members of the Confessional Church, such as Dietrich Bonhoeffer, denounced the Nazi persecution of Jews. Niemöller survived his incarceration in Dachau and spent the rest of his life as a prominent anti-war advocate. Bonhoeffer was less fortunate. He was imprisoned in Buchenwald and then moved to Flossenbürg, where he was condemned to death by SS Judge Otto Thorbeck and hanged on April 9, 1945—just two weeks before the Flossenbürg concentration camp was liberated by the U.S. Army.

Nanne Zwiep, a pastor of the Dutch Reformed Church who denounced the Nazis and anti–Semitism from his pulpit during the German occupation of the Netherlands, died in Dachau from exhaustion and malnutrition. Norbert Čapek, a native of Bohemia, moved with his family to the United States in 1914, where he discovered the Unitarian denomination. He and his wife went to Czechoslovakia in the 1920s and established a Unitarian Church in Prague. Čapek's wife returned to the United States when the war broke out, but Norbert remained in Europe. He was arrested for listening to foreign broadcasts and sent to Dachau, where he died from exhaustion and malnutrition.

Homosexuals were among the pre-war inmates of Dachau. Sex between men had been illegal in Germany since 1871, just one year after the creation of the modern German state. Homosexuality certainly existed among the Nazis; indeed, Nazi party co-founder and S.A. "Brownshirt" organizer Ernst Röhm was openly gay, as were many other members of Röhm's inner circle. A year after the 1934 Nazi party purge in which Röhm and his entire Brownshirt staff were murdered by the SS, the Nazi party revised the 1871 law. The measure stipulated that "a male who commits a sex offense with another male or allows himself to be used by another male for a sex offense shall be punished with imprisonment." The prison sentence could be as long as ten years.

The inmate population of Dachau had risen to over 13,000 by 1937. To accommodate so many prisoners, the SS forced inmates to construct a series of buildings that dramatically expanded the complex. Relatively few Jews were imprisoned in Dachau during its early years.

Anticipating the liberation of Dachau by American forces, Himmler sent a telegram to Eduard Weiter, the camp's commandant, ordering that inmates be evacuated. A second telegram instructed Weiter to kill the entire inmate population with gas bombs rather than allow them to be liberated. Weiter ignored the order—not from compassion but out of fear that the Americans might retaliate by killing the region's German civilians. He informed the camp's SS that Dachau would be surrendered to the Americans with the Red Cross serving as a mediator. Anxious to save their own skins, guards and other camp personnel discarded their uniforms, donned civilian clothing—much of it prisoners' garb obtained from the camp's clothing depot—and fled Dachau the night before its April 29, 1945, liberation by the U.S. Army's 42nd Infantry Division, known as the Rainbow Division. Weiter himself had fled from the camp, and Dachau's commandant, Heinrich Wicker, had assumed Weiter's position only the day before. Nonetheless, about 130 armed personnel remained in Dachau when the Rainbow Division arrived. An SS officer, accompanied by a member of the Red Cross holding a white cloth that had been tied to a broomstick, emerged from the camp's gates.

Soldiers who entered the camp were stunned by the camp's foul smell. When the inmates realized that these new arrivals were American troops, they came forward and soon mobbed their liberators. Meanwhile, Lt. Col. Donald Downard and other members of the Rainbow Division had discovered a string of thirty-nine open boxcars on the railroad tracks outside the camp. Downard and his men estimated that the boxcars contained at least two thousand bodies. They found a man who was still alive. He appeared to be about six feet tall but weighed less than one hundred pounds. Downard managed to get the man in his jeep and was taking him to a first-aid station when the vehicle was hit by gunfire. Downard's driver lost control of the jeep and it crashed. The emaciated man had been wounded by gunfire from an SS sniper, who had tried to kill this inmate before he could be liberated by the Americans.

Inmates took the Americans on a gruesome tour of Dachau and shared their accounts of starvation, beatings and torture. The camp's women inmates told of their repeated rapes by the SS. The GIs were appalled by the sight of barracks packed with corpses and inmates too weak to walk. Inmates armed themselves with sticks and other weapons of opportunity and began hunting down SS personnel that had remained in the camp. Horrified by what they had found, the Americans made little or no attempt to restrain this vigilante justice. Some inmates begged the GIs for knives and guns, and their liberators willingly obliged them. An estimated 25 to 50 SS personnel were killed by inmates.

Men of the 42nd found some SS guards in a tower next to the main gate of the inmate stockade. The guards were taken prisoner and shot by the Americans after being taken from the tower.

Joshua M. Greene's *Justice at Dachau* contains a succinct account of the arrival of U.S. Army's 45th Infantry Division, known as the Thunderbird Division, at Dachau and its lethal encounter with the SS. Commanded by Lt. Col. Felix Sparks, the men of Thunderbird were outraged by the corpse-laden boxcars and entered the camp seething with rage.

Four SS men approached the GIs with hands raised. William Walsh, a 1st Lieutenant in the 45th, pushed them into a boxcar and shot them with his .45. According to a report by the Office of the Inspector General, Seventh Army, Pvt. Albert Pruitt then entered the boxcar and finished off the Germans with his rifle.

Thunderbird men apprehended other SS members and lined them up against an eight-foot brick wall outside a coal yard. Walsh ordered his men to shoot them if they moved. A light machine gun was set up and pointed at the SS, who surely realized that lining up captives against a wall was the standard procedure for an execution by shooting. Walsh, however, had not ordered an execution—but he *had* commanded his men to fire if the prisoners moved. When the SS evidently moved in an attempt to escape what they thought was their certain execution, the GIs guarding them followed Walsh's order and opened fire. Sparks, who had been exploring the camp, ran to the brick wall, kicked the 19-year-old GI who had been firing the machine away from the weapon and asked, "What the hell are you doing?" Walsh fired his pistol into the air to get the attention of the other men and ordered them to cease fire. The machine gunner, who Walsh later noted was crying hysterically, replied, "Colonel, they were trying to get away." In his account of the event, Walsh stated that he was skeptical of the 19-year-old's claim. He relieved the young GI from machine gun duty and ordered an NCO to man the weapon. Walsh then resumed exploring the camp. It should be noted that the machine gunner was not the only GI who fired his weapon at the prisoners. An investigation of the shooting revealed that soldiers armed with a Browning Automatic Rifle, M-1 carbines and either a .45 caliber pistol or .45 caliber submachine gun also opened fire.

2. The Necessity of the War Crimes Trials

Greene's narrative of the Dachau killings also includes an account of GIs finding a Nazi dining alone in the SS mess hall. The Americans asked him how he and his fellow SS could have done such things. The SS man shrugged and muttered something about human swine. According to Greene, the Americans shot him while he was holding a spoonful of beans.

Lt. Col. Joseph Whittaker, Seventh Army assistant inspector general, sent a secret memo titled "Investigation of the Allied Mistreatment of the German Guards at Dachau," dated June 8, 1945, to the office of the Seventh Army's commanding general. The memo, which outlined the known facts of the case, contained this potentially damning paragraph:

> Troops entering this camp passed the famous train with its cars of dead bodies. Inside the camp other indications of Nazi treatment were evident. The sight of these numerous victims would naturally produce strong mental reaction on the part of both officers and men. Such circumstances are extenuating, but are the only extenuating facts found.

The report concluded with the recommendation that "this report be forwarded to the Commanding General, Third Army, for such action as he may deem appropriate."

Whittaker's statement that "the sight of these numerous victims would naturally produce strong mental reaction on the part of both officers and men" doesn't even begin to convey what the Americans who liberated Dachau saw and the mindset it produced. Walsh in 1989 gave this eyewitness account.

> The scene near the entrance to the confinement area numbed my senses. Dante's Inferno seemed pale compared to the real hell of Dachau. A row of small cement structures near the prison entrance contained a coal-fired crematorium, a gas chamber, and rooms piled high with naked and emaciated human corpses. As I turned to look over the prison yard with unbelieving eyes, I saw a large number of dead inmates lying where they had fallen in the last few hours or days before our arrival. Since all the many bodies were in various stages of decomposition, the stench of death was overpowering.
>
> During the early period of our entry into the camp, a number of Company I men, all battle hardened veterans, became extremely distraught. Some cried, while others raged. Some thirty minutes passed before I could restore order and discipline.... The dead, numbering about nine thousand, were later buried with the forced assistance of the good citizens of the city of Dachau.

The horrors of Dachau were confirmed by Vincent Tubbs, a war correspondent for the *Afro-American*. According to Glenda Elizabeth Gilmore's *Defying Dixie: The Radical Roots of Civil Rights, 1919–1950*, Tubbs reported that he smelled Dachau before he actually saw it. He described the stench as a combination of burning brown sugar and the sour stench of unwashed bodies. Tubbs corroborated accounts that the Nazis had tried to burn living prisoners as the Americans approached in an attempt to destroy all evidence of the camp's atrocities. He reported seeing some prisoners who had been tied to logs in the woods and then set afire. Although Tubbs was a journalist rather than a soldier, he was seen as a liberator by one survivor who gratefully kissed his hand.

Whittaker wrote in his report that the horror witnessed by the soldiers who liberated Dachau comprised extenuating circumstances, which are legally defined as unusual or extreme facts that are in existence prior to the perpetration of an offense. Just as Dante's *Inferno* paled "compared to the real hell of Dachau," extenuating circumstances hardly describes what was seen by the American soldiers who liberated that camp.

Despite Whittaker's report, none of the Americans involved in the killing of the Dachau guards were tried. General George Patton, who had been appointed as military governor of Bavaria, dismissed all charges.

The Dachau shootings became a point of contention in 1986 with the publication of *Dachau: The Hour of the Avenger: An Eyewitness Account* by Howard Buechner, who had served as a surgeon in the Third Battalion of the 157th. Buechner had been specifically cited in Whittaker's report for not taking measures to offer medical assistance to the SS guards who had been wounded during the shooting at the brick wall. According to Whittaker, Buechner had visited the area, saw the bodies after the shooting, and observed that some of the men were still alive. However, he didn't examine them to determine whether their lives could be saved and made no attempt to aid them.

In his book, Buechner claimed that the liberators of Dacha killed 560 German soldiers, including 346 in a mass execution conducted in the coal yard. Buechner's book is a favorite to this day among Holocaust "revisionists" and other extremists who use it to try to convince the gullible that the Allies, not the Nazis, were the real villains of World War II.

Buechner's attempt to rewrite history didn't sit well with Felix Sparks. His 1989 statement on the liberation of Dachau noted that the shooting of some of the SS guards who had been lined up against that brick wall has given rise to wild claims in various publications that most or all of the German prisoners captured at Dachau were executed. Nothing could be further from the truth. The total number of German guards killed at Dachau during that day most certainly did not exceed fifty, with thirty probably being a more accurate figure.

2. The Necessity of the War Crimes Trials   27

There is no hard evidence to suggest that the killings of the Dachau SS guards—referred to by historians as the "Dachau liberation reprisals" and by right-wing extremists as the "Dachau Massacre"—played any role in the selection of the camp for the war crimes trials. Still, it was an appropriate choice. The American soldiers who had allowed the liberated inmates of Dachau to kill SS guards as well as fellow inmates who had functioned as "informers" for the Nazis clearly violated the Declaration of St. James, which explicitly rejected the notion that war criminals should be punished by acts of vengeance committed by civilians. Those GIs who, outraged by what they found at Dachau, summarily executed SS guards also flouted the Declaration of St. James, which demanded that the guilt or innocence of accused war criminals be determined through organized channels of justice. By holding the war crimes trials on the site of the Dachau concentration camp, the U.S. Army repudiated the liberation reprisals that had occurred there and affirmed its commitment to the rule of law.

The crematory at Dachau might have been used once again after the camp's liberation. Telford Taylor noted that while he believes the Nazi war criminals who were tried and convicted at Nuremberg were cremated at or somewhere near Munich after their hangings, some historians maintain that their corpses were taken to Dachau.

3

Report of the Deputy Judge Advocate for War Crimes

By order of the United States Forces European Theater (USFET), the commanding general of the Western Military District, which was the territory occupied by the U.S. Third Army in Bavaria, was empowered to appoint military courts "predominantly at the site of the former concentration camp, Dachau, for the trials of war criminals not heard at Nuremberg," according to the document *Interrogation Records Prepared for War Crimes Proceedings at Nuremberg 1945–1947.* This authorization was made in a letter dated July 16, 1945, and titled "Trial of War Crimes and Related Cases."

This document noted that the commanding general of the Eastern Military District, which was the territory occupied by the U.S. Seventh Army in Hesse, Baden-Wuerttemberg and Bremen, was also authorized to conduct war crimes trials. In a letter dated October 14, 1946, however, USFET revoked this authority "in order to streamline operations." This revocation meant that all war crimes trials "were tried at the site of the former concentration camp Dachau because centralization of war crimes activities appeared necessary in light of the large body of cases and investigations."

The U.S. Army divided these cases into four categories: main concentration camp cases; subsequent concentration camp cases; flier cases; and miscellaneous cases.

> The first category comprises 6 cases and about two hundred defendants, mainly staff members and guards at Dachau, Buchenwald, Floseenburg, Mauthausen, Nordhausen, and Muehldorf concentration camps. The second category includes about 250 proceedings against approximately 800 guards and staff members of the outcamps and branch camps of the major camps. The third category encompasses more than 200 cases in which about 600 persons, mostly German civilians, were prosecuted for the killing of some 1,200 U.S. nationals, mostly airmen. The

fourth category consists of a few cases, including the Malmédy Massacre Case, in which 73 SS men were tried for murdering large groups of surrendered U.S. prisoners of war; the Hadamar case, in which a number of Hadamar Asylum staff members stood trial for the killing of about four hundred Polish and Russian nationals; and the Skorzeny Case, in which some members of the German Armed Forces were charged with wearing U.S. Army uniforms while participating in the Ardennes Offensive.

Kasich supplied me with many documents from his extensive personal collection. *Report of the Deputy Judge Advocate for War Crimes, European Command, June 1944 to July 1948* was an especially valuable resource. Submitted by Lt. Col. Clio E. Straight, Deputy Judge Advocate for War Crimes, to Col. James L. Harbaugh, Jr., who served as Judge Advocate, European Command. Signed by Straight and dated June 29, 1948, the report was formerly classified and contains a wealth of material on the War Crimes Group that Kasich and his fellow veterans served with such pride.

In late December of 1944, Straight noted, the War Department issued a directive that established a branch in the Office of the Judge Advocate General that would have as "its primary function the investigation of alleged war crimes, and the collection of evidence relating thereto, including, for transmission to the governments concerned, evidence relating to war crimes committed against nationals of other United Nations." This directive, he wrote,

> was implemented by the European Theater on February 24, 1945 and established war crimes branches in the judge advocate sections of their headquarters; that those branches function under the supervision of the judge advocate in carrying out the responsibilities of the War Crimes Group (then located in Paris, France), but under the operational control of the army group commanders; that "Reports of War Crimes" be submitted; those in the combat zone to be channelled [*sic*] through army judge advocates and those in the communications zone to be forwarded direct to the War Crimes Group "and that full and complete Investigations of War Crimes" be submitted as to all war crimes incidents involving American nationals as victims. Direct communications between war crimes agencies was authorized.

This directive also established procedures for gathering evidence of war crimes.

> The principal commands in the communications zone and air force commands were directed to screen all patients in general hospitals as well as all U.S. military or civilian personnel arriving at any assembly or staging area in order to identify those in possession of information regarding war crimes. All those in possession of such information were to be interrogated under oath. It was prescribed that the screening and interrogating be effected by personnel under the supervision of

the staff judge advocate of the various commands. The principal objective of the plan was to perpetuate in the form of sworn testimony all evidence which could be furnished by recovered prisoners of war and all military and civilian personnel prior to their departure from the theater to other theaters of war or to the Zone of Interior.

All commissioned officers that had been assigned to duty with the War Crimes Group or the war crimes branches of other theater headquarters were "detailed to conduct such investigations in connection with alleged war crimes as may be directed by the commanding general of the command concerned." The directive also ordered military intelligence personnel to forward all information that pertained to war crimes to the war crimes branch of the headquarters to which they had been assigned.

Straight's report offers valuable insights regarding the prelude to the war crimes trials. For example, he wrote that the decision by the Combined Chiefs of Staff not to try suspected war criminals prior to the cessation of hostilities with Germany was "probably motivated by concern as to reprisals." That assertion is followed by this paragraph.

> On 15 November 1944, FM 27–10, War Department, U.S. Army, "Rules of Land Warfare," was amended by Change No. 1 which eliminated a provision in paragraph 347 providing that members of armed forces will not be punished for war crimes "committed under the orders or sanction of their government or commanders," and which added paragraph 345.1 providing that the fact that war crimes were committed pursuant "to order of a superior or government sanction may be taken into consideration in determining culpability, either by way of defense or in mitigation of punishment."

Clearly, the innocuously titled "Change No. 1" empowered Allied prosecutors to try and convict German military personnel with war crimes. The tired refrain of "I was only following orders" could result in a reduced sentence but not in acquittal.

"In carrying out the assigned war crimes mission," Straight wrote, "the Judge Advocate operated through the War Crimes Group, which formed a part of his office, until 1 November 1946. On that date," he noted, "the War Crimes Group was organized as a unit, designated as '7708 War Crimes Group.'" After this date, Straight served not only as "such staff officer of Headquarters, European Theater, but also as Commanding Officer, 7708 War Crimes Group." During its early phase, the War Crimes Group was located with Theater Headquarters in Paris. It was "virtually impossible to obtain personnel within the European Theater to staff the War

The headquarters of the 7708 War Crimes Group at Wiesbaden, Germany (courtesy Bill Kasich).

Crimes Group, the war crimes agencies in subordinate commands, and the War Crimes Investigating Teams." When it became obvious that Paris was too far removed field war crimes agencies, the War Crimes Group was moved to Wiesbaden, Germany "by intermittent air lifts, as office space and quarters for the personnel became available."

The 7708 War Crimes Group during this period was understaffed and overworked.

Shortages of personnel for other judge advocate work in the armies was so severe that war crimes personnel were used for functions other than investigation of war crimes and aiding in the screening of those in detention. Similarly, although the War Crimes Group was also seriously understaffed ... personnel thereof, including court reporters and lawyers, were utilized for long periods of time in connection with prominent and extended courts-martial cases then being tried.

The Third United States Army was relieved of all responsibility for war crimes trials in late 1946. Europe Theater now assumed this duty and promptly established a War Criminals Prison at Landsberg, Germany. War crimes tribunals were moved to Dachau. The personnel who had been assigned to the War Crimes branch of the Third United States Army were transferred to the War Crimes Group and the War Crimes Investigating Teams were placed under the control of the War Crimes Group. The group itself was headquartered at Augsburg because that city was "the closest point to Dachau where anything approaching suitable facilities for the headquarters was availalbe [sic]."

The move, made by rail in November of 1946, was followed by "renovating the facilities for offices, barracks, quarters, messes, clubs, motor maintenance shops, etc.," which was completed until late January of 1947. Members of the War Crimes Group did much of this work themselves and the lost time "severely interfered with the war crimes operation." Straight also noted that "the undermanned Munich Military Post could not furnish many of the minimum types of housekeeping services at the Freising Sub-post. Moreover, electric current was only available spasmodically, water supply including that for fire protection was almost non-existent during drought periods, and adequate billets and housing were not available."

The headquarters of the War Crimes Group was moved once again, this time to Munich, in September 1947. Straight wrote that facilities at the Munich location were "very satisfactory" and the military post in that city provided "excellent housekeeping services."

Straight's report provides insight into the importance of documents in identifying war crimes and establishing the guilt of those responsible for them. "All commands were assigned the general responsibility of collecting and forwarding evidence relating to war crimes," he noted. Teams were sent to "the principal document centers to acquaint personnel with the nature of the war crimes material desired and to offer supervisory services in document screening." The amount of material was staggering. Straight stated that "several tons of records, including death books, etc., were collected in

3. Report of the Deputy Judge Advocate for War Crimes

Office hours of War Crimes Group members involved a great deal of paperwork (courtesy Bill Kasich).

connection with a few of the major concentration camps." In one of our interviews, Bill Kasich remarked that the Germans had been meticulous record keepers. One of the ironies of both the Dachau and Nuremberg trials for him was that the Nazis' own voluminous records had played such a critical role in the prosecution of the Third Reich's war criminals.

Contrary to popular belief, however, still photographs and film footage played a far less significant role in the war crimes trials. Straight observed that during the last few weeks of the war, "a large number of atrocity scenes were recorded in still pictures and on motion picture film by combat photographers." While such stills and film footage would seem to comprise superb documentation of Nazi war crimes, Straight noted that

> no war crimes personnel were available to assist in or direct this work and no plan existed as to the preservation for war crimes purposes of this evidence from this unanticipated source. Consequently, no attempt was made to support the same by the sworn testimony of those in position to testify as to the accuracy of the scenes depicted. Later, all such pictures and motion picture films were made available by the Army Pictorial Service for screening for evidence of war crimes, after which efforts were made to return them for the sworn testimony of the combat photographers who shot the scenes or others who were present and familiar with the facts. However, little was gained by these efforts because (1) most of the pictures

and films depicted scenes of mere general interest, (2) they were shot by personnel who had no conception as to the elements of proof in war crimes cases, and (3) most of those able to testify as to the scenes depicted could not be located.

Straight concluded that "while such uncoordinated mass photography may establish that war crimes and mass atrocities have been committed on a vast scale, they are seldom of value as proof of the connection of particular individuals with specific crimes." Documents from Nazi sources as well as eyewitness accounts of war crimes, while more valuable than photos and films, also presented problems. As Straight pointed out, "This war crimes material was in many languages and some of that which eventually proved to be the most valuable was very fragmentary and often merely bore on the fact of the commission of a war crime, or merely contained faint leads as to the place of the commission, the identity of the perpetrator, the victim, or the witnesses."

War crimes "had been committed on a scale unknown to modern history," and the amount of material required to document them was enormous. "Near the completion of the war crimes trials program," Straight noted in his report,

> about 18 tons of documents which were no longer of war crimes interest and the information collected in the personal date files of those detained in the War Crimes Enclosure were transferred to agencies under the supervision of the Assistant Chief of Staff, G-2. All war crimes material considered essential for retention, including the case folders in connection with tried and untried cases, the card indices, etc., necessary in utilizing the same, and the records of trial in cases tried, were transferred to the custody of the Judge Advocate Division, European Command, as of 20 June 1948.

The fact that investigators were able to accumulate such a surfeit of war crimes documentation is all the more astonishing in light of the difficulties they faced. Members of the military, who had valuable testimony to share, were scattered by redeployment. "Civilian witnesses, many of whom were imported slave laborers and other displaced persons, were also scattered," Straight observed. The war criminals themselves "made every effort to conceal their identity."

The judge advocate's office developed a strategy for gathering testimony from witnesses who, in all likelihood, would be far removed from the Dachau courtrooms when accused war criminals were placed on trial.

> Inasmuch as it was evident that in many instances the witnesses would be scattered throughout the world before most of the war crimes cases could be brought to trial and, in view of the fact that the extrajudicial sworn testimony of witnesses

was admissible in evidence by the procedural applicable to the trial of war crimes cases, the investigative instructions provided that all statements would be under oath, preferably in question and answer form supplemented in instances where the circumstances so dictated with the sworn narrative statements of the witnesses in their native languages.

In the "Trials" section of his report, Straight cited "some of the more interesting cases" that were tried. These included the "Hadamar Murder Factory Case" (*United States v. Klein et alia*), "in which the accused were charged with killing several hundred nationals of other United Nations in the course of the operation of an euthanasia institution." Straight's description of the psychiatric hospital located in the German town of Hadamar as a "euthanasia institution" is much too charitable. The term euthanasia, which is derived from the Greek word meaning "good death," is generally defined as terminating someone's life in order to end that person's suffering. Euthanasia is often referred to as "mercy killing," since bringing about the suffering person's death can justly be regarded as an act of mercy. There was nothing merciful about the killings conducted at Hadamar, nor did Hadamar's victims experience anything even remotely resembling "good deaths." They were not suffering excruciating pain from lingering terminal illnesses. Hadamar's victims were physically or mentally disabled, and therefore judged unworthy of life by the standards of Nazi Germany. People with disabilities were regarded as an embarrassment by those obsessed with portraying Aryans as the master race. Men, women and children were murdered by lethal injection, or gassing in facilities designed to look like showers—a grim foreshadowing of the Nazi final solution for Jews. Indeed, many T-4 personnel were later transferred to the staffs of concentration camps.

Institutions such as Hadamar owed their genesis to the *Euthanasie Programme*, which was established by the Nazi government in late 1939. Since the headquarters of this program was located in Berlin at Tiergartenstrasse 4, its code name was simply T-4. Opened in 1941, Hadamar's popular characterization as a "Murder Factory" is chillingly accurate. Between January and August of 1941, at least 10,000 physically and mentally disabled persons were gassed. This extermination of those regarded as unworthy of life was not without German critics. In a letter dated September 5, 1940, a Dr. Wurm of the Wüerttemberg Evangelical Provincial Church sent a letter to the Reich Minister of the Interior regarding the Nazi policy of killing persons with disabilities, which Wurm identified as "the systematic extermination of lunatics, feeble-minded and epileptic persons."

He noted that "this practice has reached tremendous proportions: recently, the inmates of old-age homes have also been included." Wurm correctly concluded that "the basis for this practice seems to be that in an efficient nation there should be no room for weak and frail people." He warned the Reich Minister of the Interior that this program was demoralizing the German people by fostering "the feeling of legal insecurity ... which is regrettable from the point of view of national and state interest."

Another clergyman was even more blunt in his condemnation of this program. The bishop of Limburg, in a letter dated August 13, 1941, and sent to the Reich Minister of Justice, wrote that "all God-fearing men consider this destruction of helpless beings a crass injustice." He concluded this missive with the plea, "I beg you most humbly, Herr Reich Minister ... to prevent further transgressions of the Fifth Commandment of God."

These pleas fell on deaf ears. The T-4 program continued to kill those judged to be unproductive citizens of the Reich. While Hadamar closed in 1941, it reopened the following year and remained in operation until the end of the war. Between 1942 and 1945, over 4,000 person were murdered at Hadamar.

The "crimes against humanity" indictment had not yet been adopted at the time of the Hadamar trial, which prevented Allied prosecutors from charging the staff with murdering their fellow Germans. During the course of the war, however, some 476 Polish and Soviet civilians who had contracted tuberculosis were sent to Hadamar to be killed. Existing international law recognized the murder of Allied civilians as a war crime and seven staff members were convicted in the Wiesbaden courtroom, where Leon Jaworski (1902–1982), who decades later gained fame during Nixon's Watergate scandal, served as prosecutor.

Alfons Klein, who served as chief administrator at Hadamar, as well as two male nurses were sentenced to death. All three were executed on October 15, 1946. The other defendants received prison sentences. The case of Irmgard Huber, the chief nurse at Hadamar and the case's sole female defendant, was particularly significant in terms of establishing personal culpability during the perpetration of war crimes. After her arrest by the Allies, Huber protested that she had never killed any patients at Hadamar. When her claim was corroborated by co-workers and other witnesses, she was released. Later, however, it was established that Huber had played a significant role in selecting patients for murder and had maintained control of the supply of drugs used to administer lethal overdoses to patients. She had also played a prominent role in falsifying the death certificates of patients. She was rearrested and placed on trial with Klein and the other Hadamar defendants. Huber was sentenced to 25 years imprisonment. She was later sentenced to serve additional prison time by a German court for her actions at Hadamar but was released in by the United States in 1952 in response to pressure from the West German government. Huber lived in the town of Hadamar until her death in 1983.

Straight also cited *United States v. Stroop at alia* as another interesting case tried at Dachau. Sometimes referred to as the "Superior Orders Case," the *United States v. Stroop*, et alia centered on "the execution of a common design to kill surrendered American airmen through Wehrkreiss [a German military district] XIII." Straight noted that "the accused ranged from Lieutenant General Stroop, Higher SS and Police Leader of Wehrkreiss XII, down to and including the trigger men in several incidents of such illegal killings."

While SS General Jürgen Stroop is infamous as the commander of the German troops who destroyed the Warsaw Ghetto in 1943, he was tried at Dachau for his role in the murder of nine members of the U.S. Army Air Corps who were shot down in his military district and then summarily executed. During his trial at Dachau, Stroop falsely claimed he had never authorized the killing of the American airmen and had no knowledge of these murders. The presiding military tribunal didn't buy his protestation of ignorance and non-responsibility. Stroop was convicted and sentenced to death by hanging. He managed to escape the hangman's noose when he was abruptly flown to Poland to stand trial for war crimes committed in that nation, including the liquidation of the Warsaw Ghetto.

Straight's characterization of United States v. Stroop as "one of the more interesting cases tried" was written decades before the publication of Kazimierz Moczarski's *Conversations with an Executioner*, a book that takes its readers inside the mind of a Nazi war criminal. Moczarski had served in the Polish Home Army, which was the underground resistance to Poland's German conquerors. The Soviet Union saw the Polish Home Army, which had maintained loyalty to the Polish Government in Exile during the war, as a threat to Soviet domination of Poland in the post-war era. Consequently, Moczarski was imprisoned—and Stroop became his cellmate in a Warsaw prison. Ironically, the Polish Home Army had ordered Moczarski to assassinate Stroop during the war for his crimes against Poland.

Stroop and Moczarski spent 255 days as cellmates, during which time the Nazi talked freely about his life and military career. He remained steadfast in his allegiance to Nazi doctrine and insisted that Aryans, particularly those of Nordic stock, comprised a master race. He expressed no remorse for his actions and maintained that he was simply following orders from Himmler, who had characterized all American airmen as murderers and terrorists.

"Among the trials," Straight wrote, "were 222 cases involving 642 accused and approximately 1244 American nationals as known victims." He cautioned readers that the 1,244 figure is misleading. "These trials are exclusive of mass atrocity cases in which an undetermined number of American nationals were victims." Straight speculated that this "undetermined number" of "additional American victims" was probably in the hundreds.

No less than 489 cases, which involved 1,672 accused war criminals, were tried. Eight war crimes were in session simultaneously at the War Crimes Enclosure at Dachau during most of 1947. Straight informed readers that "the marked increased rate of completion of trials during 1947 is to some degree assignable to the fact that a vast amount of investigation and apprehension work had to be completed before cases could be referred to trials in large numbers and to the fact that a greater number of personnel was made available for the mission, it was primarily assignable to the centralized operational control of all aspects of the operation during the third phase," which Straight had earlier defined in his report as the point when "lower commands were relieved of responsibility in connection with the development and trial of war crimes cases." This degree of centralization, which meant holding all trials at Dachau as well as assigning officers to the War Crimes Group for continuous service on war crimes tribunals, eliminated delays and difficulties in appointing courts and scheduling trials.

Nonetheless, certain problems remained that hampered the efficiency of the War Crimes Group as well as the Dachau trials. The report conceded that

> ...many operational difficulties were encountered, e.g., the facilities at Dachau did not permit appropriate segregation of suspects and witnesses. The technical barriers and restrictions on moving to and from the other Occupational Zones and countries created by regulations imposed by the United States and other Occupation Forces constituted a very severe impediment to the procurement of witnesses from countries of western Europe and their movement to Dachau. Parenthetically, it should be mentioned that at no time could investigations be made in or witnesses obtained from Russia, areas under its control, or from Russian dominated countries. Similarly, the difficulties of coordinating war crimes activities with Czechoslovakia gradually increased. No investigations could be made

therein during the third phase and near the end of the trials program it was nearly impossible to procure witnesses therefrom.

In other words, the growth of Cold War tensions between the United States and Soviet Union severely interfered with the prosecution of war criminals. Straight's mention of "gradually increased" difficulties of "coordinating war crimes activities with Czechoslovakia" reflects the growing communist presence in that nation's national government in the post-war era that culminated in complete communist domination in 1948. The level of cooperation necessary between the world's two superpowers to bring Nazi war criminals to justice no longer existed.

Straight devoted Section VII of his report to an examination of the legal aspects involved in the war crimes trials. "It was directed by the Joint Chiefs of Staff in their directive 1023/10, 8 July 1945, that such courts should, to the greatest practicable extent, adopt fair, simple and expeditious procedures designed to accomplish substantial justice without technicality." He then noted that this directive had stood on solid legal ground. "The propriety of instructions of this character by the executive branch of the government was upheld by the Supreme Court of the United States in the case of In re Yamashita, 66 Supreme Court Reporter 340."

Straight evidently assumed that anyone who read this report would be familiar with this case and made no mention of its details or judicial importance. As commander of Japan's Twenty-Fifth Army, General Tomoyuki Yamashita invaded the British colony of Malaya in late 1941, a campaign that culminated in the British surrender of Singapore on February 15, 1942. Yamashita's forces captured 130,000 British, Australian and Indian troops, the largest surrender of a British-led military force in history, earning him the nickname the "Tiger of Malaya."

Yamashita's army committed a major war crime on Valentine's Day when his troops entered Alexandra Military Hospital in Singapore. The Japanese had been enraged by the fact that retreating British soldiers had fired at them from the hospital grounds and were determined to take vengeance. A British officer who approached the Japanese holding a white flag of surrender was bayoneted. Japanese soldiers then indiscriminately killed approximately 50 medical personnel and patients, including those undergoing surgery. The next day about 150 medical personnel and patients were marched to a nearby industrial area. Those too weak to walk, as well as those who fell during the forced march, were bayoneted. Prisoners who reached the industrial area were bayoneted or hacked to death with machetes. A few Allied soldiers managed to survive the massacre.

A second atrocity soon followed. The Japanese were aware that the Chinese who lived in Singapore and Malaya were loyal to either the British Empire or the Republic of China—both of whom were at war with Japan. Consequently, Chinese who were thought to comprise the greatest threat to the occupying Japanese, such as civil servants and members of the Singapore Overseas Chinese Anti-Japanese Volunteer Army, were marked for extermination. This war crime is generally called Sook Ching, which is Chinese for "purge through cleansing." The Japanese army's word for this event is translated as "purging of Chinese." Another Japanese term for the killings translates as the much more innocuous "great inspection of Singapore." Japan today refers to this war crime as the "Singapore Chinese massacre."

The killings began in late February of 1942. Documented incidents include the shooting of about 66 Chinese men at Changi Beach. As many as four hundred Chinese men were shot to death at Punggol Beach. At least eleven major massacre sites have been identified. The Japanese attempted to carry their extermination program throughout Malaya. The massacres ended in early March of 1942. Estimates of those killed during the purge vary from the fewer than 5,000—the official Japanese version—to the Chinese Singapore community's estimate of 50,000 to 100,000. The third war crime perpetrated by troops under Yamashita's command occurred in 1944. After a term of service in the Japanese puppet state of Manchukuo, Yamashita was transferred to the Philippines. With recapture of Manila by American-Filipino forces imminent, Yamashita ordered all Japanese to evacuate the city in January of 1945. However, about 17,000 Japanese marines and soldiers remained in the city and fought the advancing Allied forces. Angry and feeling humiliated upon being driven out of Manila, the Japanese vented their rage upon the city's civilian population. A Japanese order dated February 13, 1945, commanded troops to conserve ammunition while killing Filipinos and to place their bodies in houses that were to be burned. The order also allowed for the option of dumping Filipino corpses into the river. Residents of Manila were mutilated by bayonets and machetes. Many of the massacres occurred in schools and convents. Countless women were raped. Historians estimate that approximately 100,000 Manila civilians were killed, although some civilian deaths can be attributed to American artillery and air strikes.

Yamashita and what remained of his army in the Philippines surrendered to the Americans when Japan finally capitulated after the atomic bombs were dropped on Hiroshima and Nagasaki. He was tried as a war criminal by an American military tribunal in Manila. The prosecution based its case on Yamashita's failure to maintain sufficient control over his troops. It was ultimately his responsibility, prosecutors argued, to prevent Japanese forces under his command from committing massacres and other atrocities. The military tribunal condemned Yamashita to death.

Yamashita's defense attorneys protested the verdict: first, to the Supreme Court of the Philippines and, secondly, to the U.S. Supreme Court. Their client, they argued, had been convicted not for committing war crimes but for having failed to prevent troops under his command from committing war crimes. They also maintained that the military commission lacked the legal authority to try and convict Yamashita. The defense attorneys also strongly objected to the fact that the commission allowed the admission in evidence of depositions, affidavits and opinion and hearsay evidence during Yamashita's trial. In doing so, however, the commission was merely following the orders of General Douglas MacArthur who, the Supreme Court noted in announcing its decision, had "directed that the commission should admit such evidence 'as in its opinion would have probative value in the mind of a reasonable man' and in particular in might admit affidavits, depositions or other statements taken by officers detailed for that purpose by military authority."

The U.S. Supreme Court, which heard the case argued from January 7 to January 8, 1946, delivered its decision on February 4 of that year. Speaking for the majority, Chief Justice Harlan Fiske Stone wrote in part:

> it is not denied that such acts directed against the civilian population of an occupied country and against prisoners of war are recognized in international law as violations of the law of war.... The question is then whether the law of war imposes on an army commander the duty to take appropriate measures as are within his power to control the troops under his command for the prevention of the specified acts which are violations of the law of war and which are likely to attend the occupation of hostile territory by uncontrolled soldiery, and whether he may be charged with personal responsibility for his failure to take such measures when violations result.

The court concluded that soldiers would likely commit violations of the law of war "if the commander of an invading army could with impunity neglect to take reasonable measures" for the protection of the civilian population of the occupied territory. Yamashita bore responsibility for the men under his command.

Regarding the use of affidavits, depositions, opinions and hearsay testimony during Yamashita's trial, the court stated that "we cannot say that the commission, in admitting evidence to which objection is now made, violated any act of Congress, treaty or military command defining the commission's authority." The commission's rulings regarding evidence presented by the prosecutors "are not reviewable by the courts but only by the reviewing military authorities." The Supreme Court's decision effectively sealed Yamashita's fate. "We therefore conclude," Stone wrote, "that the detention of petitioner (Yamashita) for trial and his detention upon his conviction, subject to the prescribed review by the military authorities were lawful, and that petition for certiorari, and leave to file in this Court petitions for writs of habeas corpus and prohibition should be and they are Denied."

Yamashita's attorneys appealed for clemency to President Harry Truman, who declined to intervene. The Tiger of Malaya was duly hanged in a prison camp located south of Manila on February 23, 1946. In his final message to the Japanese people, Yamashita wrote that he had "been judged by rigorous but impartial law" and postulated that "the foolish methods of war that Japan adopted will be regarded as the illusions of an idiot."

Straight's report didn't overemphasize the importance of the Yamashita's decision for the Dachau trials. Military tribunals indeed possessed the authority to try war criminals. These military tribunals also possessed the authority to allow affidavits, depositions and even hearsay to be admitted as evidence. Stone and a majority of the justices of the U.S. Supreme Court had effectively upheld the legality of the July 8, 1945, directive by the Joint Chiefs of Staff, which had authorized "fair, simple and expeditious procedures designed to accomplish substantial justice without technicality."

A major revision to the Legal and Penal Administration section made by Headquarters, United States Forces, European Command, which Straight cited in his report, also served to streamline justice at Dachau. The new regulations, implemented on March 27, 1947, read in part:

> The procedure for the trial of cases laid down in these rules may be modified to the extent that certain steps in the trial may be omitted or abbreviated so long as no rights granted to the accused are disregarded. Opening statements in particular may frequently be omitted. No greater formality than is consistent with a complete and fair hearing under these rules is desirable and the introduction of procedural formalities from the manual of Courts Martial or from trial guides based thereon is discouraged except where specifically required by these rules.

These new regulations facilitated speedy justice while ensuring the accused of a fair trial in which "no rights granted to the accused are

3. Report of the Deputy Judge Advocate for War Crimes

disregarded." Another section of the new regulations further ensured accelerated justice while protecting the rights of the accused.

> The proceedings shall not be invalidated, nor any finding or sentence disapproved, for any error or omission, technical or otherwise occurring in such proceedings, unless in the opinion of the Reviewing Authority, after an examination of the entire record, it shall appear that the error or omission has resulted in injustice to the accused.

Straight gave examples of laws that had been adopted at various international conventions and how those laws had been utilized—and interpreted—at the Dachau trials. A judicial decision stemming from the Geneva Convention of 1929 significantly augmented the legitimacy of the Dachau trials. Article 63 stated that "sentence may be pronounced against a prisoner of war only by the same courts and according to the same procedure as in the case of persons belonging to the armed forces of the detaining power." Citing this article, attorneys for some of the defendants at the Dachau trials argued that their clients, as prisoners of war, were entitled to be tried in the same military courts as American military personnel. Straight noted that "it was concluded that Article 63 applied only to a sentence pronounced against a prisoner of war for an offense committed while he was a prisoner of war and did not apply to a violation of the law committed while he was a prisoner of war and did not apply to a violation of the law of war committed prior to his status as a prisoner of war."

The legitimacy of the Dachau trials, Straight wrote, was further reinforced by the successful resolution of the question as to whether American Military Government Courts had jurisdiction to try war criminals for offenses committed during the war (1939–1945) but before the United States entered the war in 1941. He observed that

> The opinion was expressed that the courts had jurisdiction over such offences. The reason given was that jurisdiction of a sovereign state to try war criminals is derived from the common law of nations under which jurisdiction to try war criminals is an incident of the sovereign power of an independent state. Such power is full and complete, except where restricted by the body of principles comprising the law of nations. It was pointed out that it is axiomatic that a state, adhering to the law of war which forms a part of the law of nations, is interested in the preservation and the enforcement thereof. And this is true, irrespective of when and where the crime was committed, the belligerency or non-belligerency status of the punishing power, or the nationality of the victims.

Straight briefly dealt with the so-called "Superior Orders" defense in which the accused offers evidence that the offense was committed "pursuant to orders of a superior." Compliance with orders from a superior, he noted, didn't constitute a defense to the charge of having committed a war crime, although under certain circumstances it might be taken into consideration in sentencing. Regarding those defendants who tendered the defense that they were merely soldiers who were following orders, Straight wrote:

> An accused who seeks relief on such grounds assumes the burden of establishing (a) that he received an order from a superior directing that he commit the wrongful act; (b) that he did not know or, as a reasonably prudent person, would not have known that the act which he was directed to perform was illegal or contrary to universally accepted standards of human conduct; and (c) that he acted, at least to some extent, under immediate compulsion. Having satisfactorily established these elements, the amount to which his sentence should be mitigated depends upon the character and extent of immediate compulsion under which he acted.

These criteria were in no way unrealistic. They were necessary to ensure that convicted war criminals received sentences that reflected the heinousness of their crimes. The implementation of justice at Dachau also benefited from the rejection of the argument of "military necessity as a justification for killing prisoners of war." Straight noted that in the 1947 case of *United States v. Kluettgen*, it was stated that "if military necessity went so far as to justify killing a prisoner of war, it would result in the destruction of most of the elementary restraints on war handed down from antiquity and it would permit governments and commanders deliberately to confuse military necessity with strategical interest and military convenience."

Straight then addressed the issue of evidence in a war crimes trial and immediately established the unique quality of the Dachau trials. "Neither the rules of evidence as known in American municipal criminal law not those prescribed for courts-martial are applicable to war crimes trials," he observed.

The general rules of evidence applied were as follows:

> a. A Military Government Court shall in general admit oral, written and physical evidence having a bearing on the issues before it, and may exclude any evidence which in its opinion is of no value as proof.
>
> b. The Court shall in general require the best evidence available.
>
> c. Hearsay, or other evidence deemed to be of probative value or helpful in arriving at a true finding, is admissible.
>
> d. Evidence of bad character of an accused shall be admissible before findings only when the accused has introduced evidence as to his own good character.

Point (d) represented a good-faith effort to ensure that the accused received the fairest trial possible. So did the stated policy of extending the American judicial principles of reasonable doubt and presumption of innocence, which Straight noted in his report. "While the rule in American municipal criminal law as to reasonable doubt and presumption of innocence was not applicable as such to war crimes trials," he wrote, "in the absence of a suitable prescribed standard, the rule requiring that an accused be presumed innocent until proven guilty and that proof of guilt be established beyond a reasonable doubt was adhered to in the war crimes trials." By extending the principles of reasonable doubt and presumption of innocence to accused war criminals when these principles were not, as Straight observed, applicable to war crimes cases, the War Crimes Group conclusively demonstrated that these trials were grounded in the quest for justice, not vengeance.

Extrajudicial sworn statements made by either the accused or witnesses were admissible as evidence. Straight's report frankly noted that it was "not required that foundation evidence to establish that sworn statements, including those by the accused, be offered to show that such statements were voluntarily procured." This rather disturbing admission is followed by Straight's comment that "the question of whether extrajudicial sworn statements or confessions were voluntary or whether they were made under circumstances which might have induced accused or witnesses to state untruths was held to be a question for the court to determine." Extrajudicial sworn statements or confessions by one accused war criminal were admissible as evidence against another accused. Straight wrote:

> This conclusion was based primarily on the general rules of evidence applicable to war crimes trials under which any evidence deemed to be of probative value is admissible. Moreover, an analogy was drawn to the rule in American municipal criminal law under which an extrajudicial confession is admissible against the maker as an exception to the hearsay rule. As the hearsay rule is inapplicable to war crimes trials, there is no basis for excluding such evidence.

In our interviews, Bill Kasich was quite emphatic about the circumstances under which sworn statements and confessions were made. The court needn't have concerned itself, as Straight put it, "whether sworn statements or confessions were voluntary or whether they were made under circumstances which might have induced accused or witnesses to state untruths." Kasich assured me that the American interrogators he knew and worked with neither bullied nor beat anyone.

When a plea of guilty is entered by the accused, Straight wrote, the court heard "such statements for the prosecution and the defense and such evidence as it required to enable it to determine the sentence to be imposed." The absence of the accused during his/her trial, whether due to illness or other reasons, "did not invalidate the proceedings as long as he was adequately represented by counsel." The decision by the International Military Tribunal at Nuremberg to try Martin Bormann *in absentia* provided a precedent that allowed the Dachau courts "to proceed during the temporary absence of the accused." Straight also noted that any requests by the condemned men for a soldier's traditional execution by firing squad fell on deaf ears. "It was held that there was no reason for permitting a war criminal sentenced to death to choose a form of execution less ignominious than the prescribed manner of execution of death sentence by hanging."

Straight then addressed a somewhat controversial topic: the backlog of cases that of cases earmarked for review and recommendation. He wrote:

> The number of cases in connection with which Reviews and Recommendations had not been submitted to the Judge Advocate for his action as Reviewing Authority, or for recommendation to the Theater Commander and to views expressed by the Deputy Judge Advocate in his Reviews and Recommendations, gradually increased throughout the war crimes trials. A backlog of 216 unreviewed cases existed on 31 December 1947. This gradual increase in number of unreviewed cases resulted from a number of factors, including the almost total absence of personnel assigned to the War Crimes Group with prior experience fitting them for dealing with the novel questions of international law involved in the cases, the unfortunate but necessary recurrent burdening of the Deputy Judge Advocate with administrative matters, and the great urgency placed upon the early completion of the other aspects of the program, i.e., investigations, apprehensions, and the screening of those in detention, which resulted in unusually strong demands for the utilization of most of the more capable personnel on other aspects of the operation.

Since experienced personnel were unavailable, "lawyers therefore were selected from within the War Crimes Group and trained on the job." This training successfully provided the personnel needed to address the backlog. "Following the completion of the war crimes trials," Straight wrote, "efforts were concentrated on the reviewing of records of trials. The last Review and Recommendations was forwarded on 28 April 1948."

Straight noted that the Combined Chiefs of Staff had postponed the granting of extraditions and surrender requests until after the cessation of hostilities with Germany. "Few deliveries," he observed, "were effected prior to 1946." Since utilizing conventional diplomatic channels to return

3. Report of the Deputy Judge Advocate for War Crimes

war criminal suspects to the nations in which their crimes had been committed would have been time-consuming and hindered by delays, requests for extradition and surrender were

> accomplished on prescribed forms and filed with the Military Governor, U.S. Zone of Occupation, Germany, addressed to the attention of the Judge Advocate, who was empowered and directed to act on behalf of the Military Governor on requests for the extradition and surrender of war criminal suspects and witnesses to war crimes, as well as on requests for the taking of depositions or for the delivery of evidentiary material in the U.S. Zone of Occupation.... This authority of the Judge Advocate was redelegated to the Deputy Judge Advocate and such requests in practice were routed to the latter's office.

The report drew a distinction between actual war criminals and "renegades and quislings," who were not war criminals but "by virtue of their high positions held or their international notoriety attained, presented potential diplomatic level problems." Since "no special procedure was prescribed for processing extradition requests as to them, such requests were handled under the procedure prescribed for the extradition and surrender of war criminal suspects."

Unfortunately, Straight's report made no mention of specific individuals who fell into this category. "Renegades," within this context, meant citizens of Allied nations who threw in with the Germans during the period of wartime occupation. Such collaboration with the enemy could have taken the role of civilian employment by the German army, or agreeing to work as informants who provided the Germans with information about the resistance movement. The most extreme example of renegades would have been citizens of an occupied nation that agreed to take up arms and fight alongside the German army, such as the Charlemagne Division of the Waffen-SS that consisted of about 20,000 French volunteers who fought on the eastern front. The Charlemagne Division suffered horrendous casualties fighting the Soviet army. Those who survived the war were despised as collaborators by the French people after liberation. Many who had served as officers were executed, while enlisted men drew prison sentences. A few survivors of the Charlemagne Division were given the option of enlisting in the French Foreign Legion and then sent to Indochina in an attempt to regain control of that colony, which had been occupied by the Japanese during the war. Other examples of renegades included Ukrainians, Cossacks and other USSR nationals who agreed to fight the Soviet armies when their nations were occupied by Nazi Germany.

"Quislings" were those citizens of a nation that had been conquered and occupied who agreed to serve in the government of a puppet state. The word comes from Vidkung Quisling, a fascist politician who served in Norway's pro–German government after that nation had been invaded and conquered by Nazi Germany. He helped to raise a military unit of Norwegian volunteers to fight alongside the Germany army, cooperated with Nazi efforts to arrest and deport Jews to concentration camps and attempted to enroll Norwegian children in a program modeled after Germany's Hitler Youth camps.

Quisling remained in close contact with Hitler throughout the war. He was arrested in Norway after that nation's liberation. Quisling argued at his trial that he had consistently acted in such a manner as to ensure the continued independence and economic well-being of Norway. He was convicted for treason as well as a variety of other charges and sentenced to death. Still protesting his innocence, Vidkung Quisling was executed by firing squad on October 24, 1945. His place in history was secured when his name became a synonym for a traitor who holds a high-ranking position in a puppet government. The War Crimes Group had nothing to do with the apprehension and prosecution of Quisling, although Straight had no problem using quisling as a pejorative term in his report.

Phillippe Pétain would have fallen into Straight's quisling category. A general who vanquished the Germans at the battle of Verdun during World War I and received the honor of being named Marshal of France, Pétain was brought into the French cabinet in an effort to bolster resistance when Germany invaded France in 1940. When the cabinet was shuffled and Pétain became prime minister, he sought a cease-fire with Germany and became the head of state of unoccupied France, which popularly became known as Vichy France since its headquarters was in the resort city of Vichy.

Pétain, a lifelong reactionary who detested liberal values, wielded dictatorial powers and transformed the French republic into an authoritarian state with fascist overtones. Vichy France repudiated the traditional motto of republican France—liberty, equality and fraternity—and adopted as its motto "work, family, fatherland." Pétain and his fellow collaborationists imposed strict censorship on the press, imprisoned dissidents and passed anti–Semitic laws. Vichy France even had its own militia, the Milice, which actively hunted down members of the French resistance. French armed forces in overseas colonies were instructed to fight Allied armies if they entered colonial territory.

When the German army occupied Vichy France in late 1942, Pétain theoretically remained in power but only as an obvious puppet of the Germans. Petain and his Vichy collaborators retreated into Germany after the liberation of France. Shortly before the surrender of Germany, however, Pétain voluntarily returned to France, where he was placed under arrest and tried for treason during the summer of 1945. Upon conviction, he was sentenced to death with the court's recommendation that he be spared execution due to his age. Charles de Gaulle, leader of the Free French forces after the fall of France and president of that nation's provisional government after liberation, honored the request. Pétain was sentenced to life imprisonment and died in 1951 at the age of 95 while incarcerated on a small island off the Atlantic coast of France. The old man remained in exile after death and was buried in a cemetery near the prison. Ironically, Pétain remained a Marshal of France even after being found guilty of treason and exiled to an island prison, since the French court that convicted him lacked the authority to revoke it.

In a section of the report titled "Furnishing Leads to Other nations," Straight wrote that a "very substantial portion of the individuals surrendered were covered by extradition and surrender requests" from other nations in contact with the War Crimes Group. Such requests were carefully examined to determine whether "the described crimes constituted violations of the law of war." Straight candidly admitted that "requests were not granted which covered individuals wanted in connection with the American war crimes operation."

Extradition and surrender requests from countries that were not members of the United Nations presented a problem for the War Crimes Group. An "appreciable number" of such requests "were received from Hungary and Austria, involving both their own nationals and Germans." Austria had been annexed by Nazi Germany in 1938, while Hungary had declared war on the Soviet Union in 1941 and became an ally of Germany. While Straight might have wanted to cooperate with these nations in their desire to apprehend and try individuals who had committed war crimes within their borders, his hands were tied. He wrote:

> The directive concerning extradition and surrender did not deal with such requests and explicit instructions were not forthcoming from the War Department. Under such circumstances the War Crimes Group pursued the policy of not granting such requests by former cobelligerents [sic] of Germany, except requests covering their own nationals in instances where the request was coupled with compelling circumstances.

As far as Western nations were concerned, however, Straight wrote that "coordination of the extradition program presented no problems which were not susceptible of ready solution." Initially, deliveries of war crimes suspects who had been cleared for extradition "were made from various detention installations" and the War Crimes Group decided that using one delivery point would be more efficient. Consequently, Straight initiated "the program of congregating all individuals of war crimes interest to the United States or other United Nations in the War Crimes Enclosure, Dachau." Such centralization, he noted, "permitted of an accurate and final check as to the identity of the individual proposed for delivery." The last deliveries of war crimes suspects occurred in January 1948. "Future extraditions are limited to exceptional cases and staff responsibility thereof is that of the Legal Division," Straight wrote. Records of the War Crimes Group that relate to the extradition program were delivered to the Legal Division in February 1948.

Straight's report provides a succinct history of the War Crimes Group and ends with five specific recommendations and a surprisingly brief conclusion. He began by suggesting that a "central recording agency" be created following a situation similar to the conclusion of World War II when alleged war crimes must be investigated. There was a "dire need," he wrote, for the existence of

> an effective central agency for the recording of information as to names, physical description and other pertinent data as to wanted war criminal suspects and witnesses to war crimes, the dissemination of information as to such wanted individuals to the pertinent agencies of the nations concerned, the recording of information as to the installations in which such individuals are detained, and the dissemination of such detention information.

Straight cautioned that such an agency must not be "burdened with any additional functions" if it is expected to give "adequate and sufficiently prompt service, irrespective of the type and quality of facilities and personnel available to it." Straight argued for the prompt development of cases in the second point of his conclusions.

> The only opportune time for the collection of evidence ... and the apprehension of perpetrators of war crimes is soon after their commission. Sources of evidence must be exploited before they are dissipated. Witnesses must be interrogated and perpetrators must be apprehended and detained before they are scattered.

Such favorable circumstances for the prosecution of war crimes can be achieved, Straight believed, if a particularly bold suggestion were followed. "Experienced lawyer investigators," he wrote, "must follow close behind the advancing armies in such numbers as to ensure prompt development of cases." Straight emphasized that these investigators must be lawyers. "This work of gathering the sworn testimony of witnesses for actual presentation to war crimes tribunals is not investigative work, as that phrase is ordinarily used, and should be done by experienced lawyers."

Straight's third recommendation called for the "centralized detention of war criminal suspects and unfriendly witnesses. Centralized detention," he maintained, "is essential to the efficient and expeditious development of evidence in war crimes cases" and noted that, during hostilities, "prisoners of war thus detained need not be deprived of the rights to which they would otherwise be entitled under the Prisoners of War Convention." Straight concluded this recommendation with a rare loose end. "Concern as to reprisals on the part of the enemy should not serve as a deterrent to such a congregation" of war criminal suspects and unfriendly witnesses, he stated, but offered no suggestions as to how such reprisals can be averted.

The fourth recommendation dealt with the need for the centralization of operational responsibility. The experiences of the War Crimes Group demonstrated that

> not much can be expected from other agencies or individual officers or soldiers, excluding the victims of heinous crimes, in the making of "Reports of War Crimes." It is impractical to assign investigation and apprehension responsibilities to agencies already burdened with assigned primary missions. Effective combat operations are of such dominant interest to the commanders of lower commands and tactical units, as well as personnel thereof, during operations against the enemy that it is futile to expect personnel under the operational control of such commands to receive effective direction and support. The same is true as to war crimes personnel under the operational control of subordinate commands during an occupation period. All aspects of a war crimes operation, including the imperativeness of centralized correlation and continuous reanalysis [sic] of evidence procured, dictates that there be centralized operational control and direction of the mission and the personnel working thereon. Otherwise, progress is haphazard, attention is not focused on cases of comparative major importance susceptible of development for successful prosecution, and trials are not held promptly.

Straight's final conclusion was simple and straightforward. "The centralized operational directive," he wrote, "can best be carried out through a unit similar to 7708 War Crimes commanded by the officer having initial responsibility for the legal aspects of the operation and the preparation of the basic reviews as to records of trial." Straight obviously regarded the 7708 War Crimes Group as having succeeded in its mission.

The report concluded with three brief recommendations. "Advance planning, together with the organizing and staffing of the Judge Advocate's war crimes unit responsible for all aspects of the mission in advance of the opening of a theater of operations," Straight wrote, "is essential." His second recommendation appears rather mundane but evidently reflected two sources of major annoyance for the 7708 War Crimes Group. "A war crimes unit of this type should be relieved of a maximum amount of housekeeping responsibilities," Straight wrote, "and care should be exercised in advance of and during the operation to assure that it receives adequate administrative and supply support." Straight's final recommendation concerned the operational framework of a war crimes unit. "By agreement of nations," he stated, "there should be a general recodification of the law of war incorporating recognized principles as applied and elaborated upon in recent trials."

The text of *Report of the Deputy Judge Advocate for War Crimes, European Command* is followed by seven pages of footnote references and appendices. No mere summation, however meticulous, does the report justice. It deserves to be read in its entirety.

4

Bill Kasich

*A Nineteen-Year-Old
in Post-War Germany*

DURING THE COURSE OF our interviews at my book shop, Bill Kasich always arrived with voluminous material that related to his work with the War Crimes Group. One photocopied article, titled "7708 War Crimes Leaves Augsburg for Freising" that he brought to our first interview, provided a succinct overview of the group and its mission. The newspaper in which the article had been published wasn't identified on the photocopy, nor was the date of the edition included. From the content of the article, however, it is easy to construe that the newspaper was a U.S. Army periodical produced in Augsburg, Germany, and the article appeared in mid–July of 1947. There were obviously several holes in the original copy of the article, and two paragraphs were fragmentary. The first two paragraphs state:

> The War Crimes Group departed from Augsburg Tuesday, July 10, to set up their new headquarters in Freising. The Group has been in Augsburg since November 20th, 1946, having moved to the Arras Kaserne here from Wiesbaden. The entire Group moved to Freising, with the exception of the Wac [sic] Medical Detachment, which departed for Frankfurt.
>
> The Group was activated in November 1946 with personnel absorbed from the USFET [United States Forces European Theater] War Crimes Group.

The article further states the Group "is comprised mainly of specially trained men and women who have been considered experts in their lines" as civilians. Their duties in the Group "range from typists to highly trained professional investigators and lawyers." The reporter described the Group as

> perhaps the most unusual unit in the entire United States Army because of its functions. It is actually carrying on the "second phase of the war," so to speak, and is trying to exact the "winning of the peace" insofar as apprehending and trying war criminals is concerned.

> The duties of the 7708 War Crimes Group are gigantic when it is recalled that the results of the trials will greatly determine the fate of the future Germany, all Europe, and the world.

This reporter only slightly exaggerated the importance of the work performed by Bill Kasich, who was still in his teens at the time, and the other members of the War Crimes Group. He also noted, "Another unique feature of the 7708 Group is its foreign liaison detachments from virtually every European country, who work hand-in-hand with U.S. authorities in the prosecution of Allied war criminals." Kasich confirmed this international connection in one of our interviews. The building that housed the War Crimes Group had three floors, he told me. "We had two floors and the third floor was liaison." Kasich noted. "Officers from other countries: Poles, British and others. The French didn't have any (office) there. I think they had a separate building."

I observed that many history buffs and even some professional historians are unfamiliar with the work of the War Crimes Group, so much of its work must have been of a sensitive nature. "Yeah," Kasich replied, "they don't even know who we are. Everything was secret, top-secret." A bit later during this first interview, he told me, "I had three stamps: confidential; secret and top-secret. I used the top-secret more often than the secret." In a later interview, Kasich described a typical work day.

> We prepared all of the briefs and gave them to our prosecutors. I'm not taking pride, but I do know more than any prosecutor who tried these cases because we looked at every document that went through. We worked from eight o'clock to, I think it was, five-thirty: eight and a half hours. Most of the other divisions had an hour for lunch. Apprehension and Clearance Section was given orders. We went to the cafeteria and came right back. We came [to work] before everybody else. We worked half a day on Saturday to prepare all of these cases.

I asked whether the War Crimes Group did all the legwork. "We did all of this. Yes, yes," Kasich replied. "And we had to prepare. When Nuremberg called, we had to send them documents."

During one of our interviews, I asked Kasich about this brief encounter with one of the most powerful men in the Third Reich—Hermann Göring. "I can still visualize his eyes. Scared eyes. He was scared to die." Kasich, who recalled that he sat in seat #80 in the courtroom, gave me this account of his five-word message to Göring.

> And I looked at him and said, "You son of a bitch!" Then he looked at me and frowned a bit. He looked at me. Then he looked away, then he looked back up again and I said the same thing to him: "You son of a bitch!" And he knew English.

Göring also made quite an impression on Ralph Schulz, according to a memoir he contributed to the Nashville [TN] Holocaust Memorial. Schulz regarded Göring as delusional and believed "everyone there would just snap to attention, follow his orders, and accept his testimony." Göring "genuinely believed he had served the German people with honor." Schulz would later tell me that Holocaust survivors who were present at Göring's trial surely found it difficult to hear the testimony. Nonetheless, "there was healing for them, too," since they could see that Göring had been "brought to justice."

Bill Kasich, proud member of the 7708 War Crimes Group (courtesy Bill Kasich).

Kasich's contempt for the Nazi war criminals prosecuted at Nuremberg and Dachau didn't include the desire to see them executed, however. When I asked whether he had witnessed any executions, Kasich replied:

> I refused twice. No, three times. The French asked me because I was well-known for what I did for Nuremberg. I sent the massacre of Dubno to them [the Nuremberg prosecutors]. And the French asked me to witness shootings. And I refused because I'd learned that even then as young as I was that human life is worth everything. It was what I would term sacred. And even if you're guilty, I'm against the death penalty. My wife isn't, but I am. Because for the simple reason, I know they deserve it but you're still taking a life. And then they asked me at Nuremberg if I would be a witness [at the executions] at Nuremberg because of the office [7708 War Crimes Group]. Now it was [Col. Clio] Straight that sent in the fellow that asked me. He said, "Would you like to witness the hanging at Nuremberg?" I said no. Now maybe I should have gone, but I saw the pictures when they came back. It was horrible. Just the pictures. Von Ribbentrop was the one that took it

the hardest. He had his tongue out. His eyes bulged. And you know he wanted to live, but they took his life. They were cremated and we don't know where their ashes were dumped because at that time, they thought they [Nazi sympathizers] would make a shrine out of it.

As horrible as were the photographs of the dead war criminals that Kasich saw, the executions themselves were ten times more grisly. In his article, "The Nuremberg Hangings—Not So Smooth Either," Tom Zeller, Jr., of the *New York Times* quoted Donald E. Wilkes, Jr., a professor of law at the University of Georgia Law School, who noted that many of the condemned men fell through the trap door of the gallows with insufficient force to break their necks, which caused them to suffer slow, agonizing deaths from strangulation.

Ribbentrop and Sauckel each took 14 minutes to choke to death, Wilkes wrote, while Keitel took 24 minutes to die. Wilkes chides Master Sgt. John C. Woods, the U.S. Army's "experienced" hangman for botching the executions. If Wilkes had conducted a bit more research, however, he would have discovered that Woods's experience as a hangman had been grossly exaggerated—by Woods himself.

Born in Wichita, Kansas, in 1911, John C. Woods had joined the U.S. Navy in 1929. He deserted a few months later, only to be apprehended and court-martialed. Before being dismissed by the navy, Woods was examined by a medical board that concluded Woods was "obviously poor service material." This board diagnosed Woods as suffering from "Constitutional Psychopathic Inferiority Without Psychosis." Woods's problems with accepting responsibility and obeying authority continued. He joined the Civilian Conservation Corps in 1933 but was dishonorably discharged that same year for refusing to work and being AWOL for six days.

Inducted into the army in 1943, Woods lied about having experience as an assistant hangman in the United States. The army never bothered to check his claims and made Woods a hangman, in which capacity he served as either the primary or assistant hangman in the executions of over thirty U.S. soldiers who had been sentenced to death. Army records indicate that Woods bungled at least eleven of these hangings. After the war, Woods was indeed given the responsibility of hanging Nazi war criminals, including the most prominent Nazis convicted at Nuremberg. He also served as the hangman at Landsberg prison, where those convicted at the Dachau trials were executed.

Ironically, Woods's bungling led to his own death in 1950 while stationed at the Marshall Islands. He was accidentally electrocuted while trying to repair an engineer lighting set. Woods took great pride in his role as the world's most famous hangman and often inflated the number of hangings in which he had participated.

Göring met death at Nuremberg, but not at the end of a hangman's rope. He committed suicide by taking a cyanide capsule in his cell. Historians for decades have speculated how Göring acquired the capsule. Some considered the possibility that he had always had it with him, hidden in a hollow tooth or within a dental crown. Others thought the poison had somehow been slipped to him by a Nazi attendant, who could have concealed it in a bar of soap. Göring's wife was also a suspect. She could have concealed the capsule in her mouth and slipped it to him during a farewell kiss when she last visited him before his scheduled execution.

The mystery was supposedly solved in 2005 when 78-year-old Herbert Lee Stivers, who had been an army guard assigned to watch Göring during the Nuremberg trials, told the *Los Angeles Times* that he had delivered the fatal capsule to Göring. As a nineteen-year-old Army private, Stivers had been one of the U.S. soldiers who escorted the defendants in and out of the courtroom and stood behind them during the trials. Stivers had struck up a friendship with Göring, who spoke reasonably good English, and the two of them talked about sports and Charles Lindbergh, the famous American aviator, who Göring had come to know before the war.

Stivers, like many American GIs, had a German girlfriend, Hildegarde Bruner, to whom he gave candy bars, peanuts and cigarettes, which she and her mother sold on the black market. One day outside a hotel that housed an officers' club, Stivers was approached by a beautiful woman who began flirting with him. The woman, who said her name was Mona, asked Stivers if he got to see the prisoners. He replied yes and proved it by showing her his autograph of Baldur von Schirach, one of the war crimes defendants. The flirtatious woman asked if she could have it. Stivers eagerly forked it over. He obtained Göring's autograph the next day for his new girlfriend. She told Stivers that she had a friend who wanted to meet him. "The following day," Stivers told the *Los Angeles Times* reporter, "we went to his house." Stivers said that he met two men in this house, who gave their names as Erich and Mathias. They told him that Göring was a very sick man who wasn't being given the medicine he needed. Stivers twice smuggled notes from these men to Göring. The notes were hidden in a fountain pen.

One day Erich gave Stivers a capsule to pass along to Göring. Erich purportedly told Stivers that it was medicine and, if it worked, they would give him additional capsules to smuggle to Göring. Stivers did as he was told. Two weeks after receiving this "medicine," just hours before his scheduled execution on October 15, 1946, Göring committed suicide by poisoning himself with a cyanide capsule—presumably the "medicine" that had been smuggled to him by the hapless Stivers.

Suspicion never fell on the young GI, who was never interrogated by Army intelligence but merely asked if he had observed anything suspicious. Stivers told the media in 2005 that he "wasn't thinking of suicide when I took it to Göring" since he hadn't seemed especially despondent, despite facing death by hanging. "I would never have knowingly taken something that I thought was going to be used to help someone cheat the gallows," Stivers said. Although an Army investigation concluded that Göring must have had the cyanide all along, Stivers believed that the "medicine" he smuggled to the Nazi must have been the poison.

Not everyone was convinced by Stivers's confession. The British historian Ann Tusa, author of *The Nuremberg Trial*, noted that several people have stepped forward over the years to claim involvement in Göring's suicide. Tusa said that Stivers's account was "possible but I would be cautious."

Stivers's insistence that three German nationals manipulated him into facilitating Göring's suicide in order to save him the ignominy of death by hanging at the hands of the victorious Allies in no way should detract from the credibility of his narrative. As we shall see later, there was an active—and, at times, deadly—Nazi underground in post-war Germany.

Kasich's mention of the Dubno Massacre merits elaboration. Telford Taylor, chief counsel of the American team of prosecutors at Nuremberg, included an account of this atrocity in his memoir *The Anatomy of the Nuremberg Trials*. In one of our interviews, Kasich referred to a Hermann Graebe, a German civilian contractor who witnessed the massacre and made affidavits that were introduced as evidence at Nuremberg. "His [Graebe's] choice of words is so powerful it makes you cry," Kasich told me. Taylor extensively cited Graebe's eyewitness testimony of the murder of some 5,000 Jews by the SS and German-allied Ukrainian militiamen in the Dubno community of German-occupied Ukraine. Graebe's account of family members forced to strip naked and bidding each other farewell with a few words and a kiss can indeed make one cry.

Jews were forced to walk a few steps into a vast pit that became their mass grave. They were then shot. Graebe stated that this pit was already about two-thirds full when he saw it and estimated that it contained approximately 1,000 bodies. He heard no pleas for mercy. The Jews knew that they could expect no mercy from the SS and their Ukrainian allies. Some of the Jews in the pit who had already been shot were still moving, according to Graebe. They showed their murderers that they were still alive by lifting their arms and moving their heads. SS personnel directed about twenty Jews at a time to enter the pit. Each new contingent of victims laid down among the bullet-riddled bodies and awaited death. Graebe recalled that those who were about to die often caressed those who had been shot but were still alive while speaking words of comfort to them. The shooting was done by a member of the SS who sat on the edge of the pit and wielded a submachine gun. The SS man casually dangled his feet into the pit and smoked a cigarette while he went about his work.

Hartley Shawcross, the British chief prosecutor at Nuremberg who had earlier secured the convictions of John Amery and William ("Lord Haw Haw") Joyce for treason, read from Graebe's account of the Dubno Massacre during his opening statement. Göring became so angry that he tore off his earphones so that he could no longer hear the interpreter's translation.

I mentioned to Kasich that I recently had heard Whitney Harris (1912–2010), one of the Nuremberg prosecutors, speak at the Ethical Society of St. Louis. Harris had told the audience that the ashes of the executed war criminals were dumped into a river, possibly the Isar. Kasich replied that the speculation when he was in Germany was that it was the Danube. He expressed regret at having not taken me up on my invitation to attend Harris's address. "I'd like to talk to him someday," Kasich said. "See, he has a different perspective because he was at Nuremberg. And I have a wider perspective of it because we handled all the mass murders, the killings, the concentration camps."

I asked Kasich if he had served in World War II. "No," he replied. "I was drafted in 1945. I was in a troop movement in Camp Roberts [located in California] and my papers went to the Pentagon and the Pentagon assigned me to the Judge Advocate division." When I asked about what kind special training he had been given. I was surprised when he replied, "Nothing. No special training at all." Before being drafted, Kasich had been a student at the University of Illinois and played on its football team. He completed his education after leaving the army and embarked on a career as a teacher at a grade school in Litchfield.

I inquired how many suspected Nazi war criminal cases were investigated by the 7708.

> There were about 50,000 we had to go through.... And there were millions of papers and documents. Of course I didn't go through that many. I went through thousands and thousands [including] wanted reports. We had the responsibility to assist Nuremberg. Now that [the proceedings at Nuremberg] was a piece of cake as far work goes because everything was funneled to them and all they had to do was go through the papers and find what was relevant. Now that's the reason I was transferred to Apprehension and Clearance Section because the noise coming from Nuremberg that we weren't doing our job. I was assigned to Ralph Morgan's outfit, which was the Apprehensive and Clearance Section.

Kasich again contrasted the War Crimes Group with Nuremberg in a later interview. He stated:

> And because Nuremberg, as far as I am aware, they didn't do any of the screening and all the documents were sent to them. They didn't have a force like we had. Actually, Nuremberg was a piece of cake compared to what we were doing because we were doing the nitty-gritty. All of the hard stuff. We did all of the investigating and made sure we had the right person.

"You were responsible for making both sets of trials happen?" I asked in surprise. "Yes. And no one questioned us. If someone was to be detained, you put your initials on it [the document authorizing detention]. And they went to detention. Detention would look up to see if they were already detained in prison, some [other] confinement, and then it would come back to us and we would make the wanted reports and send out copies."

During our first interview, I asked about the apprehension of war crimes suspects. "John Cashman, one of our agents, he talked to more German generals than anyone else. It's a shame he's dead—he died in 1982—because he knew so much. Every morning, when he was in the office, he and three colonels would have a meeting and John did all the dirty work. Out in the field, transporting criminals."

Kasich mentioned Cashman during our second interview as well. "He [Cashman] told me that sometimes they give up very easily. He remembered one time he went into this farmhouse and he [the suspect] got his coat, kissed his wife and he went willingly. Some of them committed suicide as soon as they knew we [War Crimes Group personnel] were coming. Then, some shot it out."

John Cashman once asked Kasich to take a ride with him. Kasich had no idea why but accepted the invitation. They went down a country lane and Cashman told the driver to turn right.

> We came down to a little ravine and there was a factory there making signs. [Cashman] knew. He had been there before. Then he said, "We're going to take

a respite." So he took out his .25 [semi-automatic pistol] and he shot at a tree.... I told him, "John, I'm hungry. We've got to get going. What the hell are you doing here?" He said, "Oh, we're going to take a little rest."

I knew that the standard military sidearm at that time was the Colt Model 1911A1, which was a .45 semi-automatic pistol, and asked Kasich whether Cashman had a .25 or .45.

25. He kept it in his boot all the time. I said, "What do you keep that in your boot for?" He said, "If I get into a situation, that's for me." When he was going to blow his brains out because he didn't want to suffer. They [the Nazi underground] knew who he was. They knew who I was. Because the girls would always when I was walking down the street say, "Hi, Bill!" They would smile and they were beautiful girls.... I was leery because I knew what they were up to. But John took chances. So we stayed there for a while.... I was hungry [and] said, "What the hell! I'm going to see what I can find to eat." And I was so darn hungry that I took a big turnip and I started gnawing on it.

Kasich grew increasingly impatient during what he saw as a pointless excursion.

I said, "John, let's get the hell out of here." He said, "No, wait a little while." So he said, "It's time to go." We got in, turned around and went up the hill to the first right. He ... told the jeep driver, "Stop right here." I said, "Why?" He said, "We've got a flat tire." I looked and said, "John, you don't have a flat tire." He said, "Keep your mouth shut and follow orders." And he said, "Put a clip in your .45." So I slipped a clip in the .45 and he told the driver to change the tire.

Kasich and Cashman approached a nearby house.

"...three beautiful girls came out." They said, "What do you want?" He [Cashman] said, "I want to know if you've got a jack. We've got a flat tire." So the father came out. By the way, you knew he was a military man by his mannerisms and everything else. And he said, "We don't have a jack." So the driver said, "John, I got it fixed." So I walked off and that was a mistake, turning my back on him. But I didn't know what was going on. John, didn't tell me, which was stupid on his part. And after coming home, after years and years, I said [to myself], "What the hell! He [Cashman] was casing the place. He was going to come back to see if the guy was home because they were going to pick him up [as] a war criminal." And I'm quite sure that the guy knew what was going on.

While Kasich never participated in the apprehension of war crimes suspects, he "went three times to deliver prisoners because we were short of help." During another interview, Kasich suddenly stopped reading from some material that he had been sharing with me to narrate an incident that he regarded as indicative of how some Germans had been capable of compartmentalizing their minds during World War II.

> We [members of the 7708 War Crimes Group] went to Paderborn, [in] the British sector, to pick up [General Alfred] Jodl's outfit. We ate with the English at that time. I don't know if it's changed now but the privates had to eat with the privates, the corporals with the corporals and so on. Well anyway, the next day.... I was on a [truck] with Jodl. We had to have an officer [sign the necessary paperwork] before they [the British] would release a prisoner to the Americans for transport. The papers had to be signed by an officer.... I was assigned to this one with Jodl in the back of the truck. But as we were loading, I think it was about five prisoners pointed to themselves and said to me, "Kultured. Kultured." Thinking just because they were cultured, they read the right poetry or saw the right play or the right book, that this would be an excuse to free them.

While making this journey with the Americans, Jodl was angered by the Allied destruction of a particular town. "Jodl spotted the town and he looked at me and he said, 'Schweinehund Amerikans!' American pig-dogs. We bombed his city [in] Germany. While he was on the Eastern Front, they [Jodl's troops] burned villages and towns. Just burned them completely."

Kasich wasn't intimidated by Jodl's rank or reputation and responded to the insult.

> And I looked at him and I leaned to him and I said, "I had nothing to do with it." And I had an M-1 rifle [the standard American military rifle of that era], no bullets in it. And they [Jodl and the other prisoners] knew I didn't have any bullets in it. So I looked at the other men and they kind of smiled to hear me talking that way, talking back to a German officer. Even in surrender, they wouldn't dare talk that way to a general. But, to me, he was just another human being. And I didn't have any trouble with him. None whatsoever. And they [Jodl and the other prisoners] could have thrown me out of the back of that truck at any time they wanted to. But they didn't.

I asked if they offered no resistance because they knew it would have been futile. Kasich replied, "Well, they could have got orders from him [Jodl] to behave themselves." Kasich theorized that Jodl never suspected that he actually would be prosecuted as a war criminal, since his military background would have made him a valuable asset to the Americans when relations with the Soviets began to sour. If that indeed was Jodl's assumption, he was badly mistaken.

Alfred Jodl (1890–1946) had served as an officer during World War I and remained in the German army following the war. As the operations chief of the German armed forces during World War II, Jodl carried out Hitler's notorious Commissar Order, which the Führer issued on June 6, 1941, just before the German army invaded the Soviet Union. The order stated, in part:

> The [German] troops must be aware that: (1) In this battle, mercy or consideration of international law is false. They [communist commissars] are a danger to our own safety and the rapid pacification of the conquered territories. (2) The originators of barbaric, Asiatic methods of warfare are the political commissars. So immediate and unhesitatingly severe measures must be taken against them. They are therefore, when captured in battle, as a matter of routine to be dispatched by firearms.

The order noted that the commissars could be easily identified by "their special badge—a red star with a woven hammer and sickle on the sleeves." When captured by German troops, the commissars were to be "separated from the prisoners of war immediately.... When they have been separated, they are to be finished off."

Jodl also carried out the Commando Order, which Hitler signed on October 18, 1942. The Commando Order specified that Allied commandos operating in Europe and Africa. The order stated, in part:

> I [Hitler] order therefore:—From now on all men operating against German troops in so-called Commando raids in Europe or in Africa are to be annihilated to the last man.... To hold them in military custody—for example, in P.O.W. camps, etc.—even if it is only a temporary measure, is strictly forbidden.

While Jodl showed no mercy for commissars and commandos, he undoubtedly saved the lives of many German troops during the last days of the war. Grand Admiral Karl Dönitz, Hitler's successor, had instructed Jodl to drag out Germany's negotiations with Eisenhower's deputies for as long as possible. This tactic allowed large numbers of German soldiers to flee Soviet forces, from whom they could expect no mercy, and surrender to the American and British armies. Eisenhower, who was aware of why Jodl was stalling, finally demanded that the German general sign the instrument of surrender or he would seal the Western front. Jodl scrawled his signature at 2:28 a.m. on May 7, 1945. According to Joseph E. Persico in *Nuremberg: Prelude to Judgment*, Jodl later learned that his foot-dragging had allowed over 900,000 German soldiers to escape the Soviets.

Jodl's anger at American military personnel that Kasich observed stands in stark contrast to his rationalization for following Hitler's commissar and commando orders. While imprisoned and awaiting trial, Jodl was interviewed by Augustus "Gus" Gilbert, the prison psychologist who talked with the Nuremberg defendants in an effort to understand how men who had been judged clinically sane could engage in such acts of barbarism. For Jodl, orders were orders. Had he disobeyed Hitler's orders, Jodl told Gilbert, he would have been arrested—and rightly so, he added. Jodl was utterly baffled that Gilbert as well as the Allied prosecutors and judges couldn't grasp the simple fact that disobeying orders hadn't been an option for him. It evidently never occurred to him that the "Schweinehund Amerikans" who had wrought such destruction on Germany during the war had merely been, like himself, soldiers following orders and therefore undeserving of his hatred.

Gilbert asked Jodl about the death camps. The general claimed to have had little knowledge of what occurred within their walls and professed to be horrified upon learning the full story. According to Persico, Jodl asked Gilbert what kind of beasts could have committed such acts. Gilbert replied that the concentration camp atrocities had been committed by Germans obeying orders.

Jodl remained unrepentant during his trial and declared in his final statement to the court that the Wehrmacht had served the German people and their fatherland. He felt no shame and would leave the courtroom with his head held high, regardless of the court's verdict. True to his word, Jodl indeed left his head high after being found guilty on all counts: criminal conspiracy; waging aggressive war; war crimes; and crimes against humanity. He was hanged on October 16, 1946.

5

Ralph Schulz
Seminarian Turned Record Keeper

BILL KASICH PROVIDED ME with the names of several veterans of the War Crimes Group who were willing to share their experiences with me. Ralph Schulz had relatives living in Alton, so I thought it quite feasible that I might have the chance to interview him at some future date. I dropped him an e-mail to introduce myself and we began a correspondence. In an e-mail dated 5/8/01, Schulz wrote, in part:

> My time with the War Crimes Trials Group was not [as] spectacular as Bill Kasich's, although I feel it was most interesting and a great opportunity for a 20-year old guy interested in the world's affairs at the time. I intend to document whatever I send you, but all my documentation is in Louisville [Kentucky], and I have not been there since we first talked. Hence my obvious reticence and slow response.
>
> We had very limited resources and personnel. All our commissioned officers were Majors and above because of their standing in the legal profession. Therefore we noncoms were assigned jobs far above our duties in the TO [table of organization]. For instance, many of the duties I was assigned were supposed to be discharged by a Captain. We had almost no Captains or Lieutenants, so Sergeants like me were pressed into service.

Schulz was quite frank in his criticism of the army brass.

> In addition, many (I am inclined to say MOST) upper-level personnel on site at that time were more interested in pursuing the opportunities of our role as "victors," than in mundane duties. Time was short for everyone, so alert persons used their time and resources to exploit more obvious opportunities whenever possible. Duty was not the PRIMARY concern for everyone with other promising opportunities, so those of us who didn't share upper-level opportunities had the privilege of enacting roles and duties normally reserved for higher ranks. We did our jobs well because we were proud to be part of an important job, and we had been chosen because we had proven to be serious and successful in prior assignments.

He alluded to some of his responsibilities with the War Crimes Group and then concluded, "Those simple facts tell you something about our personnel shortages in Germany at that time and the obsession of our commissioned officers ... in pursuit of their advantages which we rarely shared." Schulz claimed he didn't particularly mind.

> However, I was very happy to pursue my duties, take my pictures and movies, and bask in the Swiss pastries and travel advantages of my limited roles. I had easy promotions, exposure to travel and important events and freedom to indulge my interests. I had come to the Army directly from a Catholic seminary, where I studied for the priesthood for five years, so I was little interested in the temptations of the flesh, and most interested in my engrossing work.

Schulz never mentioned during any of our subsequent communications whether his experiences in the War Crimes Group played a role in his decision not to continue his studies for the Catholic priesthood upon returning to the United States following his discharge.

He closed his e-mail by saying that he was "interested in helping ... but I want to document what i [*sic*] say. I hope we have the opportunity to visit in person when I have corroborating evidence at hand, but I cannot promise even that for the moment." Schulz noted that he was "an unwell grandfather of twenty" and had "duties which are both demanding and important to me and my family.... Please consider my intentions rather than my performance. I will do what I can."

I received another e-mail from Schulz on May 5, 2002, that confirmed that Myron Smith, a veteran of the War Crimes Group who had been extremely active in organizing its reunions, had died of cancer. "Yes, unfortunately Smitty died of cancer during January [of 2002]," Schulz wrote. "He was the glue that brought us together after half a century, and spent all of his energies in retirement on our behalf." He closed his e-mail in a manner that indicated he would share his memories with me.

> We are dwindling away, and we are as eager as anyone to keep some memories alive. My family and I are arranging to preserve any items I have, but most are simply pictures, 8mm movies of inconsequential workday items, sports, etc. We were there, but our exposure to matters of state were very limited. I wish you well in your endeavors.

I finally had the opportunity to interview Ralph Schulz on July 30, 2002, when he visited his relatives in Alton, Illinois. It was our only interview. I began by asking Schulz what was his theory as to why he and the other men were selected for service with the War Crimes Group. "We've discussed it many times," he replied. "Smitty's theory was that we were superior intellect." The members of the 7708 possessed IQs "over 130 and Smitty's theory was that we were selected on that basis." I asked about other theories.

> One of the young men ... his duties were the simplest. He sat at a typing table and people brought him reports. And he typed them and passed them on. His theory was that we were there because we all knew how to type. Now that's one extreme to the other. But it is true that we all knew how to type and it is true that we all had some administrative experience. Our educational experiences were very diverse. I had one year of college and the beginning of a second year when I went in.

Schulz was a sergeant and his duties included the monumental task of transporting all war crimes files from Wiesbaden to Augsburg. "My duty, for which I have the orders still, was to take all our files," which took eighteen trucks to hold. The files were covered by tarps because "no one was supposed to know what was in there." Schulz's service with the War Crimes Group included duty that surely equaled the responsibility for safely transporting all those files. He worked with the documentary crews that filmed the trials at the Hall of Justice in Nuremberg. The crews always had a great deal of blank film left over, he told me, and he was able to use it to make brief films himself. Schulz recalled that there was a darkroom in the Red Cross building, which was located near the courthouse in Wiesbaden. The mention of this darkroom kindled a memory that puts the Red Cross in a rather negative light.

A young German who had been through the denazification process worked as a technician in this darkroom. Schulz recalled him as being quite gaunt. "He had a wife and child," Schulz said, and slept in an overcoat because he had no blanket. "We had a pile of blankets half the size of this room," Schulz affirmed—and our interview was conducted in a rather large room. "Many of them tattered by field use and this man had nothing." Schulz was "almost sent home" when he took pity on this young German and gave him one of the army's old blankets. "I was lectured by one of the Red Cross women that it was disloyal for me to give him a blanket," he said. The German "helped us immensely. He was a full-time paid attendant and they couldn't find anyone else to hire who had been cleared by the courts," Schulz told me. "So they didn't fire him but they did reprimand me for giving him the blanket."

Schulz shared another memory that placed the Red Cross in a more favorable light. During the Christmas season of 1946, he said, he helped to organize parties for "our German kids," as he called them. These parties, which included "lots of activities" for children, were held in one of the Red Cross buildings.

Like many other American military personnel, Schulz had German roots. One of Schulz's grandparents had been born in Germany and his father had asked him to do some genealogical research while he was stationed in that country. His father had been "very disappointed when I didn't find anything," he recalled. Schulz's possessed a working knowledge of the German language, which put him in demand as an interpreter. Talking about Germans who provided testimony regarding war crimes, he recalled: "Those were not people who were given to making up stories because they were scared for their lives. And many of them [the witnesses] that we worked with were so scared. They would not have lied to us because they were afraid. We were SS people to them. That's the way they identified us."

Schulz meant that the German people, after living under Nazi tyranny, had come to look upon anyone occupying a position of authority over them as a potential threat, who held their lives in the balance. Germans who were taken into custody by the War Crimes Group merely to be interviewed often became panic-stricken because they assumed they were being taken to their deaths. Schulz recalled seeing German villages from hilltops and they would appear to be bustling with activity. When they entered the village, however, "all the shutters would close. You'd drive through the town and there was nobody there.... The witnesses didn't know what we were there for and one of the reasons I was sent on these missions was because I spoke a little German."

Schulz would speak to the witnesses they wished to take into custody merely for questioning in an attempt to calm them down. He told them not to worry. "You're not going to be accused of anything," he reassured them. Schulz's words were generally in vain, however. He began to say "But they didn't believe us most of the time" but stopped his sentence after "most" and finished it as "any of the time." He recalled the witnesses' families "were all wailing and carrying on" and were always overjoyed when this family member was returned to them unharmed after being questioned by war crimes investigators.

He recalled one witness who proved to be especially difficult after being taken into custody.

> I had one man try to commit suicide on me one night. [He] set fire to his mattress. I was captain of the guard that night. In the middle of the night they called me [because] he had set fire to the mattress. He was locked in a cell ... for his own

safety. We had to get in there to put out the fire. We opened up the jail cell and he came at us with a knife as long as six inches. Didn't know where and how he got it.

The knife-wielding man was "just a witness, not a suspect," Schulz emphasized. Evidently, "he didn't understand that."

Schulz wasn't reluctant to talk about the military personnel of the other Allied nations. "The Russians always stayed to themselves," he stated. He also strongly implied that the USSR, which had suffered such devastation at the hands of the Third Reich, desired vengeance, not justice. "The Russians wanted to kill everybody," he told me. "They didn't want us to have anybody [in custody awaiting trial for war crimes]. If we had a suspect, we had to be careful not to let him be encountered by the Russians." Schulz recalled that the British also "stayed to themselves a lot." This veteran was unwavering in his criticism of the French. "It sounds bad today but nobody had any respect for the French." I asked whether the French were unprofessional.

> Yeah, and everybody had a concerted attitude that they were dirty and unkempt. Didn't take care of their quarters. The English were just the opposite—took pride in everything. The French, all they wanted to do was drink and carry on. They were off by themselves and that's the way they wanted it. We felt like they didn't have any real pride.

He also shared some colorful memories of the Polish Guard:

> We all feared the Polish Guard so much that we didn't even give them ammunition. They were really something else. We had a full platoon of them at Dachau to guard the outside. Each one had one cartridge. They were supposed to fire them into the air to alert the guard if something happened. They fired them indiscriminately. We feared them more than we feared the Germans.

The Polish Guard was a paramilitary unit that was formed by the U.S. Army after World War II. It consisted of Polish refugees who had fled their homeland after its occupation by the Soviet Union. According to Wojciech Jerzy Muszynski's "The Polish Guard Companies of the U.S. Army After World War II," the creation of the guard served a dual purpose. It gave employment to refugees who were often destitute and enabled the demobilization of thousands of U.S. soldiers, since Polish Guard members could be used to serve as guards at prison camps, army offices, warehouses and other sites that required security. Muszynski noted that many Polish Guard members as well as Polish leaders in exile hoped that the guard would serve as the nucleus of a "Polish Legion" that would fight alongside the United States in the event of a war with the Soviet Union.

I recalled Schulz's statement, quoted in the *Telegraph* article, about how after so many years he could "still remember the smell of the remains of the innocent people who were killed at Dachau" and asked him to describe the odor. "I would describe it as very heavy, almost stifling," he answered. "And when you went in the front entrance ... it was the worst. You went past there as quick as you could." Schulz and other military personnel found another scent in the vicinity that temporarily took their minds off the stench of Dachau. "There was a little place that had bakery goods on the way to Dachau and we used to go there and it was kind of"— Schulz paused for a moment as he searched for the right words—"it would get us out of some of that atmosphere." He recalled, "They [the bakery's staff] didn't like us coming, but we'd buy pastries."

Schulz stated that seeing the graves and crematory at Dachau was one of his two most vivid experiences while serving in the War Crimes Group. His other most memorable experience was a half-hour briefing by the officer to whom he reported. Early in our interview, Schulz remarked, "I reported to a full-bird colonel, believe it or not," who then noted that he had only been a sergeant. A "full bird colonel" is army slang for a full colonel and distinguishes him or her from a lieutenant colonel, which is the rank just below colonel. "Full-bird" refers to the silver eagle insignia worn by a colonel, but not by a lieutenant colonel. Schulz referred to this officer as Colonel Eichmann during our interview but never mentioned his full name. Both Schulz and I remarked that this U.S. officer who had been assigned to a war crimes unit had the same last name as one of the most infamous Nazi war criminals. Research following the interview revealed that the Eichmann to whom Schulz reported was Ottomar W. Eichmann, who served as one of eight American officers who was assigned to preside at the war crimes trial of Otto Skorzeny. Colonel Andrew G. Gardner served as president. According to *Records of United States Army War Crimes Trials; United States of America v. Otto Skorzeny et al.*, the German commando's defense team "challenged Gardner and Eichmann as prejudiced against their case because they felt that these individuals had been specifically selected to achieve convictions and to hand out stiff sentences." The challenge was overruled. While Gardner was indeed a full bird colonel, *Records of United States Army War Crimes Trials; United States of America v. Otto Skorzeny et al.* lists Eichmann as a lieutenant colonel.

The fact that Eichmann wasn't a full bird colonel did nothing to lessen the intensity and impact of the lecture he gave Schulz shortly after his arrival in Germany regarding the importance of the work being performed by the War Crimes Group. Eichmann emphasized the critical importance of the files that contained the documentation of war crimes. Schulz told me that Eichmann stressed the fact that these files contained "the only evidence we had regarding these atrocities." Schulz then noted that "atrocities was the word we used at the time," rather than war crimes. Eichmann made it clear to Schulz that the content of these files made him much more than a mere glorified file clerk. He would be playing a significant role in an important historical event: the prosecution and conviction of defendants accused of having committed atrocities.

"I'm going to make you responsible for those files," Eichmann told Schulz. "That's a heavy responsibility and if we don't keep them right this will go all over the world that we didn't do our job right." By the end of that half hour, Ralph Schulz understood that the eyes of the world were focused on him, a young man who had just completed his first year of college, and he would be held partially responsible if the war crimes trials failed because he hadn't properly maintained the records. Schulz was well-informed when he went to Germany and was aware of the nature and extent of Nazi atrocities. "I knew how bad it was before I got there because I had read enough about it," he told me. "I fully expected what I saw so it didn't actually affect me as much as the responsibility, the duty." The duty to which Schulz was referring, of course, was maintaining those files. "I don't think we ever intentionally destroyed one sheet of paper," he said. "Everything we had went into a file."

Schulz's job with the War Crimes Group ensured that he would have an excellent knowledge of Nazi atrocities. I couldn't resist asking him what he thinks upon reading contemporary writers who deny the Holocaust. Schulz replied that he immediately stops reading the book or article and puts it down. "When they deny the reality that I've seen with my own eyes, I can't take any more of that," he told me. Interesting, Schulz attributed such Holocaust denial to motives other than anti–Semitism or a desire to rehabilitate the reputation of Hitler and Nazi Germany. Such authors, in his opinion, are simply "getting something down on paper that they've been paid to write."

I sent Schulz an e-mail on June 2, 2004, in which I reintroduced myself as "the guy who interviewed you back in 2002 for my book on the War Crimes Group." I explained my long absence by noting that I was going through a messy divorce but still intended to write that book someday. "If there is any additional information you would like to e-mail or snail-mail me," I wrote, "I'd be delighted to hear from you!" Schulz replied to my e-mail just two days later. He expressed sympathy for what he called the "meat grinder" I was going through and closed his missive with two poignant paragraphs.

> WCG [War Crimes Group] has lost a lot of people, and we are down to a few. We have had annual meetings, with this one in California for 2004. Each person has done his own thing on preserving the experience, but few are now capable to recording more. I have recorded conversations with two Nashville groups: Holocaust people and Middle Tennessee University, both of who [*sic*] recorded 90-minute sessions and took photos of us. Haven't done anything else. Keep up the work: there will come a time when no one will be around who knows what WCG is or was!

I never heard from Schulz again. He died in Nashville, Tennessee, on November 10, 2005.

6

The Malmédy Massacre

I ASKED RALPH SCHULZ what he recalled about the Malmédy case, which he described as "more combat-oriented than most of our cases." He remembered "some of the depositions and interviews that they had in the files" and the fact that "these people would brag about the fact that they had done these things." The Malmédy defendants "were proud of it" and "had contempt for the people who were accusing them."

Bill Kasich expressed profound contempt for the Malmédy defendants, especially General Josef "Sepp" Dietrich and Colonel Jochen Peiper. Dietrich served as commander of the Sixth Panzer Army. Peiper commanded *Kampfgrüppe Peiper*—Battle Group Peiper—and spearheaded the Ardennes Offensive, which is popularly known as the Battle of the Bulge.

The accounts of Malmédy Massacre survivors make for harrowing reading. Charles Appman (1919–2013) was driving a truck near Malmédy, when rounds from a German machine gun shattered the windshield. He jumped out but was soon taken prisoner. Appman recalled that he and his fellow American soldiers were robbed of their valuables before being herded into the field. The massacre began when a German shot an American with his pistol. The German then used his pistol to shoot another American. "Then almost immediately they opened with machine-gun fire," Appman said. "I hit the ground with the rest and made believe I was dead. I lay there while they searched the bodies, and I could hear the German laughter with immediate fire at the moaning ones."

While Appman lay on the ground and pretended to be dead, he could hear the Germans firing pistol shots into the wounded. "I could hear them calling, 'Hey Joe, Hey Jim' and then 'wham.' They would give somebody the coup de grace." He tried to hold his breath, since exhaling in the cold air would have alerted the Germans he was alive. The American lying on top of Appman was also still alive. A German finished him off with a bullet. Appman recalled that he felt the man quiver before dying.

Appman might have survived the massacre because of a mystical experience he had while lying among the dead and dying. Fear as well as the bitter cold caused him to shake. Suddenly, Appman saw a bright white light. "I knew it was God, and it calmed me, and I stopped shaking," he said.

When he heard another survivor say, "Come one! Let's get out of here!," Appman rose and began running. The Germans fired on them. Appman's obituary quoted his son as saying, "He could see machine-gun bullets kicking up the snow as they were running. He crawled under a barbed wire fence but got caught by the collar on his shirt. Someone came back and unhooked him." Upon reaching safety, Appman discovered how close he had come to being killed. A bullet had passed through his coat and sweater but missed striking him. Appman's son was quoted in the obituary as saying that his father, while physically unscathed by the Malmédy Massacre, bore psychological scars. "Today they would call it post-traumatic stress disorder," he said. "He just dealt with it. He didn't know what it was."

Stephen Domitrovich was the last living survivor of the Malmédy Massacre when I wrote this book's first edition. He died on October 20, 2019, at age 94. He told a reporter for his local newspaper that he was driving an ambulance in a column of vehicles heading out of Malmédy. The vehicle immediately in front of him was a weapons carrier. When the column came under fire from a German aircraft, he pulled over and jumped into a ditch.

He was captured by a German soldier, who placed his rifle to Domitrovich's head. The 20-year-old GI asked for his rights under the Geneva Convention. It was a cruelly ironic request in light of what soon transpired. "After a while, they walked me up and into a field," Domitrovich recalled. "We had to cross a fence with our hands over our head ... there were 147 of us." A fellow GI described by Domitrovich as a "buddy" said they'd be going to Germany, which seemed to be a logical assumption since the men were now prisoners of war. These Americans had no idea the Germans intended to kill them in cold blood.

When the Germans began shooting their prisoners, Domitrovich heard men crying out, "Mom! God! Mom! God!" Someone told him to fall and he dropped to the ground. The Americans continued to cry out as they were shot. The Germans then walked among the sprawled bodies to finish off the wounded, one of whom was the GI lying next to Domitrovich. The young man was Domitrovich's buddy, who had told him they'd be going to Germany.

"I laid there real quiet and pretty soon a German came up to me," he

6. The Malmédy Massacre

The Malmédy Massacre was the 7708 War Crimes Group's most high-profile case.

told the reporter. "He looked at me." Whether the German thought Domitrovich was dead or took pity on him is unclear. In any event, he didn't shoot the young American. "Why that German left me, I don't know." He told the reporter, "I was praying like mad."

When the Germans departed, Domitrovich and some other survivors left the field and walked to a house, where the Belgian residents directed them to some other Americans. The survivors were taken to a hospital in Liege, Belgium. While hospitalized, he was haunted by memories of his ordeal. Domitrovich recalled "screaming and screaming all night long." He again cheated death. After his release, a German V-1 rocket—popularly referred to as a "buzz bomb"—hit the room where he had been hospitalized.

Upon return to his unit, Domitrovich again drove an ambulance. Ironically, his duties included transporting wounded German soldiers to an American hospital.

The trial of the 73 defendants began at Dachau on May 16, 1946, and concluded exactly two months later. The Review and Recommendations of the Deputy Judge Advocate for War Crimes, dated October 20, 1947, lists the charge as "violation of the law and usages of war" and specified that the defendants in conjunction with other persons not herein charged or named, at or in the vicinity of MALMÉDY, HONSFELD, BUELLINGEN, LIGNEUVILLE, STOUMONT, LA GLEIZE, CHENNEUX, PETIT THIER, TROIS PONTS, STAVELOT, WANNE and LUTREBOIS, all in BELGIUM, at sundry times between 16 December 1944 and 13 January 1945, willfully, deliberately and wrongly permit, encourage, aid, abet and participate in the killing, shooting, ill-treatment, abuse and torture of members of the Armed Forces of the United States....

"The accused," the report noted, were all members of the Waffen SS and "involved in the execution of a common plan, which contemplated the application of terroristic methods in combat during the Ardennes Counteroffensive." The SS had adopted such "terroristic methods" from Genghis Khan, according to the report. "At least during the year 1937 some effort was made to teach all SS officers in the military academies the significance of the tactics applied by Genghis Khan in warfare." The report cited the book *Genghis Khan and His Legacy* by Michael Prawdin that was utilized as "source material" and given to "all SS men who graduated from officer candidate school." Khan's tactics emphasized "that the first attack ... had to carry panic and terror to the remotest part of the country. The invaded country was to be paralyzed with fear."

Genghis Khan indeed had admirers in the Third Reich. Ukraine-born Michael Charol, who adopted the *nom de plume* Michael Prawdin, had moved to Germany after the Bolshevik Revolution, and garnered international attention for his two books dealing with Genghis Khan. Himmler tremendously admired these works and ordered their publication in a one-volume edition for distribution to SS members.

Emulation of Genghis Khan aside, there might well have been another motivation for the barbarity shown by the SS at Malmédy. Danny Parker, an authority on the massacre, noted that Peiper had been enraged by the Allied bombing of Düren, Germany, in autumn of 1944. Peiper had seen the devastation firsthand when his regiment had entered the city to lend humanitarian assistance. He later claimed to be outraged by the wholesale slaughter of civilians and stated that he would have castrated the bombing's perpetrators with a broken bottle. Düren, Peiper said, left his soldiers angry and obsessed with thoughts of revenge.

The report extensively quotes the Nuremberg International Military Tribunal to emphasize the ruthlessness of the SS. The most relevant paragraph, from Volume I, page 272, allowed Hess and Himmler to damn the SS with their own words.

6. The Malmédy Massacre

Hess wrote with truth that the Waffen SS were more suitable for the specific tasks to be solved in occupied territory owing to their extensive training in questions of race and nationality. Himmler, in a series of speeches made in 1943, indicated his pride in the ability of the SS to carry out these criminal acts. He encouraged his men to be "tough and ruthless," he spoke of shooting "thousands of leading Poles" and thanked them for their cooperation and lack of squeamishness at the sight of hundreds and thousands of corpses of their victims. He extolled ruthlessness in exterminating the Jewish race and later described this process as "delousing." Those speeches show that the general attitude prevailing in the SS was consistent with those criminal acts.

The clear implication is that the Waffen SS possessed no moral qualms about murdering Allied troops who wished to surrender. In order to corroborate this contention, the report cited a meeting between Dietrich and Hitler held on December 12, 1944, at Bad Nauheim. Hitler spoke for two or three hours "and stated in substance that the decisive hour for the German people had arrived; that the impending battle [the Battle of the Bulge] must be won at all costs; that the fighting must be hard and reckless; that the troops must act with brutality and show no humane inhibitions; that a wave of fright and terror should precede the troops; and that resistance of the enemy was to be broken by terror." Dietrich's Order of the Day, issued on or about December 14, 1944, reflected Hitler's declarations and stated in substance that "our troops have to be preceded by a wave of terror and fright and that no human inhibitions should be shown." This order, the report noted, "was to be read to the troops immediately prior to the offensive."

The implementation of this Order of the Day took the form of "the shooting of unarmed, surrendered American prisoners of war and unarmed civilians ... at various points along the route of advance." The report listed thirteen locations of such incidents, including "Crossroads, located about four kilometers southeast of Malmédy and about four kilometers north of Ligneuville." This section of the report serves to remind readers that the Malmédy massacre was merely one of several incidents in which American soldiers who had surrendered to the Germans were gunned down. At Büllingen, for example, "8 or 10 unarmed American soldiers came out of a house with their hands above their heads, waving a white cloth about 60 by 70 centimeters in size." When they came within 10 meters of a German vehicle, they were machine-gunned to death. "In the vicinity of Cheneux," the report stated, "two American soldiers in a jeep were attacked by machine gun fire, one American being killed." The surviving soldier pretended to be dead but was captured by Paul Zwigart, one of the defendants, and taken from the jeep. "While his hands were clasped over his head, the American prisoner of war was shot to death a few meters from the vehicle in which the commanding officer of Combat Group Peiper was riding."

As many as 15 American prisoners of war were murdered at La Gleize, the report stated. Ironically, the massacre was said to have occurred at a stone wall surrounding a cemetery and church. "While their hands were clasped behind their heads, a German personnel carrier stopped opposite them and the crew proceeded to fire upon them with machine guns, machine pistols, carbines and pistols." On the other side of this stone wall—"directly in front of the church," according to the report—as many as 30 American prisoners were shot to death. It was determined at the trial, however, that the La Gleize massacre didn't occur. Charles Whiting, in his book *Massacre at Malmédy*, noted that a priest testified La Gleize didn't even have such a stone wall.

The report stated that "numerous shooting incidents took place" when Combat Group Peiper entered Stoumont. "On one occasion while seven surrendered and unarmed American prisoners of war were being evacuated to the rear of the German lines by a paratrooper, elements of the 11th SS Panzer Company relieved the paratrooper of his charges and proceeded to shoot and kill the seven unarmed prisoners near the edge of a pasture, using pistols and fast firing rifles."

The report devoted five paragraphs to the Malmédy massacre in a section titled "Crossroads." Certain elements of "Combat Group Peiper arrived at a road intersection between Malmédy and Lignouville, known as the 'Crossroads,' between 1200 and 1400 hours, 17 December 1944." A house stood south of the intersection on the west side of the road leading to Ligneuville. As many as 30 American trucks were parked at this crossroads.

> These trucks, part of the equipment of the American 285th Field Artillery Observation Battalion, had been subjected to such intense small arms, mortar, and artillery fire from the Germans that they could not proceed. Personnel from this American column were taken captive by Combat Group Peiper and herded into a pasture which was south of the house and barn located near the Crossroads. Before being sent into the pasture the American prisoners of war were searched and their valuables and cigarettes were taken from them. The number of prisoners herded into this pasture was variously estimated at figures ranging from 80 to 200 men. The American prisoners of war were lined up in an "oblong company formation," unarmed, and with their hands raised in surrender. Among these prisoners of war were American medics with arm bands, and red crosses painted on their

6. The Malmédy Massacre

helmets. One medic, Corporal Indelicate, was shot and killed while engaged in bandaging a wounded American.

The prisoners lined up in an "oblong company formation" brings to mind the image of a coffin, which proved to be a harbinger for what happened next.

> German armored vehicles, a tank, and half-tracks were moved into positions from which the crews could fire upon the unarmed American prisoners of war in the pasture. German armored vehicles proceeded along the road opposite this group of American prisoners. One of the vehicles stopped and a German soldier took deliberate aim and fired into the prisoners, hitting at least one of them. This was repeated and another American prisoner of war fell from this group. At about this time machine guns, machine pistols, and other automatic weapons were fired from the armored vehicles into the groups of prisoners standing in the pasture.... Most of these American prisoners were hit by this automatic weapon fire.

The American prisoners were either cut down by the German's bullets or attempted to take cover by throwing themselves on the ground. It was a futile gesture. "After the firing ceased," the report stated, "groups of German officers and men moved among the prostrate forms of the American prisoners of war shooting those who appeared to be still alive." These prisoners did nothing to provoke such an attack. "There was no conduct on the part of the prisoners that prompted the shooting, such as making an effort to escape or offering resistance." After affirming that this massacre "was carried out by elements of various units of Combat Group Peiper," the report stated that "some survivors, even though wounded, were able to escape and receive medical aid." This section of the report concluded by noting "Smaller groups of six to eight American prisoners of war who were unarmed and surrendered were shot in this same vicinity by elements of the same units."

Parker, in his book *Fatal Crossroads,* noted the findings of John A. Snyder, the American army captain who examined the bodies of the Americans slain at Malmédy. Twenty of the victims were shot in the head at a range close enough to leave powder burns. Three had died from blows to their heads. Close to a dozen met death with their hands over their heads— an unmistakable gesture of surrender.

The description of the massacres of unarmed prisoners of war by Combat Group Peiper is followed by "Evidence for Defense," which promptly challenged the contention that German soldiers had been ordered to kill prisoners. "On 25 November 1944," the report stated, "troops of the Sixth SS Panzer Army were given orders regarding training.... One of those orders contained instructions regarding the treatment of prisoners of war and was to the effect that as many prisoners of war would be taken as possible in order to gain information concerning the disposition of enemy units." Orders also stated that "prisoners of war should not be mistreated even though they gave only their names, rank, and serial numbers...." A special order, signed by the Sixth Panzer Army's chief of staff, contained a single paragraph "regarding loot and prisoners of war, which were to be collected rapidly by special units attached to advance elements of the corps." The defense contended that there was no order in this paragraph to kill prisoners. Instead, "prisoners of war were to be sent back to prisoner of war collection points from where they were to be brought to prisoner of war collecting stations for interrogation." Kraemer testified that "neither the Army Order of the Day nor any other order contained a statement that prisoners of war were to be shot." He stated that he heard reports of prisoners being shot from his staff officers, who in turn had heard such reports.

The "Evidence" section of this report makes for fascinating reading. It begins:

> In its opening statement the prosecution stated that tricks, ruses, stratagems and stool-pigeons, and ceremonies were utilized in procuring many of the extrajudicial sworn statements of accused and witnesses. Also, in nearly all instances the prosecution, an incident of the introduction of an extrajudicial sworn statement, placed the individual or individuals who procured the same on the stand and disclosed the methods used in the pretrial interrogation. The defense contended throughout the trial and its Petition for Review that the various extrajudicial sworn statements were not admissible because they were procured as a result of trickery, threats of violence, and other methods of coercion and duress. The defense introduced evidence indicating that violence or threats of violence were used to obtain extrajudicial sworn statements from accused KRAEMER, PEIPER, CHRIST, HENNECKE, TOMHARDT, SIEVERS and MOTZ-HEIM. It also introduced similar evidence as to the interrogation of witnesses Trott and Agather.

The report stated the prosecution called witnesses to the stand who denied the accusations of abuse. During one of my interviews with Bill Kasich I noted that Halow, in *Innocent at Dachau*, wrote about Gustav Petrat appealing his conviction on the grounds that his interrogators beat him and even threatened him with execution. "Baloney!" Kasich replied. Were the interrogators fair guys? "Fair guys," Kasich said. "Just like the rest of us. You just sat there and asked question. You didn't beat anybody." I asked about Halow's contention that the Dachau prosecution used "professional witnesses," who routinely gave testimony that incriminated the defendants in trial after trial. "No! No! No! No! We had to abide by civil authority."

Kasich stated that the evidence used at the war crimes trials "was gained just like any other evidence." He also noted, "The witnesses that I knew of, they had to be credible." All potential witnesses were interrogated and "These interrogators were pretty smart." They could "tell who's lying and who's telling the truth." I asked Kasich whether the war criminals who claimed they had been beaten by their American interrogators were just trying to beat the rap. "They were just trying to get themselves off the hook," he said. "In fact, one would beat on the other" before apprehension. "One [concentration camp] trusty would scar [himself] or do something to another [trusty] to convince the Allies that he was beaten by the Nazis ... that he was [just another] inmate."

The Review and Recommendations of the Deputy Judge Advocate for War Crimes gives details of the alleged threats of violence that the accused claimed were directed at them. Friedrich Christ maintained that during an interrogation conducted on March 19, 1946, he was told he stood accused of giving orders at La Gleize and Stoumont that prisoners were to be shot. When Christ denied this, he was "cursed terribly" and warned that if he didn't tell the truth, he would be hanged in Bruchschal. Christ also claimed interrogators told him that his mother would be informed of his hanging as well as denied both work and ration cards. Interrogators also allegedly threatened him with death by saying "if he did not talk he would be sent to Stoumont and be shot while trying to escape." The prosecution denied all charges of abuse—including the cursing.

Heinz Tomhardt claimed to have a hood placed over his head and then subjected to be beaten on the face and stomach. He also said that he was subjected to sleep deprivation while housed in a so-called "death cell." Fritz Kraemer stated that he had been "handcuffed, shacked and required to remain in one cell for three hours" and then placed in a "punishment cell for 20 to 24 hours." Kraemer claimed he was forced to stand at attention for two hours during his first interrogation, during which he was told: "You are a war criminal and will be treated as such. We won't put on a show of trial for every German. We have enough ways and means of getting rid of you in a quiet manner. If you are in the same boat with the Nazi General Dietrich, then you will have to pay the consequences."

By "show of trial," Kraemer probably meant "show trial," a term that came into popular usage in the 1930s, when it was employed to describe a series of widely-publicized sham trials held in the Soviet Union. It was always a foregone conclusion that the defendant in a show trial would be convicted. In any event, the prosecution denied Kraemer's accusations.

Anton Motzheim also lodged charges of brutality during his interrogation. "Mr. Thon came in and said that he, MOTZHEIM, had shot a prisoner of war." Motzheim denied this accusation and made a sworn statement affirming his denial. "Mr. Thon then became very angry and beat the accused." Motzheim claimed that things soon got a lot worse for him.

> Lieutenant Perl and Mr. Thon then beat the accused for one-half hour. When the accused still refused to admit any shooting, Lieutenant Perl kicked him four times in his sexual parts and Mr. Thon kicked him on the leg. This lasted for one-half hour. A black hood was then placed over his head and he stood in the corner of his cell for an hour. At 1600 hours the next day he was taken to a cell and Mr. Thon came and told him there was only one chance. If he did not say that he shot a prisoner of war, he would be hung. Sergeant Pluschke was brought in and said that he had told them that the accused had said to him that he shot a prisoner of war in Stoumont. Mr. Thon then gave the accused a sheet of paper and a pencil and he started writing. The accused further testified that the words in the statement to the effect that he assumed the prisoner wanted to surrender were not his words, but those of Mr. Kirschbaum, the interpreter.

Both Perl and Thon denied beating Motzheim, while Kirschbaum stated that he didn't supply Motzheim with a confession sentence about assuming a prisoner wanted to surrender. Another interrogator testified that Motzheim had said that he had shot an American who was attempting to surrender.

It's an article of faith among right-wing extremists that the defendants at the Malmédy trial were tortured into signing statements admitting their crimes. Freda Utley, a former communist who journeyed to the other end of the political spectrum, condemned the Dachau trials in general and the Malmédy case in particular in the chapter titled "Our Crimes Against Humanity" in her 1949 book *The High Cost of Vengeance*. Utley claimed that defendants were consistently subjected to physical and psychological torture in order to make them write incriminating statements that were dictated to them by their interrogators. She contended that the war crimes investigators and prosecutors utilized methods comparable to those employed by the SS and Gestapo. In the same paragraph, she likened the procedures of the Dachau courtrooms to those found in the courtrooms of the post-war communist regimes in Hungary and Bulgaria that were trying and convicting Catholic and Protestant clergymen. Placing war criminals on the same moral plain as Christian clergymen reveals the depth of her hatred for the Dachau and Nuremberg trials and the men and

6. The Malmédy Massacre

women who made them happen. Halow cited *The High Cost of Vengeance* in *Innocent at Dachau* and praised it as a valuable work of scholarship. *The High Cost of Vengeance* was translated into German and published under the title *Kostspielige Rache*. The Internet swarms with neo–Nazi web sites that decry the prosecution and conviction of the Malmédy defendants. Every account the author examined on these sites emphasized that the interrogators, such as William Perl, were Jewish. "Jews specialized in torture techniques," one site claimed. Multiple neo–Nazi sites maintain that well over a hundred of the defendants at Dachau and Nuremberg allegedly had their testicles crushed.

Perl is consistently portrayed as the very incarnation of evil on these extremist web sites. Born in Prague in 1906 when that city lay within the borders of the Austro-Hungarian Empire, William Perl earned a law degree at the University of Vienna. He became involved with the Zionist movement and began transporting Jews to what was then the British Mandate of Palestine in 1937. This was a dangerous and illegal enterprise. Britain was determined to limit the number of Jews who emigrated to Palestine, since it didn't want to alienate the region's Arabs.

When Hitler invaded and annexed Austria a year later, Perl was interrogated by Adolf Eichmann, then an obscure SS lieutenant. Eichmann pointed his pistol at Perl and demanded to know the whereabouts of a Jew he was seeking. Perl refused to give up the Jewish fugitive but managed to interest the future architect of the Holocaust in a plan to evacuate Jews from Vienna and settle them in Palestine.

Eichmann's eventual rejection of his plan failed to deter Perl. He went to the German Finance Ministry in Berlin and received permission to exchange German marks for British pounds, which enabled him to pay Greek seamen to smuggle Jews into Palestine. Perl's obituary in the *New York Times* quoted a 1990 interview with that newspaper, during which he admitted "that the most painful part of his work had been selecting the healthiest evacuees for the scarce shipboard space. He said he was still haunted by the image of a sick Hungarian woman and her family whom he had barred from a transport. 'I convicted them to death,' he said."

Perl was arrested by the Germans in 1940 while in Greece. He always believed that he owed his arrest to the British, who wanted to end his smuggling of Jews into Palestine. While on a train to Berlin as a prisoner, he slashed his wrists and was put off the train. He eventually made his way to the United States and enlisted in the U.S. Army as a private shortly after Pearl Harbor. Lore Rollig Perl, his wife, had converted to Judaism from

Roman Catholicism shortly before their 1938 marriage. Unable to join her husband in the United States, she remained in Europe. She was arrested for aiding Jewish children and imprisoned in Ravensbrück concentration camp. Perl risked arrest and creating an international incident when he rescued her in 1945 from Soviet sector of Vienna.

Perl and his family settled in the United States after the war, where he earned a doctorate in psychology from Columbia University and counseled soldiers. After retiring from the army, Perl became a psychologist for the District of Columbia's welfare department, taught at George Washington University and maintained a private practice in psychology.

He became involved in activities to protest the treatment of Jews in the Soviet Union. A federal grand jury in 1976 convicted Perl of conspiring to shot out the windows in the apartments of two Soviet Embassy officials in Hyattsville, Maryland. The conspiracy conviction was overturned on appeal, but Perl was sentenced to three years of probation on a firearms charge. Perl died in his Maryland home in 1998 at age 91.

Colonel Willis Everett, the principal defense attorney for the Malmédy accused, asked the court to allow condemned defendants to be executed by firing squad rather than hanging. The court refused. Forty-three of the seventy-three defendants, including Peiper, received death sentences. After thoroughly reviewing the case, Straight and his staff recommended prison sentences for eighteen of the condemned men. Everett, deeply dissatisfied with the interrogations of his clients and the conduct of the trial, unsuccessfully attempted to file a writ of *habeas corpus* with the U.S. Supreme Court, which refused to hear the case. He then brought his petition to James C. Davis, a Georgia congressman who was a close personal friend. Davis in turn brought Everett's petition to Walter S. George, one of Georgia's United States senators. George took the petition directly to Secretary of the Army Kenneth Royall, who ordered a stay of executions until the Malmédy case had been reviewed.

Royall established a three-person committee to investigate and review every death sentence that had been handed down at the Dachau trials and upheld after being reviewed. Judge E. Leroy van Roden would prove to be the most controversial member of this committee. In his book *Crossroads of Death,* James J. Weingartner stated that van Roden seemed to have been an anti–Semite and regarded the post-war trials of accused war criminals as an attempt by Jews to exact revenge on the Nazi persecutors. In any event, van Roden publicly expressed his condemnation of the work conducted by the 7708 War Crimes Group in an article titled "American

Atrocities in Germany" that he wrote for the February 1949 issue of *The Progressive* magazine. The author found van Roden's article posted in its entirety on a web site associated with David Irving.

Van Roden claimed that the German people had no idea whatsoever that atrocities were being committed in the concentration camps that existed in Germany and its occupied territories. "After this investigation, and after talking to all sides, I do not believe that the German people knew what the German Government was doing," he wrote. "I am convinced the German populace had no idea what diabolical crimes that arch-fiend, Himmler, was committing in the concentration camps." The following section is devoutly quoted by neo–Nazis, whose agenda includes discrediting the Dachau trials—and, by implication, the Nuremberg trials as well.

> Our investigators would put a black hood over the accused's head and then punch him in the face with brass knuckles, kick him, and beat him with rubber hose. Many of the German defendants had teeth knocked out. Some had their jaws broken.
> All but two of the Germans, in the 139 cases we investigated, had been kicked in the testicles beyond repair. This was Standard Operating Procedure with American investigators.

Weingartner observed that van Roden's anti–Semitism made him prone to accept uncritically the most outrageous allegations of abuse by interrogators. Clearly embarrassed by the negative attention drawn by his article, van Roden later tried to minimize his role in writing it. When testifying before a U.S. Senate subcommittee charged in 1949 with investigating the Malmédy trial, he cited the report of the Royall committee, of which he had been a member, which concluded that there was no clear evidence of systematic use of improper interrogation techniques.

The senate investigation gave Senator Joseph R. McCarthy of Wisconsin his first national platform. McCarthy had been elected to the senate in 1946 and sought to exploit an issue that would lift him from national obscurity. He was still a year away from making his speech in Wheeling, West Virginia, when he claimed to possess a list of 205 communists who had infiltrated the U.S. State Department. McCarthy was harshly critical of the Malmédy trial, possibly in an attempt to appeal to Wisconsin's sizable German-American population. He might also have been trying to curry favor with the powerful *Chicago Tribune*, which had many Wisconsin readers. That influential Chicago daily has been extremely critical of the post-war trials in general and the Malmédy trial in particular.

The subcommittee's report noted that mock trials were employed by interrogators "in not more than 12 cases of the several hundred suspects interrogated by the war crimes investigation team." There was no consensus regarding any alleged abuse of suspects. "The evidence given concerning these trials is extremely conflicting, even among the persons who alleged they were subject to a mock trial." The War Crimes Group prosecution team maintained that the results of these mock trials were "very unsatisfactory" and stated they were used "only on the less intelligent and more impressionable suspects."

The report detailed the procedure of a typical mock trial:

> There was a table within a room, which was covered with a black cloth and on which was a crucifix and two lighted candles. Behind this table would be placed two or three members of the war crimes investigation team, who, in the minds of the suspects, would be viewed as judges of the court. A prisoner would be brought in with his hood on, which was removed after he entered the room. Two members of the prosecution team, usually German-speaking members, would then begin to harangue the prisoner, one approaching the matter as though he were the prosecutor or hostile interrogator, and the other from the angle of a defense attorney or friendly interrogator. The subcommittee could find no evidence to support the position that the suspect was told, specifically in so many words, that anyone was his defense attorney. However, there is no question that the suspect quite logically believed that one of these persons was on his side, and may have assumed that he was his defense counsel. The subcommittee does not believe that these mock trials were ever carried through to where a sentence was pronounced, nor was any evidence found of any physical brutality in connection with the mock trials.

The subcommittee's report concluded that use of mock trials was "a grave mistake." This dubious interrogation technique, the report noted, had been Perl's idea "and had been patterned after German criminal procedure with which the suspects were familiar." For Perl, born in Austria and trained as a continental lawyer, "the procedures seemed proper to him." The report exonerated the war crimes prosecution team for keeping the prisoners in separate cells since it was necessary "to keep the suspects separated until interrogation was completed." The Malmédy suspects suffered no deprivations during their confinement. "The preponderance of evidence," the report stated, "showed beyond a reasonable doubt that such confinement was under the most favorable conditions that the circumstances permitted, and that during this time the men were fed, were warm, and suffered no more inconvenience than one would normally except to find in an ordinary civilian prison in the United States."

The report succinctly dismissed the prisoners' allegation that they were denied drinking water and forced to drink from their toilets during

6. The Malmédy Massacre

the entire period of their incarceration. This charge was contrary to the testimony of the attending medical personnel as well as the guards and interrogation teams. It was also contrary to the testimony of the Malmédy accused themselves.

> Several suspects who were questioned by the subcommittee testified that they received regular food, a change of underwear once a week, shaving equipment and washing water every morning, but no drinking water. On cross-examination those who alleged they received no water gave conflicting answers, and admitted they received other liquids with their meals. One, who claimed he never received drinking water during his entire stay at Schwabisch Hall, had previously testified he had been on bread and water for 4 days.

The report dismissed the accusation that investigators had disguised themselves as priests for the purpose of obtaining confessions from suspects. This particular accusation originated with one Otto Eble, a witness who also claimed that interrogators placed burning matches under his fingernails to force him to say whatever they wanted him to say. A medical examination found no evidence of such abuse. "The doctors who examined him stated that in their opinion the man was a pathological liar and was incapable of telling the truth," the report stated. It further noted that Eble had four convictions for embezzlement. Eble had played a key role in promoting the allegations of abuse:

> As will be noted throughout this report, many of the most flagrant charges which have been so widely publicized in this case can be attributed first to the affidavit prepared by Eble, second to the cloak of authority given to his statement through the media of the publications and speeches of Judge Van Roden, and third by the organized dissemination of this information both in our country and abroad by the National Council for the Prevention of War.

The senate subcommittee surmised that efforts to destroy the credibility of the Malmédy trial and other Allied prosecution of war criminals didn't necessarily reflect altruism or a passion for justice. "Through competent testimony submitted to the subcommittee, it appeared that there are strong reasons to believe that groups within Germany are taking advantage of the understandable efforts of the church and the defense attorneys as well as in other ways to discredit the American occupation forces in general," the reported stated. "One ready avenue of approach has been through the attacks on the war-crimes trials in general and the Malmédy case in particular.

> The subcommittee is convinced that there is an organized effort being made to revive the nationalistic spirit in Germany through every means possible. There

is evidence that at least a part of this effort is attempting to establish a close liaison with Communist Russia. These matters, of course, must be judged against the back drop of the current situation in Europe and their probable effect in the event of a war involving Russia and the United States. Everything done to weaken the prestige of the United States and our occupation policies will play an important part in any emergency.

The subcommittee acknowledged that the withdrawal of American occupation forces from Germany might well precipitate "a general amnesty program to release these former Nazis and SS officers," which the committee saw as part of "a larger plan to associate such individuals with the Communist forces of Europe." Such apprehension is quite understandable when viewed in the context of the times.

The committee made six recommendations, three of which can be construed as specifically motivated by negative reports regarding William Perl. "The State Department and the Department of Defense employ no civilians on military-government work who have not been American citizens for at least 10 years," the report stated in Recommendation 2. "Provisions should be made to waive such requirements in individual and specific cases except for positions involving important questions of administrative or judicial policy." Recommendations 3 and 4 read:

> 3. Military personnel engaged in war-crimes work should meet the same citizenship requirements.
> 4. The Department of Defense should institute a reserve program leading to the creation of a pool of trained investigators and lawyers for war-crimes work who would be committed to serve beyond the cessation of hostilities. Since legislation on this point is required, it should be submitted promptly for the consideration of the Congress. Only through the availability of such trained personnel can procedural mistakes and mistakes of judgment be avoided.

Was justice served at the Malmédy trial? Yes and no. Parker makes it quite clear in *Fatal Crossroads* that any number of possible participants in the massacre were never even apprehended, let alone placed on trial. Parker, James Weingartner and other historians have noted that SS Major Werner Pöetschke, who might well have been the officer who gave the actual order to execute the American prisoners of war at Malmédy, escaped capture and trial. He was killed on March 24, 1945, while fighting in Hungary.

Although 43 of the men convicted for committing war crimes at Malmédy were sentenced to death, not even one walked to the gallows. After reviewing the sentences handed down by the court, Clio Straight and his staff recommended only 25 be carried out. Colonel James Harbaugh,

6. The Malmédy Massacre

Theater Judge Advocate, assigned Colonel Howard Bresee, chief of his office's review branch, to review the Malmédy sentences. Bresee's report, completed on February 8, 1948, severely criticized the interrogators' techniques—especially the alleged "mock trials"—as well as rulings made by the bench, which Bresee thought hampered the defense. He concluded that in no less than 29 of the 73 cases evidence had been insufficient to sustain conviction. Still, the report recommended that 12 death sentences be carried out.

General Lucius Clay, military governor of Germany, commuted six of the remaining 12 death sentences to life imprisonment in the spring of 1949. Clay's decision was based in part on the need to establish a favorable relationship with the new nation of the Federal Republic of Germany, popularly known as West Germany, which came into existence on May 23, 1949. The United States was now locked in a Cold War with its World War II ally, the USSR, and saw a pro–Western West Germany as a bulwark against the spread of Soviet influence in Europe. Commuting the death sentences of six German war criminals would do much to secure this new nation's allegiance to the West.

General Thomas T. Handy, Commander in Chief–European Command, commuted the death sentences of the last six condemned Malmédy men to life imprisonment in 1951. A "life imprisonment" sentence for a Malmédy war criminal proved quite short indeed. All were eventually released from Landsberg Prison. Peiper, the last of the lot, left Landsberg on December 22, 1956, after eleven years of confinement.

In an interview with Charles Whiting when he was conducting research for his book on the Malmédy massacre, Peiper described himself as a fatalist, who was sitting atop a powder keg. The old Nazi proved to be something of a prophet. On the night of July 13, 1976, Peiper's house was set afire by parties unknown. He died of smoke inhalation while trying to save some of the home's objects. Bill Kasich thought this quite ironic. He pointed out that Peiper's troops had a reputation for burning down any building in their path. They carried blowtorches that had been converted into short-distance flamethrowers, which gave them the nickname "the Blowtorch Battalion." Kasich regarded Peiper's death by fire and smoke as nothing less than poetic justice.

7

Otto Skorzeny
"The Most Dangerous Man in Europe"

BORN IN VIENNA IN 1908, Skorzeny joined the Nazi Party of that nation in 1931 and worked as a civil engineer before volunteering for the German army during World War II. He was wounded while fighting on the Eastern Front and awarded the Iron Cross. While recuperating from his wound, Skorzeny studied commando operations in preparation for his return to active duty. His string of successes allowed Charles Foley to title his 1953 biography of Skorzeny *Commando Extraordinary* without fear of hyperbole.

Skorzeny's most celebrated mission occurred on September 12, 1943, during Operation *Eiche* (German for "oak"), when he and a commando team rescued deposed dictator Benito Mussolini, who was being held at the Campo Imperatore Hotel in the Apennine Mountains of Italy. Mussolini, under arrest since being deposed two months earlier, had been moved from place to place by his Italian captors. After determining Mussolini's location, Skorzeny and his commandos boarded German transport gliders, landed on the mountain and liberated Mussolini without a single shot being fired. The dictator was flown to German-occupied Italy and installed as the titular head of the Italian Social Republic, a puppet state of Nazi Germany. Mussolini gave Skorzeny a watch to express his gratitude. In its obituary for Skorzeny, the *New York Times* reported, "The watch vanished after the SS officer surrendered himself to the Allies at the end of the war." Not according to Charles Foley, who interviewed Skorzeny in Spain years after the war. Foley wrote that the old commando proudly wore the watch and removed it so Foley could examine the memento. The letter M, for Mussolini, was inscribed on the back of the gold timepiece, along with the date of its presentation to Skorzeny.

The sheer audacity of the raid astonished the Allies and provided

Nazi Germany with new fodder for its propaganda machinery. Skorzeny received a promotion as well as the Knight's Cross of the Iron Cross, the highest award that Nazi Germany could bestow for battlefield courage and military leadership.

Skorzeny further ingratiated himself to Hitler by his role in hunting down Germans who played a role in his attempted assassination, which occurred on July 20, 1944, at the Wolf's Lair, Hitler's headquarters in East Prussia. Count Claus von Stauffenberg left a briefcase containing two bombs in a conference room, where Hitler was meeting with his military advisors. The resulting explosion claimed four lives and left virtually all the survivors wounded. Hitler, shielded from the main force of the blast by a leg of the heavy, solid-oak table, suffered only minor injuries. Arrests of everyone thought to be associated with the plot began immediately. Skorzeny, ever loyal to Hitler, arrived at the War Office in Berlin with troops and began a comprehensive search of the building. He was determined to root out every participant in the conspiracy and halted the hasty executions of suspects until they could be tortured into revealing any accomplices. Such calculated ruthlessness did not go unnoticed by Hitler, who warmly thanked Skorzeny for saving the Third Reich.

Skorzeny also distinguished himself in October 1944 during Operation Panzerfaust, when he kidnapped the son of Admiral Miklós Horthy, the regent of Hungary. Hitler had learned that Horthy intended to sign a truce between his nation and the Soviet Union. Since Romania had recently concluded a truce with the USSR, Hungary's defection would have isolated approximately one million German troops who were fighting in the Balkans. Horthy's son was lured to what he thought would be a meeting with envoys from Josip Broz Tito of Yugoslavia, who supported the Allies. Upon arriving for the purported meeting, he was beaten and arrested by Skorzeny and his commandos. The young man was concealed from the public by being rolled up in a carpet, flown to Vienna and transported to the Mauthausen concentration camp. Unaware that his son had been kidnapped, Horthy announced on Hungarian radio that he had signed an armistice with the Soviet Union.

When Skorzeny and his forces launched an assault on Buda Castle, the seat of Horthy's government, Horthy realized that resistance was futile and ordered Hungarian troops to stand down. Upon learning that his son had been taken hostage and would be released if he would resign as regent, Horthy signed a letter of resignation. Nazi sympathizers now ruled Hungary, but Horthy's son remained a prisoner of the Germans until the end of the war.

In his *Memoir of the Most Dangerous Man in Europe*, published in 1950, Skorzeny recalled being briefed by Hitler regarding the German offensive launched on December 16, 1944, known as the Battle of the Bulge, as well as the role that he was to play in it. Hitler wanted Skorzeny and his men to disguise themselves by wearing American uniforms and wreak havoc behind enemy lines by issuing false orders and hampering communications. Skorzeny claimed Hitler cited Allied precedents for employing troops wearing the uniforms of their enemy during commando raids. Hitler, according to Skorzeny, dismissed him with a plea to accomplish the impossible but forbade Skorzeny from venturing behind enemy lines himself because he was too valuable to the Third Reich. Hitler named the mission Operation *Greif* (in English, "Griffin") and Skorzeny proudly noted that Hitler made him responsible for its execution.

Skorzeny was given the specially created 150th Panzer Brigade, which included two tank companies, each equipped with ten American-made M4 Sherman tanks; three reconnaissance companies, each equipped with ten American armored cars; and three battalions of motorized infantry with American trucks. His mission was two-fold, Skorzeny wrote. The 150th Panzer would exploit the breach made by Sepp Dietrich's Sixth Panzer Army, assume the lead and capture the Mass bridges located at Huy, Amay and Engis. These bridges, Skorzeny noted, had to be taken intact in order to allow German forces to advance on Antwerp.

Skorzeny knew that the success of his second objective depended in large part upon finding German military personnel who could speak English well enough to pass as Americans. In *Memoirs*, Skorzeny recalled his profound disappointment when the first hundred volunteers for the mission arrived at Friedenthal. As more men arrived, Germans Skorzeny called "professors" (his quotation marks) divided the men into categories according to their knowledge of English. Category I was supposed to consist of Germans who spoke English well in addition to being fluent in American slang. This category included only ten men, who had served in the German navy and presumably acquired their knowledge of English before the war while visiting ports in the United States or British Empire. Thirty to forty men comprised the second category, which also included a number of sailors. The third category consisted of approximately 150 men who could more or less make themselves understood in English, while the fourth contained men who had learned some English while in school. The rest of the men, according to Skorzeny, knew little English beyond "yes" and "no." In *My Commando Operations*, Skorzeny stated that only 120 of

7. Otto Skorzeny

the 2,000 men under his command were authorized to conduct actual conversations in English during Operation Greif. The rest were instructed to remain silent or, in the event that they *must* say something, to murmur or utter single-syllable words. Skorzeny admitted that his English was only passable at best.

Charles Foley recounted an incident that underscored the language limitations of Skorzeny's men. A jeep carrying four men wearing GI jackets swung into a military filling station behind the Allied lines. The driver called out that they needed petrol, rather than gas. As if that weren't damning enough, he was much too polite for a typical GI—even to the extent of using the word "please" when requesting the petrol. When the men in the jeep were asked where they were from, the driver panicked and drove off down the icy road. The vehicle soon overturned and the jeep's occupants were taken prisoner, when it was discovered that they were wearing German uniforms beneath their GI jackets. Threatened with execution for being spies if they didn't talk, one of the prisoners stated that they were under the command of Otto Skorzeny and offered what he evidently believed to be the purpose of their mission: to kidnap General Eisenhower.

Locating uniforms to complement this deception proved equally challenging, according to Skorzeny. The first batch of uniforms to reach the unit were British-issue rather than American. A freight car filled with overcoats arrived next, which were equally useless since American soldiers wore field jackets. When some field jackets were finally delivered, Skorzeny was disappointed to find them bearing the prisoner of war triangle.

Suitable clothing for the Germans was eventually located and delivered. Skorzeny saw to it that the Germans were taught nuances of GI behavior, such as chewing gum. The charges brought against Skorzeny during his Dachau trial included "wrongfully obtaining from a prisoner-of-war camp United States uniforms and Red Cross parcels consigned to American prisoners of war," according to "Trial of Otto Skorzeny and Others" in the World Courts database. In *My Commando Operations*, Skorzeny wrote about such attention to detail as training his men to open a package of American cigarettes in the manner of a GI. He neglected to mention how those American cigarettes had been obtained.

Otto Skorzeny was "a very arrogant man," Kasich stated. "He was good. He was one of the best. But he was arrogant. He knew he was good. And he let everyone know that he was good."

I mentioned the alleged plot to have Skorzeny kidnap Eisenhower. Kasich shared what he had learned about this plot.

Okay, now this is a story.... Twice John Cashman brought Skorzeny into the prison at Wiesbaden and twice John came to me and he told me, "Bill, I've got Skorzeny. I want you to talk to him." But when we went there, he was already gone. I told him [John], "Let's eat supper first and then we'll go see him." But they moved him. Second time, same thing: they moved him. And I asked John, "What did he [Skorzeny] say?" [Cashman replied] "Well, I asked him the question, 'Is it true that you wanted to capture Eisenhower?'" And I asked John, "What did he say?" And this is what John told me: "Skorzeny smiled ... looked at me and said, 'You had better generals.'" That's exactly what he said ... if they were going to capture anybody, it wouldn't be Eisenhower.

In his *My Commando Operations*, Skorzeny referred to the rumor that he had been assigned a top-secret mission to kidnap Eisenhower and revealed that it was also believed by most low-ranking German military personnel. He claimed to have been approached by Hauptmann Stielau, who told him that he knew the objective of Operation *Greif* was to kidnap Eisenhower. Skorzeny facetiously told Stielau that he was correct and to keep his voice down. On page 357, however, Skorzeny set the record straight by stating that there never was a plan to kidnap or kill Eisenhower. In *Memoirs*, Skorzeny claimed to have encouraged such rumors in the hope that they would be picked up by Allied military intelligence. In his biography of Skorzeny, Foley wrote that while the German word *Greif* refers to a mythical bird, it can also mean "grasp," which greatly contributed to the rumor that the mission's objective was to kidnap Eisenhower.

Skorzeny's men wore German parachute overalls to cover their American uniforms. Upon breaking through Allied lines, they were to discard the overalls and advance to capture the Mass bridges at Huy, Amay and Engis. According to "Trial of Otto Skorzeny and Others" in the World Courts database, Skorzeny's men "were instructed to avoid contact with enemy troops and if possible to avoid combat in reaching their objectives." When the SS Armored Division failed to break through, Skorzeny on December 18 "decided to abandon the plan of taking the three Mass bridges and put his brigade at the disposal of the commander of the SS corps to which it had been attached to be used as infantry." Skorzeny was ordered to attack in the direction of Malmédy. This order placed Skorzeny's men in the thick of combat while wearing American uniforms. These men remained in combat until they were relieved on December 28.

In *My Commando Operations*, Skorzeny claimed that he could have committed suicide or escaped to a foreign country when the war ended but refused to abandon his nation and fellow Germans during their hour of need. This assertion doesn't jibe with his post-war abandonment of the Fatherland. Skorzeny also maintained that, upon getting word to the Americans that he wished to surrender, he and three comrades were picked up in a jeep driven by a Texan, who had been instructed to drive his prisoners to Salzburg. The Texan, according to Skorzeny, stopped the jeep at an inn and ordered a bottle of fine wine, which Skorzeny paid for. As they continued their journey, the driver supposedly asked him whether he was really Otto Skorzeny. When Skorzeny confirmed his identity, the Texan admonished him to drink up with his friends since he'd surely be hanged that night.

In *The Beast Reawakens*, Martin A. Lee challenged Skorzeny's colorful version of his surrender. According to Lee, Skorzeny and a handful of German soldiers emerged from the woods to enter the command post of the U.S. Thirtieth Infantry Regiment near Salzburg, where he announced his surrender to a lieutenant. Skorzeny was a busy man before giving himself up. Lee stated that Skorzeny allegedly buried the Reichsbank treasury somewhere in the Austrian Alps. This Nazi gold has never been recovered and might have been used by Skorzeny to finance his neo–Nazi activities during the post-war era. Skorzeny also endeared himself to top SS officers by transporting their gold and jewels to secure hiding places throughout Germany. Lee wrote that Skorzeny used Red Cross ambulances to haul this loot. Skorzeny, Lee asserted, assisted General Reinhard Gehlen in burying top-secret Nazi intelligence files at several locations in the mountains of Bavaria.

Despite the U.S. Army sergeant's alleged claim, Skorzeny had no appointment with the hangman. He claimed to have been transferred from one location to another until he was finally arrested in earnest and stripped naked to be searched. Skorzeny proudly recounted his interrogation by the U.S. Army and their insistence that he was responsible for everything from plots to kill Eisenhower, Bradley and Montgomery to flying Hitler to a safe haven in some unnamed foreign country. Skorzeny concluded this account of his interrogation with a quotation about himself from Foley's *Commando Extraordinary* in which the author lauded the subject of his biography as a man who had become a character of modern mythology and was capable of performing any feat. Skorzeny's obvious glee in quoting Foley's judgment of him reminded the author of Bill Kasich's comment about Skorzeny that "he knew he was good. And he let everyone know that he was good."

Kasich mentioned a conversation John Cashman had with Skorzeny. "John asked him, because he had a scar on his cheek, 'Otto, how'd you get that scar?'" He told Cashman it was self-inflicted. Skorzeny was being sarcastic. Every reliable biographical source, including Charles Foley's *Commando Extraordinary*, states that Skorzeny received his scar as a fencer during his student days in Vienna. Martin A. Lee, in *The Beast Reawakens*, wrote that the wound was stitched on the spot without any kind of anesthetic. I shared a section of Skorzeny's autobiography with Kasich in which the German talked about his imprisonment. Forced to share a cell with a habitual criminal, Skorzeny claimed to have made it clear to his cellmate who was in charge. "Yeah, he would," Kasich replied. "He was arrogant. He was good, but he was arrogant."

Skorzeny's arrogance was tempered by some degree of discretion, however. None of his published memoirs contain an account of his participation in ODESSA, a secret network that facilitated the escape of Nazis from Allied custody and assisted them in relocating to other nations. Lee cited files in the National Archives that indicate U.S. Army Counterintelligence Corps (CIC) placed an informant in the same prison that held Skorzeny to learn more about his activities. The informant was astonished to learn that the commando had founded an underground organization known as the Skorzeny *Gruppe* (Group), which existed as a branch of ODESSA. Also known by such names as *die Spinne* (the Spider) and *Kamradenwerk* (Comradeship), ODESSA owed its genesis to a meeting of German industrialists and bankers held in Strasbourg in 1944. These power brokers realized that it was only a matter of time before Germany lost the war and a

Otto Skorzeny managed to appear debonair even while incarcerated. His trial resulted in acquittal.

network should be established that would allow Nazis to escape Allied justice. Simon Wiesenthal learned about ODESSA from a German counter-espionage agent he met at the Nuremberg trials. The agent told Wiesenthal that ODESSA had been set up in 1946.

ODESSA enjoyed the support of many Roman Catholic priests, especially Franciscans, who gave refuge to Nazis in a chain of monasteries stretching across Austria and Italy. According to Wiesenthal, a Franciscan monastery known as Via Sicilia in Rome functioned as a transit station for Nazis. Once in Italy, according to an article posted on the Jewish Virtual Library, these fugitives were out of danger and could then be settled in Nazi-friendly nations such as Franco's Spain and certain Latin American countries. Wiesenthal thought that most of these priests were motivated by a misguided sense of Christian charity than sympathy for National Socialism.

Bishop Alois Hudal, rector of the Pontificio Istituto Teutonico Santa Maria dell'Anima in Rome, was authorized by the Vatican Secretary of State to visit German-speaking civil internees in Italy. Hudal viewed Nazi fugitives as victims rather than criminals and used his position to facilitate the escape of any number of wanted men, including such notorious figures as Franz Stangl, who served as commandant officer at Treblinka, and Adolf Eichmann.

Skorzeny's ODESSA contingent at Dachau received assistance from some unlikely allies. According to CIC documents cited by Lee, the Polish Guard played an active role in helping prisoners escape—the same Polish Guard that Ralph Schulz had recalled, "We all feared ... so much" because of their propensity for firing their rifles indiscriminately. "We feared them more than we feared the Germans," Schulz told me. He evidently didn't know that the Polish Guard had forged an alliance with the German prisoners. Why this alliance? Members of the Polish Guard had fled their native land when the USSR occupied Poland, which certainly meant they would have hated the Soviets. The Germans incarcerated at Dachau also hated the Soviet Union. Reasoning that "the enemy of my enemy is my friend," these Poles threw in with the men they had been assigned to guard.

Kasich talked about transporting some of Skorzeny's men to the courthouse for trial. He was asked whether he "wanted to help John Cashman take prisoners to Dachau." Kasich replied, "Yeah, I'll go with him." I asked whether Skorzeny himself was on this bus. "No," Kasich replied. "Just his men. They wouldn't let Skorzeny in [the bus] because if he told them to escape, they would listen to him." Cashman warned his friend about their prisoners.

So as we boarded the bus, John said, "Look at their eyes, Bill, as you board." So I boarded the bus and looked at them and they looked like steel. There was no life in those eyes.... And John got in the middle of the bus and he passed cigarettes around. He said, "Take a cigarette and pass them around." And he got his .45 out of his holster and held it up and took the clip out. He said, "I'm putting the clip in my pocket. Bill, you do the same thing. Put it [the clip for his .45] in your pocket." So the next thing he told them [the prisoners] was "If you want to escape, do it now. If you escape, the next time we come after you, you'll know what's going to happen." He didn't say that we're going to shoot you, but they got the message. They didn't give us any more trouble....

When the bus made a stop for the prisoners to stretch their legs, according to Kasich, a firearm was discharged for the only time during the transport. A guard fired his Thompson submachine gun into the air, apparently in an attempt to intimidate the prisoners. Kasich told the guard, "You didn't impress these guys." He knew that Otto Skorzeny's men wouldn't be rattled in the least by a few rounds of gunfire.

Both of Skorzeny's autobiographies are replete with attempts to exonerate Nazi Germany. While recounting his imprisonment by the Allies, he mourns those accused Nazi war criminals who chose suicide after enduring alleged mistreatment by their Allied captors. For instance, Skorzeny laments the suicide of Dr. Leonardo Conti, who was appointed by Hitler to the post of Reich Health Leader and personally murdered by lethal injection as many as six persons who had been judged unworthy to live under Germany's euthanasia program. The slow deaths of these persons, some of whom required second injections, convinced Conti that gas chambers were a more effective means of murder. Conti also participated in experiments at the Dachau and Buchenwald concentration camps, where inmates were deliberately infected with malaria. About one-third of the test subjects died. Conti was captured on May 19, 1945, and hanged himself in his cell on October 6 of that year.

Despite his role in Nazi Germany's murder machine, Skorzeny in *My Commando Operations* eulogized Conti as both "good" and "brave" and informed readers that the accusations against him were unjust. When referring to the Nuremberg trials, Skorzeny put the word confessions in quotation marks and admonished historians to regard such statements, as well as the accounts given by all prisoners who were interviewed by Allied interrogators, with skepticism. Like contemporary Holocaust deniers, Skorzeny contended that many prisoners gave false testimony in order to be acquitted. Hitler's commando let readers know in no uncertain terms that he denounces these persons as liars.

7. Otto Skorzeny

"The crimes alleged by the prosecution in the four-count indictment were all violations of the laws and usages of war," according to *Records of the United States Army War Crimes Trials, United States of America v. Otto Skorzeny et al., July 13, 1945–December 13, 1948*. According to this document:

> Charge I asserted that Skorzeny and his men participated in combat wearing U.S. uniforms. Although most interpreters of international law agree that wearing of enemy uniforms is permissible in carrying out a ruse, it is unlawful to be uniformed in the garb of the enemy during actual combat. Therefore, it was crucial for the prosecution to prove that the defendants participating in combat wearing U.S. uniforms. Charge II alleged that the defendants tortured and killed more than 100 U.S. prisoners of war. Charge II stated that Skorzeny and his defendants removed, used and appropriated insignias of rank, decorations, uniforms, identification documents, and other effects and objects of personal use in the possession of U.S. prisoners of war. Charge IV alleged misappropriation of Red Cross food and clothing parcels consigned to U.S. prisoners of war.

Skorzeny and the other nine defendants pled not guilty to all charges. Three American officers were appointed as defense counsels: Lt. Col. Robert Durst; Lt. Col. Donald McClure; and Major L.I. Horwitz. Skorzeny proudly noted that three German lawyers joined the defense team, although there was no assurance that they would ever be paid for their services. Durst, according to Skorzeny in *Secret Missions*, supplemented the defense team by selecting civilians from the War Crimes Group to form a staff. Foley's biography of the commando portrays Durst as relentlessly interviewing Skorzeny and the other defendants in their jail cells prior to the trial. The prisoners supposedly wondered whether their own counsel was trying to force confessions from them. After the fourth visit, however, Durst allegedly told his clients that he was now utterly convinced of their innocence and would fight for them as though they were his own brothers.

Hitler's celebrated commando was openly contemptuous of the proceedings and succinctly expressed his scorn for all the post-war trials, both at Dachau and Nuremberg on page 444 of *My Commando Operations*, when he placed the words "war crimes trials" in quotation marks. As noted earlier, Ottomar W. Eichmann was one of eight American officers who was assigned to preside at Skorzeny's trial. Colonel Andrew G. Gardner served as president. Skorzeny professed to be disturbed upon being informed by Durst that an American army officer he designated in *Secret Missions* only as "Colonel G" would serve as president of the court. "Colonel G" would have been Col. Andrew Gardner. Skorzeny claimed that Gardner had a reputation as a hanging judge. Durst, according to Skorzeny, was unable to have Gardner replaced but succeeded in having four or five changes made in the tribunal. Skorzeny's account directly conflicts with *Records of United States Army War Crimes Trials; United States of America v. Otto Skorzeny et al.*, which states that the defense team unsuccessfully challenged only Gardner and Eichmann because "they felt that these individuals had been specifically selected to achieve convictions and to hand out stiff sentences." Col. A.H. Rosenfelt, referred to by Skorzeny as "Colonel R" in *Secret Missions*, served as lead prosecutor.

Records of the United States Army War Crimes Trials, United States of America v. Otto Skorzeny at al., July 13, 1945–December 13, 1948, states that "although members of the brigade were seen in operational areas wearing U.S. uniforms with German parachute tunics, there was little evidence that they actually participated in combat wearing these uniforms." *Trial of Otto Skorzeny and Others* notes that, in the first case, an American lieutenant testified that

> in fighting in which he was engaged about 20th December his opponents wore American uniforms with German overalls, some of them who were captured by him said, "that they belong to the 'First' or the 'Adolph Hitler' or the 'Panzer Division.'" The second case was contained in an affidavit of the accused Kocherscheid [correct spelling: Kocherscheidt], who elected not to give evidence at the trial. He said in his affidavit that during the attack on Malmédy he and some of his men were engaged in a reconnaissance mission in American uniform when they were approached by an American military police sergeant. Kocherscheid, fearing they would be recognized, fired several shots at the sergeant.

Skorzeny and the other defendants were found not guilty on all charges. The testimony of the American lieutenant, *Trial of Otto Skorzeny and Others* notes, was dismissed because "the evidence does not seem to disclose with sufficient certainty the connection with the men dressed in American uniform whom Lieutenant O'Neil captured and the 150th Brigade." The charge against Wilhelm Kocherscheidt failed to stick because there was no evidence that the German had killed or even wounded the American military police sergeant.

The authors of *Trial of Otto Skorzeny and Others* sharply criticized the court's decision regarding Skorzeny and his men donning American uniforms and insignia and then entering a combat zone. The Hague Convention, they noted, forbids their use in combat and quote the *Soldiers Handbook*, published by the War Department and distributed to American soldiers, which stated: "The use of the enemy flag, insignia and uniform is permitted under some circumstances. They are not to be used during actual fighting, and if used in order to approach the enemy without drawing fire, should be thrown away or removed as soon as fighting begins."

Kocherscheidt's attorneys argued that he had fired at the American military police sergeant because of a justifiable fear that his life and the lives of his men were threatened. As Kocherscheidt "returned from espionage mission to his own lines," they contended, "he was protected by Article 31 of the Hague Convention and therefore could not be punished afterwards for his act as a spy." The authors of *Trial of Otto Skorzeny and Others* found this argument "unsound" and question its value in securing Kocherscheidt's exoneration. After quoting Article 29 of The Hague Convention, which defines "espionage," the authors observed:

> Article 31 gives immunity to a spy who returns to his lines in so far as he cannot be punished as a spy. The accused in this case, however, were not tried as spies but were tried for a violation of laws and usages of war alleged to have been committed by entering combat in enemy uniforms. Articles 29–31 of the Hague Convention have therefore no application in this case and it would appear that the accused Kocherscheid's [*sic*] acquittal was based on lack of evidence, as he did not give evidence at the trial and the Prosecution's case rested entirely on his pre-trial affidavit.

Skorzeny and his comrades were also aided by the prosecution's failure to pursue convictions on the blatantly misuse of American uniforms, cigarettes and other items. There can be no doubt that Skorzeny stood guilty of violating the Geneva Convention. As the authors remind us: "Article 6 of the Geneva (Prisoner-of-War) Convention, 1929, provides that: 'All effects and objects of personal use, except arms, military equipment and military papers, shall remain in the possession of prisoners of war....'" and "The taking of uniforms of prisoners of war is therefore a violation of the Geneva Convention."

The defendants had also violated Article 37 of the Geneva Convention, which clearly stated, "Prisoners of war shall be allowed individually to receive parcels by mail containing food and other articles intended for consumption or clothing. Packages should be delivered to the addresses and a receipt given." The appropriation of such articles, the authors conclude, "is therefore also a violation of the Geneva Convention."

Since the court wasn't required to give any reason for its decision, the authors could only speculate why Skorzeny and the other defendants weren't prosecuted for such blatant violations of the Geneva Convention. Perhaps "having acquitted the accused of the main charge the Court applied the maxim *de minimis non cural lex*, also acquitting the accused of what were lesser violations of the Geneva Convention." Literally translated as "the law does not concern itself with trifles," *de minimis non cural lex* is a common law principle that maintains trial judges shouldn't waste their time on minor transgressions of the law. The court's failure to convict Skorzeny and his co-defendants of clear violations of the laws of war as defined by the Geneva Convention as well as the Hague Convention could be attributed to *de minimis non cural*, or it could have reflected a desire to exonerate Skorzeny.

I asked Kasich why he thinks Skorzeny was acquitted. Did the Allies think they could use a soldier with his skills somewhere down the line? "Yeah," he answered. "At the Russian front." Kasich was firm in his opinion that, as tensions between the United States and USSR grew, the American military and State Department thought Skorzeny would be a valuable asset.

> I worked on the Malmédy case ... and I followed the man [Skorzeny] all the way through. And I would ask questions about Skorzeny. In fact, they [American authorities] didn't even want to mention his name.... I followed his case all the way through. I was interested in what happened to him ... you had to admire him because of his skill. But he had a murderous skill. His purpose in life was to kill.

Skorzeny claimed that Rosenfelt came over to shake his hand even before the commando could shake hands with McClure. The lead prosecutor, according to Skorzeny in *Secret Missions*, congratulated the commando on his acquittal and assured him in no uncertain terms that he had only been doing his duty in prosecuting him. Skorzeny portrayed himself as replying that he and his men were only doing their duty as well. Hitler's commando evidently created this anecdote in an attempt to refute Rosenfelt's post-trial characterization of Skorzeny as "the most dangerous man in Europe." In *Skorzeny's Secret Missions*, he assured readers that Rosenfelt must have been misquoted by the press. In *My Commando Operations*, however, Skorzeny portrayed himself as refusing to shake Rosenfelt's extended hand after the trial because he was angry at the prosecutor's attempt to associate Skorzeny's 150th Panzer Brigade with the Malmédy massacre. Robert Durst, on the other hand, evoked a rare consistency in Skorzeny. *Skorzeny's Secret Missions, Commando Extraordinary* and *My Commando Operations* all have the chief defense counsel telling the military tribunal at the trial that he would have been proud to have men such as Skorzeny and the other defendants in a unit that he commanded.

Although acquitted, Skorzeny remained in American custody

pending any new charges. He was put to work at the U.S. Army's Historical Division, where he wrote a memoir of his mission to rescue Mussolini. Skorzeny was later sent to Darmstadt for denazification, a process that, like "war crimes trials," Skorzeny contemptuously placed in quotation marks.

In *Secret Missions*, Skorzeny offered no account of his escape from U.S. custody. Foley's *Commando Extraordinary* devoted three paragraphs to Skorzeny's escape. The obliging German driver of a transport pool car allowed him to stow away in the luggage department. Karl Radl, Skorzeny's longtime adjunct and fellow prisoner, crammed Skorzeny's six-foot, four-inch body into the small, cramped space. Three or four other prisoners clumped together in order to shield the scene from the prison camp guards. When the vehicle had reached a safe distance from the prison, according to Foley, who had extensively interviewed Skorzeny, the driver pulled over so that Skorzeny could join him in the front seat. Unnamed friends had placed a suitcase of clothes at a railway stop ten miles from Darmstadt. Donning civilian garb, Skorzeny took a train to Stuttgart and then traveled on to Berchtesgaden

If Foley accurately recorded Skorzeny's account of his escape during those interviews, Hitler's favorite commando seriously contradicted himself when relating this feat in *My Commando Operations*. Skorzeny claimed that he installed himself in the trunk of the car owned by the American colonel who was in command of Darmstadt—with no help from anyone. Rather than agreeing to help facilitate his escape, Skorzeny maintained that the driver, who had been sent to do some shopping for the camp commander, had no idea that he had crammed himself into the car's trunk.

In *The Beast Reawakens*, Lee offered a radically different account of Skorzeny's escape. On July 27, 1948, a car bearing American license plates arrived at Darmstadt. Three SS veterans, all of whom wore the uniforms of U.S. Army Military Police, emerged from the vehicle, entered the camp and informed authorities that they had been ordered to transport Skorzeny to Nuremberg for a legal hearing. Thus, Otto Skorzeny escaped from U.S. custody in an American vehicle—but not hidden away in its trunk. Skorzeny later claimed that the uniforms had been provided to the former SS men by the Americans. Citing Glenn B. Infield's *Skorzeny: Hitler's Commando* as his source, Lee noted that Skorzeny's wife confirmed the old commando's account.

Why did the United States want to free Otto Skorzeny? Lee argued that the CIA as well as army intelligence had come to see Skorzeny as a valuable asset in the Cold War. His commando exploits had become the stuff of legends and his Nazi past ensured that he was a staunch anti-communist. Moreover, Skorzeny had emphasized during his interrogation by U.S. Army that, in the eventuality of a struggle between the West and the USSR, he wanted to fight for the West. His service on the Eastern Front had given him an intimate knowledge of strategically important sites in the Soviet Union. Many Ukrainians had thrown in with Nazi Germany when Hitler invaded the USSR, and Skorzeny boasted of his contacts with Ukrainian anti-communists. Lee cited a report filed by two agents of the U.S. Army's Counterintelligence Corps that vouched for the sincerity of Skorzeny's desire to aid the West. Bill Kasich was right when he asserted that the United States coveted Otto Skorzeny's services.

Foley, whose biography of Skorzeny occasionally approaches a tone resembling hero-worship, maintained that Skorzeny, presumably from pride, refused to go into hiding and resorted to disguises to avoid capture. Dying his hair blond, he openly drove around Germany with his wife and visited old comrades. In 1949 the Skorzenys visited France, where Foley has them popping up in St. Germain-en-Laye and the Champs-Élysées and then spending a winter on a farm near Lyon. We're told that Hitler's star commando went skiing at Savoy where, according to Foley, he was amused to read of his alleged activities in the neo–Nazi underground as recounted in sensationalist newspaper articles. Foley evidently had no inkling that such an organization as ODESSA existed—and that Skorzeny belonged to it.

Skorzeny, in *My Commando Operations*, wrote that after spending two years each in Germany and France, he journeyed to Spain to pursue his career as an engineer. His service to the Third Reich comprised no handicap in that nation. General Francisco Franco, Spain's dictator, launched a revolution in 1936 to overthrown his country's legally elected republican government. The three-year civil war was a kind of dress-rehearsal for World War II. Hitler and Mussolini rallied to Franco's support and supplied him with much-needed troops and supplies, while Mexico and the USSR aided the embattled republicans. Volunteers from many nations poured into Spain, including Americans who served in the Abraham Lincoln Brigade. Congress, under pressure from isolationists as well as groups that openly favored Franco's nationalist coalition, passed legislation that banned the United States from supplying the republicans with much-needed arms and other equipment. The last republican strongholds fell to Franco's army in 1939 and he quickly established a right-wing dictatorship.

7. Otto Skorzeny

When France fell to Nazi Germany in 1940, Hitler unsuccessfully tried to lure Franco into an open alliance. Historians are uncertain whether Franco demanded too much from Hitler in exchange for joining the Axis alliance, or simply wanted to remain on the fence because he doubted whether the Axis nations could defeat the Allies. In any event, Spain remained neutral during World War II—the only fascist nation to survive the conflict. Skorzeny felt comfortable, even welcomed, in post-war Spain. A German court in 1952 declared him "denazified *in absentia*." Otto Skorzeny ostensibly became a reputable, if not quite respectable, businessman.

In *My Commando Operations*, Skorzeny remarked on his business trips to other nations, including Juan Perón's Argentina and Nasser's Egypt. He failed to mention, however, that both nations contained flourishing colonies of Nazi fugitives. In his *Modern Dictators*, Barry Rubin observed that Nasser, who came to power in 1952 after a bloodless coup that toppled Egypt's monarch, had cooperated with German spies during World War II and probably would have collaborated with Nazi Germany if Rommel had been able to conquer Egypt.

Skorzeny's memoir also contains no mention of his recruitment by the CIA to help Nasser shore up his military intelligence operations. Washington saw the Egyptian dictator as a potential ally that should be cultivated in order to keep him out of the Soviet camp during the Cold War. Since it would have been politically awkward to offer direct military assistance to a nation that openly opposed the right of Israel to exist, any aid to Nasser had to be covert. Lee wrote that CIA director Allan Dulles and Reinhard Gehlen, who had become a CIA asset, decided that Skorzeny was the right man for the job. After agreeing to accept this assignment, Skorzeny used CIA money to recruit Nazis to assist him strengthening work for Nasser, including SS Major Leopold Gleim. For war crimes committed in his capacity as the Gestapo chief in Poland, Gleim had been sentenced to death *in absentia*. Gleim found the anti–Semitism of the Arab world to his liking and decided to put down roots by formally converting to Islam.

Skorzeny and his men trained Nasser's troops in commando tactics for possible combat with British forces that occupied the Suez Canal zone. The value of receiving commando training from one as renowned in that field as Otto Skorzeny, however, quickly came to the attention of Palestinians living in Egypt. Guerrillas schooled in the techniques of unconventional warfare, they realized, could conduct more successful raids into

Israel. These Palestinians began joining the Egyptian army so they could learn the fine points of guerrilla warfare from Nazi veterans, who were surely amused by the irony of their role in training troops to kill Jews. Cairo-born Yasser Arafat, who would later enter the Palestine Liberation Organization and serve as its chairman of its executive committee from 1969 until his death in 2004, trained under Skorzeny. Lee wrote that the Nazi commando and Arafat became close friends and quoted Skorzeny's wife as saying that Arafat would have done anything for her husband.

Recalling in *My Commando Operations* a trip to South Africa, Skorzeny tried to portray himself as a human rights advocate by deploring British persecution of that nation's Boers but remained silent about apartheid. Lee observed that Skorzeny conducted a considerable amount of business in South Africa, which had become a refuge for any number of fugitive Nazis who felt comfortable living in such a blatantly racist nation. Skorzeny's business enterprises seem to have been guided by the profit motive rather than racism or the promotion of national socialism, however. When France was locked in a protracted war with Algerian rebels seeking independence for their nation, Lee noted that Skorzeny sold arms to the rebels.

Certainly one of the most curious chapters in Skorzeny's post-war existence was his brief residency in Ireland, where he arrived in 1959 and purchased Martinstown House, a 160-acre farm and mansion in County Kildare. His presence in Ireland "caused much intrigue," according Peter Crutchley in "How did Hitler's scar-faced henchman become an Irish farmer?" Skorzeny's presence and intentions ignited a firestorm in the Irish and British press, according to Crutchley, which demanded to know whether the old commando sought to found a Nazi movement in Ireland. The Austrian expatriate also became a topic of discussion in the Irish parliament. Noel Browne, who served as Ireland's minister for health, speculated that Skorzeny might well be engaged in anti–Semitic and neo–Nazi activities and argued that the aging commando "should not be allowed to use Ireland for that purpose."

Skorzeny had good reason to believe that he would be welcomed in Ireland. Palash Ghosh, in "The Irish Nationalist and the Nazi: When Eamon de Valera Paid His Respects to Adolf Hitler," observed that on May 2, 1945, Eamon de Valera, Ireland's prime minister who also served as foreign minister, visited the German Embassy in Dublin to sign a book of condolences. Just two days earlier, Hitler and Eva Braun had committed suicide in Berlin to avoid capture by the rapidly approaching Soviet army. De Valera was accompanied by his aide, Secretary of External Affairs Joseph Walshe. In addition to signing the book of condolences, de Valera and Walshe met with Eduard Hempel, Nazi Germany's principal envoy to Ireland, to extend their sympathy to the government of the Third Reich. Irish envoys in other nations also visited German embassies to express their condolences upon Hitler's death.

Spain and Portugal, both of which had remained officially neutral during World War II and both ruled by fascist dictators, also expressed condolences to Nazi Germany. Ghosh reminded readers that not a single other democratic state in Western Europe followed de Valera's example. The press of the Allied nations expressed outrage at de Valera's action. The *New York Times* editorialized, "Considering the character and the record of the man for whose death he was expressing grief, there is obviously something wrong with the protocol, the neutrality of Mr. de Valera." While Churchill and Truman were understandably angry, de Valera's gesture earned him praise from the British Union of Fascists, which lauded the Irish prime minister for "honoring the memory of the greatest German in history."

This wasn't the first time that de Valera had behaved in a manner that seemed to indicate he was something less than neutral. Imperial Japan in 1943 had established a puppet state known as the Provisional Government of Free India, which was led by the Indian nationalist Subhash Chandra Bose. Bose, who had worked with Gandhi in the Indian National Congress, was determined to win independence for his homeland. He escaped imprisonment in India and made his way to Germany, where he sought to persuade Hitler to invade India and drive out the British. Hitler refused and placed Bose on a German submarine that took him to Japanese-controlled territory. Imperial Japan made Bose the head of the Provisional Government of Free India, which exercised a limited degree of control over portions of Japanese-occupied territories in southern Asia. A dynamic speaker, Bose succeeded in raising an army of about 40,000 troops, most of whom were Indian POWs from the British army. Bose's Indian National Army fought alongside the Imperial Japanese Army, which supplied it with weapons and supplies. Bose saw himself as the Asian counterpart to the Axis dictators. Since Hitler was *der Führer* and Mussolini *Il Duce*, Bose adopted the title *Netaji*, which roughly translates as "revered leader."

The Provisional Government of Free India was recognized as a legitimate state only by the three Axis powers and their satellites such as

Manchukuo, Croatia and Slovakia. While stopping short of granting the Provisional Government of Free India formal recognition, de Valera in 1943 sent a warm note of congratulations to Bose. De Valera was undeterred by the knowledge that the Provisional Government of Free India was a creation of the Japanese and had declared war on the Allies. He felt a kinship with Bose, since the Indian's hatred of the British matched his own.

Ghosh cited the recollections of David Gray, the U.S. ambassador to Ireland in the 1940s, who expressed the belief that de Valera kept Ireland officially neutral during the war "on the bet that the Nazis would defeat the Allies." Gray even suspected that "some top Irish officials were, in fact, colluding with the Third Reich." Anti-British sentiment ran deep in Ireland. Centuries of English oppression and the carving up of the nation into a "free state," which was granted home rule, and Ulster, which remained under British control, inclined many Irish into sympathizing with Germany. A man such as Otto Skorzeny, who had fought Britain and its allies, was a hero to such people.

Skorzeny didn't inflict himself on the Irish. In fact, they openly reached out to him. "Skorzeny traveled from Madrid to Ireland in June 1957, where he had been invited to Portmarnock Country Club hotel in County Dublin," Crutchley stated. A gala reception was held in his honor. A contemporary newspaper account observed that the ballroom was packed with professional men as well as representatives of parliament and various societies. One person in attendance, Charles Haughey, later became Ireland's prime minister.

This event probably played a major role in convincing Skorzeny to relocate to Ireland. A local resident recalled him as "a big man who stood out because of the scar across his face" but not particularly friendly. His neighbors often saw him driving country roads in his white Mercedes. Newspapers alleged that Skorzeny's farm served as a sanctuary for Nazi war criminals, Crutchley noted, but no solid evidence was uncovered to support this claim. Documents at the Irish National Archives in Dublin revealed that Skorzeny was granted a temporary visa to live in Ireland with the proviso that he not enter Britain, according to Crutchley. Angered that he was banned from Britain and that Ireland, probably under diplomatic pressure from Britain, refused to grant him a permanent visa, Skorzeny finally left Ireland and returned to Spain.

There had been speculation for decades that, at some point in his life, Skorzeny worked for Mossad, Israel's counterpart to the CIA, but few scholars and journalists took such a possibility seriously. In 2016, however, the Israel-based news agency *Haaretz* published a report, based on "interviews with former Mossad officers and with Israelis who have access to the Mossad's archived secrets," that claimed Skorzeny had indeed been used by Mossad to hamper Egypt's rocket program. Technologically sophisticated rockets, fired from Egypt, comprised a deadly threat to Israel. Mossad was determined to neutralize this threat even if it meant utilizing Skorzeny, who was living in Spain at the time of his recruitment. Mossad was surely aware that Skorzeny earlier had been recruited by the CIA to shore up Nasser as well as his involvement with Palestinian guerrillas. The Israelis, however, were quite willing to work with someone as unsavory as Skorzeny if circumstances demanded it.

Skorzeny refused Mossad's offer of money for his services, claiming that he was essentially well-heeled and had no need of additional funds. He requested, however, that Mossad intervene with Simon Wiesenthal to have his name removed from the celebrated Nazi hunter's list of wanted war criminals. Mossad was unable to accomplish this request but assured Skorzeny that his name had been removed. Skorzeny might also have accepted the assignment to satisfy his lifelong craving for adventure and intrigue. He would have appreciated the irony of working for a people Nazi Germany had tried to destroy. Not that many years earlier, Skorzeny had been in the service of Egypt. Accepting an assignment to help thwart that nation's fledgling rocket program appealed to his cynicism.

The old commando provided Mossad with a list of companies that were selling Egypt materiel for its rocket program. He also personally sent a letter bomb that killed several members of Egypt's rocket team, including a German scientist. Skorzeny on September 11, 1962, killed Heinz Krug, a German scientist who played a key role in Egypt's rocket program. This assassination was committed in Germany. Krug, who had been harassed by Mossad, met with Skorzeny because he trusted his fellow veteran of the Third Reich and thought Skorzeny would provide him with protection from his enemies. Instead, the commando personally squeezed the trigger of the pistol that killed him.

Krug had worked with Werner von Braun during World War II to build rockets for Nazi Germany. Declining to join Braun and other German expatriates in the United States after the war, Krug instead joined another group of German scientists in Egypt. Mossad speculated that Krug found the opportunity to help wreak havoc on Jews—including many Holocaust survivors—was simply too tempting.

One of the great ironies of the post-war period occurred when Skorzeny's Mossad handlers brought him to Jerusalem. The commando visited Yad Vashem, the museum in Jerusalem dedicated to the memory of the six million Jews killed during the Holocaust. The old "Nazi was silent and seemed respectful," according to the Haaretz account. There was an awkward moment, however, when a Holocaust survivor pointed to Skorzeny and called him a war criminal. Skorzeny's Israeli handler defused the threat by claiming that the old commando was a relative and fellow Holocaust survivor.

Skorzeny in 1970 founded the Paladin Group, which was headquartered on the Mediterranean Sea near Alicante, Spain. The Paladin Group functioned as a commando training school that taught guerrilla tactics for men who wanted to work as mercenaries. Lee reported that Dr. Gerhard Hartmut von Schubert, who had worked for Goebbels during the war, served as Paladin's manager. Ironically, the man regarded as one of history's greatest commandos hadn't kept abreast of developments in military science. Lee cited an American mercenary who attended a few sessions and decided that the tactics taught by the Paladin Group were decidedly dated. Indeed, the only useful information the mercenary learned were the finer points of arson.

A three-packs-a-day smoker for decades, Skorzeny was diagnosed with advanced lung and bronchial cancer early in 1975 and died on July 5 of that year. Lawrence Van Gelder's obituary for the old commando, which ran in the *New York Times*, mentioned his acclaimed rescue of Mussolini while noting that Skorzeny had never repudiated Nazism. "Such was Mr. Skorzeny's reputation and his blind loyalty to Hitler," Van Gelder wrote, "that long after the end of the war—in fact, almost to the very end of his life—he was said to be involved in coups and assassination plots and the organization of a Nazi network called Die Spinne (The Spider) operating out of a seaside resort in Spain." The obituary also reminded readers that while "most publicity about Mr. Skorzeny tended to emphasize the daring of his exploits, he was accused of participation in the slaughter of thousands of Jews and anti–Nazis in Hungary and of other deaths classified as crimes against humanity." Skorzeny's "loyalty to Hitler remained unswerving," he wrote. He continued,

> Early this year, after a former French resistance fighter tried to strike him with a riding crop, Mr. Skorzeny, apparently disdainful of historical accuracy, was quoted as having said: "I am proud to have served my country and my Fuhrer who was elected by the German people with an overwhelming majority. The only thing

I lament is that all Europe—and not only Germany—is divided and torn by those powers that I had the honor of fighting."

Otto Skorzeny died an unrepentant Nazi.

Van Gelder also quoted *New York Times* critic Orville Prescott, who reviewed *Skorzeny's Secret Missions* in 1950. Prescott, whose reviews were vastly influential and played a significant role in determining whether a book sold well, wrote: "His book is a proud record of the military achievements of an insensitive, unscrupulous and essentially stupid man, who never regrets for a moment that he devoted his great abilities as a soldier to the service of a monstrous leader and an infamous state. If a new Hitler appeared in Germany tomorrow, one feels after reading this book, Skorzeny would be at his side."

According to United Press International, the obituary stated, Skorzeny's corpse had been wrapped in a white shroud strewn with carnations. The open coffin rested in the back room of a Madrid "funeral establishment." An attendant was quoted as saying, "Nobody has come to see him except the photographers." His corpse was cremated.

Although ignored in Spain, the late Otto Skorzeny received a hero's welcome when his ashes were flown to Vienna for burial in a suburban cemetery. Lee reported in *The Beast Awakens* that the memorial service drew over five hundred Nazi diehards, many of whom wore their old uniforms and military medallions. Skorzeny's eulogy was delivered by Hans-Ulrich Rudel, a highly decorated World War II dive-bomber pilot. He was purported Skorzeny's personal choice to deliver his eulogy address, which is hardly surprising. Like Skorzeny, Rudel had never repudiated his allegiance to Nazism. He was a leading member of the neo–Nazi German Reich Party in West Germany and had publicly castigated the Allies for going to war with Nazi Germany, which he saw as a bulwark against the Soviet Union. Again like Skorzeny, Rudel spent time after the war as a guest of and advisor to Juan and Eva Perón in Argentina, where he cultivated contacts with the Nazi fugitives living in that nation. Skorzeny could hardly have made a better choice for his graveside speaker.

8

Downed American Airmen
Descent into Hell

Kasich touched on the plight of Allied flight crews that crashed behind enemy lines.

> You bomb this, you bomb that. But you had a lot of pilots that came in, the jocks, that would strafe German farms, which was a mistake. It was horrible. Those people had nothing to do with it [the Nazi war crimes]. But if for some reason they would be knocked out of the sky ... the [German] army came [and] would take them into a prison camp. But most of them were pitch-forked to death. They [German civilians] came out and pitch-forked them to death. They would string them up by their penises or their testicles, then they would pitch-fork them to death and they would leave them up so the others would see.

German civilians who killed downed Allied flyers were prosecuted as war criminals. Our conversation turned to a particularly well-known case.

Kasich mentioned that many Americans believe Leon Jaworski was a prosecutor at Nuremberg. "He was not at Nuremberg," Kasich said, "He was with the Judge-Advocate." Jaworski is chiefly remembered today for serving as Watergate Special Prosecutor, a post to which he was appointed in 1973 after the Nixon administration fired Archibald Cox, the first prosecutor. Jaworski served as prosecutor in the Russelsheim massacre case *(United States v. Kluettgen)*, in which the accused war criminals were civilians rather than military personnel.

This case began on August 24, 1944, when an American B-24 bomber was shot down while taking part in a raid on Hanover, Germany. The nine-man crew parachuted from the plane and was quickly apprehended. One crew member, who had been seriously wounded by anti-aircraft fire, was hospitalized for surgery. The remaining eight members of the crew were placed on a train for transport to a POW camp. On the night of August 25, the British Royal Air Force (RAF) conducted a major bombing raid on

Russelsheim in order to knock out its Opel plant. Records indicate that 116 RAF planes dropped a total of 674 2,000-pound bombs as well as 400,000 incendiaries on the city. The damage to Russelsheim was horrendous.

The track that would have taken the American POWs to the prison camp had incurred serious damage from the raid as well. The two German soldiers acting as guards were forced to remove the Americans from the train and walk them to Russelsheim, where they could take another train. A crowd of townspeople quickly materialized, who identified the prisoners as airmen by their uniforms and assumed that they had been members of the raiding party that had devastated their city. Two women shouted: "Beat them to pieces! Beat them to death! They are the ones! They are the ones who were here last night! Kill the dogs!"

The Americans were attacked by townspeople wielding shovels, sticks, hammers, rocks and other weapons of opportunity. One airman was so badly beaten that he could no longer walk, so he sat down on the sidewalk. A piece of stone was sticking in his skull. A townsperson "went over to him and kicked him in the neck and chin," according to the account introduced at the war crimes trial. The two Germans guards did nothing to stop the attack.

When none of the flyers could walk another step, they collapsed. "They crept together to protect themselves," but were unable to fend off the attack of a townsperson who began "hitting them with a hammer, beating them to and fro." Joseph Harten, a Nazi Party official and propaganda chief in Russelsheim who was married and the father of three children under the age of eight, then shot six of the eight prisoners with his revolver. He didn't shoot the remaining two only because he ran out of bullets.

The eight prisoners were piled into a farmer's cart that was drawn to the cemetery by members of the Hitler Youth. Those who showed signs of life by moaning were beaten until their moaning ceased. The sound of an air raid siren, however, caused the crowd to flee for safety. The two American who hadn't been shot managed to crawl from the cart and leave the cemetery. They were captured after a few days and imprisoned in a POW camp for the remainder of the war.

The U.S. Army learned of the Russelsheim incident from French and Polish slave laborers. The bodies of the six murdered flyers were disinterred from the cemetery on June 28, 1945. Only four could be identified because they still wore their dog tags. All of the corpses except one had fractured skulls. "The one whose skull had not been fractured had two bullet holes," according to the official report. "Two others had bullet holes in the skulls."

Although as many as two hundred residents of Russelsheim were thought to have participated in this atrocity, only eleven—nine men and two women—were tried on July 25, 1945, in the town of Darmstadt. In reviewing the case on August 23, 1945, the Office of the Staff Judge Advocate wrote:

> That the act charged against these accused constitutes an offense against the laws of war is plain. It is provided in Chapter 6, Article 2, of the Geneva Convention of 1929, that "Prisoners of War are in the power of the enemy, but not [in the power] of the individuals or bodies of troops that capture them. They must at all times be treated with humanity and protected particularly against acts of violence...." Also, in Article 23 in the Annex to the Hague Convention of 18 October 1907, it is provided that "In Addition to the prohibitions provided by special conventions, it is expressly forbidden.... To kill or wound an enemy who, having laid down his arms, or having no longer any means of defense, has surrender at discretion." To both of these Conventions, Germany is a signatory.

The Office of the Judge Advocate also noted in its review that "military counsel was provided for the accused, who were also represented by vigorous and capable civilian counsel."

Defense for the accused argued at the trial that Nazi propaganda by Joseph Goebbels regularly incited German civilians such as the residents of Russelsheim to commit acts of violence against downed fliers. Goebbels, rather than the eleven defendants, bore the preponderance of the guilt for the murders of the American flyers. Lt. Col. Leon Jaworski, as prosecuting attorney, challenged that contention. The perpetrators were adult men and women, Jaworski noted. If Goebbels' propaganda encouraged them to commit murder and they indeed committed murder, he maintained, these men and women must be held responsible for their actions. The military commission, which presided at the trial, found Jaworski's argument for personal responsibility more convincing than the defense's attempt to shift the blame Goebbels's propaganda. Only one defendant was found not guilty. Of the ten convicted, seven received the death penalty. The two women, originally sentenced to be hanged, later escaped the noose when their sentences were changed to prison terms. The other five—including Russelsheim's Nazi propaganda chief Joseph Hartgen, who had shot four of the flyers—were hanged on November 10, 1945.

Kevin Dougherty, in a 2004 article for *Stars and Stripes*, quoted Dagmar Eichorn, a contemporary resident of Russelsheim, as saying that after the war, most residents simply wanted to put the incident behind them. Many members of the mob that had attacked the flyers still lived in the community. "It was dangerous for people to talk about it," Eichorn said.

Eichorn led the drive to build a memorial to the murdered flyers in Russelsheim, which was formally unveiled in 2004. The memorial's dedication featured a prominent guest: Sidney Eugene Brown, one of the two American flyers who managed to crawl out of that cart in the cemetery.

Schulz also mentioned the plight of Allied airmen who crashed behind enemy lines. During World War II, there had been "a lot of lynchings of airmen," he told me. The Germans themselves had inadvertently provided evidence that could be used in the prosecution of war criminals. "We had pictures of whole communities of Germans around a guy being lynched," Schulz said. When I expressed surprise, he continued, "Eight or ten pictures. Grabbing him, dragging him along, hanging him. Stripping him. Using his parachute cords to hang him with. All of that was documented by the Germans."

In retrospect, I shouldn't have been so surprised that "whole communities of Germans" so readily posed with lynched airmen. Photos of lynchings were not uncommon even in the United States, where commercial photographers captured images of lynched blacks surrounded by crowds of white onlookers that may well have included their murderers. These photographs were produced as post cards and then marketed to the public.

9

Project Paperclip

The Harvest of Nazi Technology

BILL KASICH AND OTHER MEMBERS of the War Crimes Group were puzzled by a report that an accused war criminal had escaped after being transported to Dachau.

> They [field agents for the War Crimes Group] picked him up in Stuttgart, the military government, four of our agents. They took him to Dachau. Three days later, word came back to headquarters that he had escaped and we were talking how could he escape … and Morgan [Frank Morgan, a member of the War Crimes Group] was saying "Putt! Putt!" and being eighteen at that time and now wanting to admit my ignorance I was wondering, "What the heck does Putt mean?" I didn't know what was going on until I read this book and it came back to me.

The book, which he brought to the interview, was Linda Hunt's landmark work *Secret Agenda: The United States Government, Nazi Scientists, and Project Paperclip, 1945–1990*, published in 1991 by St. Martin's Press. Kasich found the photo of Donald Putt in Hunt's book. "That's him right there," he said. "He had the authority." After I had read aloud the caption for Putt's photo, Kasich said with an unmistakable tone of disgust in his voice. "Paperclip. This is all about Paperclip."

Kasich's anger at Putt for his role in allowing war criminals to escape justice came out in our second interview as well. "He [Putt] had the authority to bring them to this country. He could override anybody. They didn't even have to go to trial. They were wanted as war criminals."

Born in Sugarcreek, Ohio, Donald Leander Putt (1905–1988) graduated from Carnegie Institute of Technology in 1928 with a bachelor of science in electrical engineering. He was commissioned a second lieutenant in the Signal Corps Reserve that same year, according to his biography on the U.S. Air Force web site. Putt completed his flying training on June

28, 1929, and received his commission as a second lieutenant in the Air Reserve. He received his Regular commission three months later.

This biography noted that from October 1944 to August 1945 Putt was assigned to U.S. Air Forces in Europe as chief of Technical Services. He returned to Wright Field in Ohio in September 1945, where he served as deputy commanding general for Intelligence of the Air Technical Service Command. In December 1946 Putt was reassigned as deputy chief of the engineering division. Two years later, he was appointed to the post of Director of Research and Development in the Office of the Deputy Chief of Staff for Materiel at the Air Force headquarters in Washington, D.C. The biography concluded its account of Putt's Air Force career in the immediate post-war era by stating that he became assistant deputy chief of staff for Development in April 1951. There is no mention of his involvement in Paperclip.

In an article titled "Paperclip," which appeared in the June 2007 edition of *Air Force Magazine*, contributing editor Walter J. Boyne rationalized the need for Project Paperclip and praised Putt for his role in its success. Even in its death throes, Boyne observed, Nazi Germany "continued to astound the world with its amazing new technological marvels." In the article's next sentence, Boyne defined these technological marvels as "rockets, jet fighters, V-1 unpiloted aircraft, lethal V-2 missiles and a host of other military advances." The Allies, he noted, "naturally wanted to exploit these developments and make the new war-making capabilities their own." This desire for deadlier military weapons spurred a "spontaneous international race to acquire equipment, documents, engineers and scientists who produced the German weaponry advance." Boyne later assured us, however, that this Nazi cornucopia of advanced technology was not limited to means of destruction. "The German intellectual capital was formidable and priceless" and "extended beyond mere advances in weaponry." Nazi Germany had excelled in the development of "wind tunnels, materials and other disciplines necessary to build an advanced scientific infrastructure."

Boyne remarked that the United States clearly won this "spontaneous international race" to harvest Nazi technology "despite the admonitions of Gen. Dwight D. Eisenhower that there were to be no dealings with Nazi Germany." Actually, Ike had been given some wiggle room on this matter by the U.S. Joint Chiefs of Staff (JCS), which on May 10, 1945, sent a top-secret, 10,000-word directive to Eisenhower in his capacity as commander in chief of the Allied forces in Western Europe. The directive commanded Eisenhower to "search out and arrest all persons who have participated in the planning or carrying out [of] Nazi enterprises involving or resulting in atrocities or war crimes." Eisenhower was ordered not to grant any "special consideration" to those arrested for war crimes.

In an article for *The Daily Beast*, Richard Rashke commented: "Nothing could have been clearer or tougher. The JCS took it all back in an 18-word sentence tacked onto the directive like an afterthought. 'In your discretion, you may make such exceptions as you deem advisable for intelligence and other military reasons.'"

Rashke reminded us that this directive applied to all Allied forces, not merely the Americans. Nonetheless, Boyne is correct in asserting that the Yanks clearly bested the British and French in gathering up Nazi scientists and engineers. While conceding that "there were many reasons for the United States' greater success in exploiting the accumulated information of its former foes," Boyne stated that "the primary cause of success was the vision of Gen. H.H. 'Hap' Arnold, Commanding General of the U.S. Army Air Forces, whose strong penchant for research and development, led to his work with Theodore von Kármán." A brilliant physicist who discerned the rising tide of anti–Semitism in Europe, Kármán immigrated to the United States in 1930. Arnold in 1944 persuaded Kármán to leave Caltech and move to Washington to head the Scientific Advisory Group, which was later renamed the Scientific Advisory Committee. Boyne stated that "von Kármán's connections in academia created the kind of climate and top cover for Air Technical intelligence personnel to scour the German countryside and gather the necessary data, equipment, and personnel."

Boyne dated the origin of this program to gather what Rashke calls "the pick of the Nazi litter" to July 20, 1945, when the U.S. Chiefs of Staff consolidated a number of intelligence-gathering operations into Project Overcast, which "provided the initial guidelines for seizing, holding, using, and returning enemy nationals." Following the surrender of Japan on September 2, 1945, Boyne wrote, "protests broke out over the use of former enemy personnel for national military purposes" and Project Overcast was renamed Project Paperclip in March 1946. The new name was derived from the practice of flagging the dossiers of the most "highly valued scientists" with paperclips.

Boyne omitted the role of Dean Acheson in initiating Project Paperclip. On August 30, 1946, in his capacity as Undersecretary of State, Acheson sent President Harry Truman a suggested revision of Project Paperclip policy, which would expand the project so as to allow up to one thousand German and Austrian engineers and scientists to immigrate to the United States. Acheson urged Truman to allow their entry in order to strengthen our nation's national security at a time when war with the Soviet Union seemed a very real possibility. Both George Kennan, a U.S. career diplomat stationed in Moscow as well as Clark Clifford, who served as Truman's White House counsel, had warned Washington that the Soviet Union posed a serious threat to the United States and world peace. After four days of deliberation, Truman gave his approval.

Acheson's 1969 autobiography, *Present at the Creation: My Years in the State Department*, is a 798-page small-print opus that one would assume covered every chapter of his entire public life. He even included a matter as mundane as the 1946 shipment of prize bulls to Mexico from a region of the United States infected with hoof-and-mouth disease and how it was successfully resolved. His suggestion that Truman revise Project Paperclip policy, however, is missing. In fact, the book—dedicated by Acheson to Truman as "The Captain with a mighty heart"—contains no mention whatsoever of Project Paperclip.

"Col. Donald L. Putt, backed by Gen. Carl A. 'Tooey' Spaatz, led an aggregation of specialist teams in Operation Lusty," which Boyne praised as "the most successful of the competing operations racing across Germany." He also noted that Operation Lusty "had the most direct effect on aeronautical research." Code named Operation Lusty for Luftwaffe secret technology, this program began following D-Day, according to Robert L. Young, historian at the Air Force's National Air and Space Intelligence Center at Wright Air Force Base. Air Technical Intelligence (ATI) teams scoured the countryside in search of enemy aircraft and aeronautical equipment. Young noted that these teams utilized master intelligence manifests known as "Black Lists." The ATI teams intensified their efforts following Germany's surrender, since they knew that "advanced German technology, including documentation, had to be obtained quickly, before it was destroyed or seized by other countries—especially the Soviet Union."

Team members nicknamed "Whizzers" sought German jets. Operation Lusty scored a major triumph when First Lieutenant Robert C. Strobell acquired 15 Me-262 German jets at Lechfield, located near the Messerschmitt factory. Faced with the challenge of training American pilots to fly these jets, Strobell turned to former enemies. Two English-speaking pilots German test pilots "proved invaluable to the Whizzers." Ludwig Hofmann and Karl Baur agreed to teach American pilots to fly the Me-262.

Young stated that Hofmann "knew Charles A. Lindbergh from prewar encounters." Lindbergh (1902–1974), who became a global folk hero after completing a solo flight across the Atlantic in 1927, visited Nazi Germany several times between 1936 and 1938 at the behest of the American military to assess its strength. Göring allowed Lindbergh to tour aviation facilities and, in what Max Wallace called one of history's greatest misinformation feats, managed to convince the gullible American that the Luftwaffe was much stronger than it actually was. Acting on behalf of Hitler, Göring presented Lindbergh with Commander Cross of the Order of the German Eagle in recognition of his celebrated solo flight and contributions to aviation at a formal dinner in 1938. When Lindbergh was urged to return his award after Kristallnacht, which occurred just a few weeks later, he refused on the grounds that it would have been rude. Lindbergh evidently regarded Göring as a friend. In *Nuremberg: Infamy on Trial*, Göring told Dewitt Poole of the U.S. State Department at Nuremberg that Lindbergh had sent him a silver dish as a gift when Edda Göring, his daughter, was born in June of 1938.

When World War II broke out in 1939, Lindbergh vehemently opposed American intervention and became a spokesman for the America First movement. During a speech delivered in Des Moines, Iowa, on September 11, 1941, Lindbergh stated that "the three most important groups that have been pressing this country toward war are the British, the Jews and the Roosevelt administration." He argued that Jews held too much power in the United States. "Their greatest danger to this country is their large ownership and influence in our nation's motion pictures, our press, our radio and our government." Anti-Semites around the nation applauded Lindbergh's words—and still do. Selections from his speeches are prominently featured on many right-wing extremist web sites. Anne Morrow Lindbergh (1906–2001), whose father served as our nation's ambassador to Mexico and was later elected to the U.S. senate from New Jersey, accompanied her husband during his trips to Nazi Germany and shared his views. Her 1940 book, *The Wave of the Future: A Confession of Faith*, is a paean to fascism. In all fairness to the Lindberghs, it should be noted that they were hardly the only prominent Americans who found favor in Nazi Germany. Baldur von Schirach, chief of the Hitler Youth and later Reich governor of Vienna, testified at his Nuremberg trial that he didn't become anti–Semitic because of Nazism. His hatred of Jews sprang from reading *The International Jew* by Henry Ford, the American automaker.

Hitler possessed no small admiration for Ford and specifically cited him as "a great man" in *Mein Kampf*. Karl Kapp, the German consul in Cleveland, and Fritz Heller, German consular representative in Detroit, presented Ford with the Grand Cross of the Supreme Order of the German Eagle on July 30, 1938—his 75th birthday. The presentation took place in Dearborn, Michigan. Ford enjoyed the dubious distinction of being the only American to receive this award, which was given to foreign dignitaries who were regarded as sympathetic to national socialism.

"Under Putt's leadership," Boyne wrote, "ATI teams swarmed over Germany as it collapsed." A special group led by Col. Harold E. Watson impressed Army Air Force leaders by "snapping up copies of the latest German aircraft, which were transported to Ohio for test and evaluation." Boyne credited teams led by Putt and other members of the Scientific Advisory Group with making the most productive long-term discoveries. These teams swept through the well-known German research centers in Stuttgart (the Gran Zeppelin Research Establishment), Göettingen (the Aerodynamics Research Institute), and von Kármán's old stomping ground at Aachen. There they met their peers, leading academics, many of whom they knew personally before the war.

Putt discovered the previously unknown Hermann Göring Aeronautical Research Center in Vöelkenrode on April 13, 1945, and immediately recognized it as a treasure trove of engineering materiel and documents. He was particularly amazed by a plane with swept-back wings, a technological advance he had never before seen. Putt was admiring the work of Adolf Busemann, a brilliant aerospace engineer, who initially suggested swept-back wings to allow planes to achieve supersonic speed at the Volta Conference held in Italy a decade earlier. The plane that so astounded Putt became the prototype for the U.S. Air Force's jet-fighters such as the North American F-86 Sabre.

"Vöelkenrode," Boyne noted, "was in the area designated for occupation by Britain," which forced Putt "to maximize his yield by doing some rapid 'midnight requisitioning' of key documents and equipment and flying it out in war-weary B-17s and B-24s."

Putt's success in his "midnight requisitioning" enterprise is reflected in a report presented by three British officers to the British Intelligence Objective Sub-Committee. The officers wrote that while "the existence of such an institute was known, its exact location was not discovered during the war." The research center "occupies an area of approximately four square miles, including an airport, and has about sixty buildings," the majority of which were "completely hidden in the woods." The exposed buildings were "cleverly camouflaged to look like farm buildings." The officers reported that "the airfield itself was also well camouflaged, being sown with different coloured grasses." The institute could not be detected from the air, even by low-flying Allied planes.

"The scope of the laboratories and the scale of the equipment was most impressive," the officers wrote. "Money appears to have been no object and was freely spent here." However, the British were not afforded the opportunity to see how that money had been spent. Putt's team had been too successful.

> When the Institute was finally taken over by the M.A.P. [Ministry of Aircraft Production], practically all buildings had been thoroughly looted and all the offices and laboratories were shambles. All easily portable equipment of any value had been removed and much of the heavier equipment had been damaged. Practically all optical equipment had been rendered useless by the removal of the lenses.

Boyne stated that "Putt's work annoyed the British but pleased his taskmaster boss, Maj. Gen. Hugh J. Knerr, who ordered him to Wright Field." He doesn't mention, however, that Putt took quite a few German scientists and engineers with him. In addition to "all the easily portable equipment of any value," Putt promised the Germans jobs at Wright Field if they would voluntarily go with him to a holding center for captured enemy personnel at Bad Kissingen. He sweetened the deal by assuring the Germans that they would be eventually be joined by their families.

The case of Emil Salmon demonstrates Putt's willingness to allow criminals to escape punishment for their crimes. One month after signing a contract with Paperclip in June 1947, a denazification court convicted Salmon of crimes including membership in an SA assault unit as well as his role in assisting the SS to burn down a synagogue. He was sentenced to six months of hard labor. Salmon, however, was a jet engineer whose knowledge and experience Putt wanted to exploit for American military aviation. Two days after his conviction, Putt ordered Salmon to be taken to the United States, where he joined his fellow Nazi scientists at Wright-Patterson.

Salmon wasn't quite out of the woods yet, however. Class II Nazis—defined as "activists, militants, profiteers, or incriminated persons"—were forbidden participation in Project Paperclip, which meant that Salmon could be denied entry into the United States. Putt persuaded Salmon to sign a formal statement that affirmed his SA activities had been limited to athletic programs. Salmon's Nazi classification was soon changed from

Class II to Class IV, a category comprised of those deemed to be merely "followers." He no longer needed to fear deportation.

Otto Bock, Gerhaud Braun, Rudolph Edse, Albert Patin, Hans Rister and Theodore Zobel comprised the first group of Germans that Putt brought to Wright Field in 1945. Their fields of specialization were: Bock (supersonics); Braun (motor research); Edse (rocket fuels); Rister (aerodynamics); and Zobel (aerodynamics). While not a scientist, Project Paperclip operatives regarded Patin as a valuable resource. He was a businessman, whose factories manufactured aviation equipment such as automatic control devices and in-flight steering mechanism. In *Operation Paperclip*, Annie Jacobsen wrote that Putt coveted this cutting-edge technology and believed that it would give the American military a ten-year leap over the Soviet Union.

Putt was aware that Patin had used French, Dutch and Russian POWs as well as at least 500 Jewish women as slave laborers during the war. His value to Project Paperclip, however, easily trumped any investigation and possible prosecution for war crimes.

The Germans lived in an area in a compound known as the Hilltop, which consisted of five single-story wooden buildings and three small cottages on a single-lane dirt road that led to the town dump. They were not allowed to leave the base unaccompanied by Army intelligence personnel. A gate surrounding the Hilltop was kept locked from 5 p.m. to 7 a.m. The Germans were allowed to exercise at the Dayton YMCA on weekends. Housekeepers, provided by Project Paperclip, tidied up their living quarters and washed their laundry. This Spartan routine, however, was more than offset by the salaries paid to the Germans, which averaged $12,480— well above the annual income of most Americans in the mid–1940s.

The number of Germans brought to Wright Field at Putt's behest through Project Paperclip grew steadily. Georg Rickhey, a tunnel engineer, arrived during the summer of 1946. When his nation had been conquered by the Allies, Rickhey had taken the nondescript job of operations manager in a salt mine located about ninety miles from the concentration camp of Nordhausen, which had been created by the SS for Dora inmates no longer capable of performing slave labor in the fortified underground tunnels of Mittelwerk, where V-1 and V-2 rockets were built. Rickhey was eventually tracked down by U.S. Strategic Bombing Survey Col. Peter Beasley, who had learned from captured documents that Rickhey had been Mittelwerk's general manager as well as its liaison with the German Ministry of Armaments. He had constructed the underground tunnels that had allowed the rocket plant to withstand so much Allied bombing and later boasted to his American captors that he had personally overseen the construction of the Führerbunker beneath the New Reich Chancellery in Berlin, where Hitler spent the last months of his life.

Rickhey's reputation for building underground fortifications that were virtually bombproof as well as his knowledge of Mittelwerk made him a prime candidate for Project Paperclip recruitment. Beasley assured Rickhey that he would recommend him for transport to the United States, where he would be given the kind of employment where his knowledge and skills would be put to good use. Rickhey cemented the deal by taking Beasley to a nearby cave where forty-two boxes of documents of Mittelwerk documents had been hidden. After a brief sojourn in London with Beasley to translate and analyze the documents taken from the cave, Rickhey arrived at Wright Field, where he struck up a friendship with Patin. The two Germans enjoyed socializing and often hosted parties that lasted into the wee hours of the morning. One particular rambunctious party of drinking and card-playing in October 1946 led to Rickhey's downfall.

Hermann Nehlson, a sixty-three-year-old Project Paperclip recruit who needed a good night's sleep to ensure his continued productivity, knocked on the door of Rickhey's residence at least twice to ask that he, Patin and a third man stop making so much racket. When the noise continued, Nehlson entered the room and plunged the card table into darkness by turning out the light. Undeterred, the drunken Rickhey lighted a candle and, according to a statement by Nehlson, joked that he and his companions would continue to play cards by the light of a good kosher candle.

Rickhey had angered the wrong man. Nehlson, who had worked as a consulting engineer for an aircraft company in Austria, had never joined the Nazi Party and opposed anti–Semitism. While recruiting him for Project Paperclip, Putt had promised Nehlson a full-time job with Erwin Loewy (1897–1959), an engineer whose New York City–based company held contracts with the Army Air Force. Nehlson and Loewy were long-time friends, and the Paperclip recruit had looked forward to the opportunity of working with one who shared his loathing for Nazism and the Third Reich. Born in what is now the Czech Republic, Loewy worked at Schloemann, a German shipbuilding firm, with his brother Ludwig until anti–Semitism compelled him to go to France in 1935. Loewy knew, however, that France couldn't resist the sweeping tide of Nazi aggression, and he went to the United States in 1939. A year later,

Erwin Loewy incorporated Hydropress, which manufactured aircraft parts. Following World War II, Loewy and some of his most gifted engineers designed the first motion simulator for the Polaris missile as well as the launch pad for the Vanguard rocket. Both achievements were accomplished without the participation of any scientist or engineer who had ties to Nazi Germany.

Putt, however, reneged on his agreement with Nehlson, who now found himself working with unrepentant Nazis such as Rickhey, who could joke about using a Kosher candle—that is to say, a candle made from the melted body fat of a Jew, who had died in a concentration camp. Angered to find such pro-Nazi sentiment among his co-workers, Nehlson wrote a letter to Loewy in which he accused Rickhey of bearing chief responsibility for the hanging of twelve prisoners at the Dora V-2 rocket factory. He had previously brought this matter to the attention of the Project Paperclip personnel at Wright Field, but was told Rickhey and other recruits were valuable resources that could not be jeopardized. Nehlson was seemingly unaware of the politics involved: Rickhey and Patin were fast friends, and the latter had ingratiated himself with Putt by serving as his personal liaison with the scientists and engineers. Nehlson may or may not have been aware that his letter to Loewy would be read by military censors, who would then pass along this accusation to war crimes investigators.

Several weeks after writing this letter to Loewy, Nehlson violated security regulations by leaving Wright Field to spend four days with his brother-in-law, who lived in Michigan. Putt, who by now regarded Nehlson as a troublemaker, had him transferred to Mitchel Field in New York. Although banished from Wright Field, Nehlson's letter to Loewy nonetheless had major repercussions for one of Project Paperclip's prized recruits. His letter's reference to Rickhey's involvement in the murder of twelve prisoners at Dora caught the eyes of military censors, who passed the letter along to Col. Millard Lewis at Army Air Forces Headquarters in Washington, D.C. The executive to the assistant chief of Air Staff Intelligence as well as Chief of the Air Intelligence Policy Division, Lewis was a 1930 graduate of West Point who had commanded the 98th Combat Wing during the Allied invasion of Europe. Unlike Putt and other Project Paperclip operatives, he was not inclined to overlook war crimes allegations—even if it meant losing a valuable recruit to prosecution and possible imprisonment or execution. Lewis notified the director of intelligence for the War Department General Staff that summarized Nehlson's accusations against Rickhey and recommended that an investigation be conducted to determine their accuracy.

Air Corps Major Eugene Smith, who was assigned to the case, interviewed Nehlson at Mitchel Field as well as Werner Voss, a former Mittelwerk engineer, who corroborated the charge that Rickhey had been responsible for the hanging of prisoners at Mittelwerk. Smith also interviewed other Mittelwerk personnel such as Arthur Rudolph, who had served as operations director. Rudolph initially denied having seen any prisoners hanged at Mittelwerk, even when Smith pointed out that the executions had occurred near his office. He finally conceded that he had seen the twelve men dangling from a crane. Decades later, Rudolph's contradictory testimony would have serious repercussions for this Project Paperclip recruit.

Smith journeyed to Fort Bliss, Texas, with the intention of interviewing Wernher von Braun (1912–1977) to see whether he had information about executions at Mittelwerk. He was dismayed to find that von Braun as well as his brother, Magnus, happened to be away when he arrived. The convenient absence of both von Brauns could have been a coincidence, or it might have been arranged by Major James Hamill, the director of Project Paperclip at Fort Bliss. Hamill, an intelligence officer with the Army Ordnance Group who had earned an engineering degree at Fordham, had personally escorted von Braun from a holding facility on an island in Boston Harbor to Fort Bliss. He had no intention of allowing this German scientist to be jeopardized. Wernher von Braun had been at the top of the "Black List," which listed the names of prominent scientists and engineers who worked for Nazi Germany that the Allied military wanted to apprehend and interrogate. He was a valuable asset.

Known today as the "father of rocket science," von Braun joined the Nazi party on November 12, 1937, and later accepted a commission in the Allegemeine SS. He was promoted three times and reached the rank of Sturnbannführer, which was the equivalent of a major in the U.S. army. While employed as technical director at the Peenemünde Army Research Center in northern Germany during the war, von Braun helped to develop the A-4 rocket. One of these rockets, fired on October 3, 1942, became the first human-made object to reach outer space when it achieved a distance of fifty miles above the earth.

Albert Speer (1905–1981), Hitler's architect of choice who also served as Minister of Armaments and War Production, recalled journeying to Peenemünde with the armament chiefs of the three branches of Nazi

Germany's armed forces on June 13, 1942, to witness the first launch of a remote-controlled rocket. Its guidance system failed, however, and the rocket crashed just a half-mile away. A second test-firing on October 14, 1942, saw the A-4 travel 120 miles and strike within two and one-half miles of its intended target. When Speer informed Hitler that the test-fire had been successful, the Führer ordered that mass production of the A-4 begin in the summer of 1943. This rocket would be a "vengeance-retaliation" weapon against the Allies, prompting it to be renamed the V-2. Technical difficulties with the V-2, however, delayed its employment by Nazi Germany until early September of 1944.

Von Braun's groundbreaking contribution to the German war effort earned him Hitler's respect and admiration. Speer invited von Braun and several other Peenemünde engineers to give Hitler a special presentation on the V-2 rocket. The presentation, held on July 7, 1943, featured a color film of a V-2 launch accompanied by an explanatory narrative by von Braun. Hitler was captivated. Speer suggested that the Führer appoint von Braun as a professor. Hitler enthusiastically agreed and even said that he would sign the necessary document in person. Speer recalled Hitler was astonished that von Braun had created such a technological marvel at age 31.

Although hundreds of V-2 rockets blew up shortly after launch or missed their targets, about 3,000 reached Belgium and England. An estimated 7,000 people were killed on the continent, while at least 2,750 Londoners—almost all of them civilians—lost their lives to this weapon of revenge and retaliation that had been created by von Braun and his staff of engineers. In addition to taking civilian lives when launched, the V-2 claimed a horrifying number of lives while in production. The Nordhausen complex of concentration camps, which included Dora, wasn't an extermination camp. It contained no gas chambers and few crematoria. Nonetheless, as many as 20,000 slave laborers condemned to work 12-hour shifts seven days a week building these rockets died from exhaustion, lack of medical care and inadequate food as well as from the brutality of their captors.

Following his arrest by American soldiers, Speer was for a time incarcerated in Kransberg Castle. In his memoir, Speer remarked on the irony of being held as a prisoner in a structure that he had fitted out and rebuilt in 1939 as a headquarters for Göring. He also noted that von Braun and his assistants joined them for a few days. The brilliant young engineer who had so impressed Hitler had received offers from both the Americans as well as the British, Speer recalled, and he and von Braun discussed these proposals. Even the Russians coveted von Braun's genius, according to Speer, and surreptitiously smuggled an offer to him.

Speer himself was regarded as quite a prize by the Americans. In his *Anatomy of the Nuremberg Trials*, Telford Taylor recalled that Speer was painstakingly interrogated by the U.S. Army as well as a string of engineers and administrators, who wanted to learn as much as possible about the Nazi Reich and its formidable war machine. The United States Strategic Bombing Survey, whose members included Paul Nitze and George Ball and even the economist John Kenneth Galbraith, relentlessly interrogated Speer.

Bill Kasich confirmed the fact that the Russians were interested in von Braun and other scientists and engineers who should have stood trial with the other Nordhausen defendants. "Actually, Nordhausen, the Russians were supposed to try it, but the ones that they wanted to try we already had in the states." In another interview, Kasich recalled some Russians entering the office where he worked. "I spoke to them [the Russians] when they came in to get the Nordhausen case. They came in and I spoke to the commander [and asked], 'What do you have to say?' He ignored me." Kasich stated in that same interview, "We worked overtime to get those documents ready [for the Nordhausen case] and who they wanted to get, we already had in this country."

Unlike von Braun and his fellow scientists and engineers, Albert Speer received no offers from Allied nations that would have allowed him to escape punishment for his service to Hitler and the Third Reich. He was tried and convicted at Nuremberg for crimes such as supporting the use of slave laborers in German war industries. Speer served twenty years in Spandau Prison in Berlin. He was released three years before the United States landed men on the moon, an achievement made possible in large part because of the scientists and engineers brought to the United States through Project Overcast-Paperclip.

Project Overcast operatives were thrilled to acquire von Braun and his staff of rocket scientists. In addition to the engineers who had designed these weapons, our nation also acquired 150 V-2 rockets that were built by the slave laborers at Mittelwerk but had never been launched. Teams of American engineers, tutored by Project Overcast recruits, test-fired these V-2 rockets from 1946 to 1949 at White Sands Proving Ground—now known as White Sands Missile Base—in New Mexico, with varying degrees of success. A number of the rockets overshot the base and fell near heavily populated areas of New Mexico, while one landed south of Ciudad Juarez, Mexico, much to the consternation of the Mexican government.

High-ranking membership in the SS and questions about his activities at Mittelwerk never hampered von Braun's career in the United States. With his team of Project Overcast recruits, von Braun developed the Redstone, America's first ballistic missile, which was essentially an improved, modernized version of the V-2, as well as the series of Saturn rockets. A massive Saturn V rocket powered the Apollo 11, which in 1969 landed our astronauts on the moon. Few Americans at the time, who felt exalted by such an achievement, realized or particularly cared that this feat had been accomplished partially through the ingenuity of a former Nazi officer whose first rockets had been constructed by slave laborers from a Third Reich concentration camp.

From 1970 to 1972 von Braun served as deputy associate administrator at NASA. He was inducted into the International Space Hall of Fame at the New Mexico Museum of Space History. His on line biography duly notes his Nazi past and concedes that "his important role in Hitler's war machine will forever cloud his legacy," but then attempts to disperse some of those clouds by including this statement at the beginning of a list of von Braun quotations:

> It is hellish. My spontaneous reaction was to talk to one of the SS guards, only to be told with unmistakable harshness that I should mind my own business, or to find myself in the same striped fatigues [the uniform worn by concentration camp inmates].... I realized that any attempt of reasoning on humane grounds would be utterly futile [On the use of slave labor to manufacture V-2 rockets during World War II].

Why did Hamill presumably go to such great lengths to prevent Smith from interviewing von Braun? According to Linda Hunt, a transcript of a meeting held in Rickhey's office in 1944 lists von Braun and Rudolph as both being present. The purpose of the meeting was to discuss transporting additional French civilians to Mittelwerk as slave laborers. These new arrivals would be required to wear the distinctive striped uniform of concentration camp inmates. The transcript makes no mention of von Braun objecting to this proposal. One can only assume that, during the course of this meeting, von Braun was following the advice of the SS guard who had told him to mind his own business on the use of slave laborers.

Putt considered Rickhey an asset to Project Paperclip and in January 1947 recommended that he be given long-term employment at Wright Field. The recommendation was approved and Rickhey signed a five-year contract with the War Department on April 12, 1947. Evidently, Putt and

Rickhey weren't terribly concerned with the ongoing war crimes investigation. On May 19, 1947, however, the War Crimes Division in Washington issued an arrest warrant for Rickhey for his role as a "principal perpetrator" in the Nordhausen concentration camp case. His new contract was abruptly canceled. By August of that year, Rickhey was in a Dachau courtroom with his fellow defendants in *U.S. v. Andrae et alia*: the Dora-Nordhausen case.

Each defendant was indicted under the general charge of "violation of the law and usages of war" as well as specific charges. Rickhey was the only civilian among the nineteen defendants, who were either SS personnel or inmate block leaders referred to as "Kapos." He possessed the audacity to write letters he termed "reports" to Putt at Wright Field, as though he had been sent on a fact-finding mission rather than to stand trial as a war criminal.

U.S. Army Major Leon Poullada, assigned to defend Rickhey, requested that von Braun and other Mittelwerk engineers such as Rudolph be brought to Dachau in order to testify. His request was denied. Project Paperclip couldn't risk allowing von Braun and Rudolph to be questioned about their presence at that meeting in Rickhey's office in 1944. Linda Hunt offered another, even more potentially embarrassing reason that Project Paperclip nixed Poullada's request: Dora concentration camp survivors who attended the trial might have recognized them. Poullada also requested that the Mittelwerk records be sent to him from Wright Field. This request was also denied.

All nineteen defendants in the *U.S. v. Andrae* case pleaded not guilty to the general charge as well as to the specific charges. The trial lasted four months. The verdicts were a decidedly mixed bag: one defendant was condemned to death; fourteen drew prison sentences; and four were found innocent—one of whom was Rickhey. As part of his defense, he had pleaded with the court to consider his cooperation with the Americans as well as his work in Project Paperclip. Unlike von Braun and most of the other Project Paperclip recruits, Rickhey possessed no knowledge of rockets and jet aircrafts. Linda Hunt called him "a sacrificial lamb." She also pointed out, however, that the U.S. Army couldn't risk angering him because he knew too much about Project Paperclip and its prized recruits.

Bill Kasich spoke of the Dora-Nordhausen trial during our first interview. "We did try them [the Dora-Nordhausen defendants who weren't taken to the United States]," he stated. "It wasn't satisfactory because the people that were to be tried were no longer there. The important people."

Rickhey's acquittal didn't include the reinstatement of his contract with Project Paperclip. He never returned to the United States and died in Germany in 1966.

Paperclip recruit Arthur Rudolph enjoyed a successful career in the United States and worked at NASA with von Braun. He served as program director for the Saturn V rocket in the 1960s. NASA awarded Rudolph the NASA Exceptional Service Medal as well as the NASA Distinguished Service Medal in recognition of his work in the U.S. space program. Life was good for Rudolph until 1982, when the Department of Justice suddenly expressed an interest in learning more about his Nazi past—particularly, what he knew about the abuse and murder of Mittelwerk's slave laborers. During an interview, lawyers from the Department of Justice confronted Rudolph with a number of documents, including his long-ago interview with Smith. The most damning evidence, however, came from the Dora-Nordhausen trial, which proved that Rudolph had received daily reports that detailed the number of deaths among Mittelwerk's slave laborers. He had clearly known that they literally were being worked to death.

Given a choice between standing trial as a war criminal or renouncing his U.S. citizenship and returning to Germany, Rudolph chose the latter. Rudolph's exposure as a war criminal generated much controversy in the United States. Congressman Bill Green introduced a resolution in the House of Representatives to strip Rudolph of his NASA medals. When Rudolph applied for a visa in 1989 to join other American scientists and engineers to celebrate the twentieth anniversary of landing on the moon, the State Department refused. Nonetheless, Rudolph enjoyed some support among Americans. In a column for the July 14, 1990, edition of the *New York Post*, Patrick Buchanan wrote "Whatever Arthur Rudolph did during World War II, his quarter-century of service to the United States entitles the old man to a public hearing before he goes to his grave." Few agreed with Buchanan, however, and the proposed "public hearing" was never granted. Arthur Rudolph died in Hamburg, Germany in 1996. Buchanan continued to champion Rudolph even after his death. In 1999, he eulogized him as "the German rocket scientist who built the Saturn that took Armstrong to the moon" and "was cleared by two post-war investigations."

An investigation by the Associated Press revealed in October 2014 that Rudolph's decision to renounce his American citizenship and return to Germany was heavily influenced by an offer he received from the Office of Special Investigations of the U.S. Justice Department. This office, which functioned as the Justice Department's Nazi-hunting unit, allowed Rudolph and dozens of other aged Nazis living in the United States to keep their Social Security benefits if they voluntarily left the United States. Such an arrangement allowed the Office of Special Investigations to rid the United States of Nazi war criminals while avoiding lengthy, expensive deportation hearings.

This course of action by no means enjoyed the unanimous support of all branches of the federal government. Both the State Department and the Social Security Administration expressed outrage at an arrangement that essentially bribed Rudolph and other old Nazis to leave the United States, according to the AP investigation. Nonetheless, dozens of war criminals received millions of dollars in benefits over the years. There were at least four living beneficiaries when the AP broke the story, including former guards at the Sachsenhausen and Auschwitz concentration camps.

The War Crimes Group and Project Paperclip were both created by the U.S. Army but for diametrically opposed purposes. Men such as Bill Kasich had been ordered to bring Nazi war criminals to justice, while Project Paperclip operatives like Donald Putt worked to exploit Nazi science and technology, even if it meant war criminals would go unpunished. Kasich felt betrayed by the army in which he served so commendably and even by his own government.

Kasich provided me with an article that appeared in the November 7, 1946, edition of the *Wiesbaden* [Germany] *Post*, a U.S. Army publication, which noted that the War Crimes Group had completed its work at Wiesbaden. The group would now move to Augsburg, "near Dachau site." The article praised the high conviction rate of the War Crimes Group. It had tried 84 cases involving 358 defendants, 330 of whom were convicted. Of those 330, 190 received death sentences.

The article cited the Malmédy case as "one of the most famous of their work" and congratulated prosecutor Lt. Col. Burton L. Ellis, "brilliant in obtaining the complete conviction of all his 73 opponents." But this unnamed reporter believed that the matter hadn't yet been concluded. "Today," he wrote, "the Malmédy Massacre trial continues in a sequel of searches un-ending and relentless for all the SS men responsible for the murder of prisoners of war." He excoriated Nazi Germany for its crimes.

> There are many cases in the War Crimes Branch; trials that involve extreme cruelty and mass murder that would take volumes to describe in their entirety ... the Auschwitz Concentration Camp in Poland, where unprintable cruelties were wrought upon men and women alike as thousands died daily ... the Flossenburg

Concentration Camp wherein thousands were held for racial prejudice, persecution of religious tendencies....

The writer then shifted his focus to the new location of the War Crimes Group.

> Most famous and dreaded of all concentration camps was Dachau. Dachau, graveyard of 138,000 mutilated and starved. Scene of mass cremations and unprintable experiments into the realm of human endurance. From originally documented statements a curt speech was made to a group of newly arrived persons at Dachau by its Nazi commandant: "...there will be no freedom or escape from here except by the chimney; those of you who are Jews step forward now, those of you who are priests may live a month, the rest of you two months!"

Not all perpetrators of the Dachau outrage had been apprehended, he noted, but "The search for all the 1500 guilty persons involved in the operation of Dachau still goes on." He concluded with a vow that surely resonated with every member of the War Crimes Group.

> As long as untried perpetrators as these exist, there will be a Justice Tribunal awaiting them once they are apprehended—to the very last man.
> The War Crimes Commission will continue its work of Justice at Dachau; it will remain ready long after the last Nazi has been tried and convicted to carry on as a new kind of Justice—the Justice of "crimes against humanity."

This army staff writer spelled justice with an upper-case J both times in that final paragraph. I believe it wasn't a typographical error. Covering the apprehension and trials of Nazi war criminals had made him believe in justice so passionately that, like the United States or God, it merited capitalization. It's easy to understand why Bill Kasich kept this article and made a point of sharing it with me. He and this reporter shared the same values.

For such men, clemency for Nazi war criminals was unthinkable, regardless of the extent that their knowledge could be exploited by the American military. Their commitment to justice wasn't shared by the Joint Chiefs of Staff and the operatives of Project Paperclip. Linda Hunt, in *Secret Agenda*, underscored the reporter's naiveté in assuming that the top brass shared his commitment to apprehending and trying the Dachau perpetrators "—to the very last man." Her book certainly corroborated the reporter's depiction of Dachau as the site of sadistic experiments that used camp inmates as human guinea pigs. The stench overwhelmed U.S. soldiers of the 363 Medical Battalion when they entered Experimental Block No. 5, where the experiments were conducted. Hunt cited Yaffa Eliach and Brana Gurewittsh's *The Liberators*, which noted that hundreds of inmates had been murdered in the block. Parts of human bodies, including arms, legs and organs of every type, were lying everywhere.

Inmates had been forced to drink seawater in order to discover ways to save the lives of Luftwaffe pilots who crashed into the ocean and lacked access to fresh water. Other inmates were subjected to freezing temperatures to find ways to ensure the survival of Luftwaffe pilots who were exposed to extreme cold while flying or parachuted from their planes at high altitudes. Nazi scientists working at Dachau kept meticulous records of these experiments, which were seized by the camp's liberators. These accounts are taken from *Criminals Before the Nuremberg Military Tribunals*, which was published by the U.S. Government Printing Office. Here is report by SS-Untersturmführer Sigmund Rascher, a Luftwaffe physician, dated September 10, 1942.

> The experimental subjects [the inmates] were placed in water, dressed in complete flying uniform, winter or summer combination, and with an aviator's helmet. A life jacket made out of rubber kapok was to prevent submerging. The experiments were carried out at water temperatures varying from 2.5 [36 Fahrenheit] to 12 centigrade [53.6 Fahrenheit]. In one experimental series, the occiput (brain stem) projected above the water, while in another series of experiments the occiput (brain stem) and back of the head were submerged in water.
>
> Electrical measurements gave low temperature readings of 26.4 [78 Fahrenheit] in the stomach and 26.5 in the rectum. Fatalities occurred only when the brain stem and the back of the head were also chilled. Autopsies of such fatal cases always revealed large amounts of free blood, up to one-half liter, in the cranial cavity.

In other cold-temperature experiments, the victims were drugged. Professor E. Holzlohner of the University of Kiel, Rascher and Dr. Finke issued this report, dated October 10, 1942: "If the experimental subject was placed in the water under narcosis, one observed a certain arousing effect. The subject began to groan and make some defensive movements.... The defensive movements ceased after about five minutes.... These cases ended fatally, without any successful results from resuscitation efforts."

In the "Reports from Other Camps" section of *The Buchenwald Report*, Hermann Haller recalled the so-called "Heavenly Chariot" of Dachau, which was a tall, closed box on wheels with instruments for measuring atmospheric pressure, temperature and altitude. This device, part of the Luftwaffe Experimental Station at Dachau, could subject a camp inmate to the physical conditions to which a pilot would be subjected at a flight above 32,000 feet, and then a dive towards earth.

Following this simulated "flight," the inmate, who was clad in a waterproof suit and fitted with a life preserver, was plunged into a pool of water. Intended to simulate a crash landing in the ocean, the water's temperature was only 33 to 35 degrees. The inmate had to survive this ordeal for at least two hours. The few test subjects who emerged alive from the water were put to bed with women, who were housed in a specific facility at Dachau. The warmth of the women's bodies could supposedly revive the test subjects, who were near death from hypothermia when removed from the water. The test subject was regarded as having successfully survived the experiment if he was able to have intercourse with at least one of the women.

Haller noted that Rauscher wasn't satisfied merely observing the external behavior of those inmates subjected to this torture. He wanted to learn its effects on their brains. Accordingly, he had the skull of a Jew, who was fully conscious at the time, split open after the simulated high-altitude flight so that he could examine it.

The first human guinea pigs for this sadistic study were recruited from the camp population with the promise of extra rations. As word eventually spread, however, this tactic no longer worked. New test subjects were selected from the barracks through deception. New arrivals at Dachau were generally preferred, however, since they had no idea what to expect following selection.

Himmler met three survivors of the Heavenly Chariot when he visited the camp and, according to Haller, personally released two of them from Dachau and then transferred them to the Luftwaffe in Berlin. After six months, the Heavenly Chariot was removed from camp, Haller stated. The water experiments, however, continued.

Ironically, Rascher was executed at Dachau—but not by the Americans. He angered Himmler, who had been his faithful patron, by attempting to pass off children he and his wife had illegally adopted as proof that racially pure Aryan parents could produce children well into middle age. Himmler had Rascher arrested and imprisoned at Dachau. He was killed on April 26, 1945, just three days before the U.S. Seventh Army 45th Infantry Division. His supposedly fecund wife, imprisoned at the Ravensbrook Concentration Camp, was shot to death when she allegedly attacked a guard shortly before the camp's liberation.

Some conspiracy theorists claim that Rascher was given a new identity by Project Paperclip and brought to the United States. There is no evidence to support this contention. It is reasonable to conclude, however, that Rascher was killed for reasons other than passing off adopted children as his own. Rascher was proud of his work at Dachau and not reluctant to discuss it. Himmler didn't want Rascher talking to the Allies about the experiments conducted at Dachau.

Luftwaffe Col. Hubertus Strughold (1898–1986), a Project Paperclip recruit who became known as "the father of American space medicine," headed the Luftwaffe's Institute for Aviation Medicine in Berlin. Strughold denied any knowledge of the Dachau experiments, but the minutes of a 1942 medical conference in Germany prove otherwise. Children, some of who had epilepsy, were taken from a psychiatric institution and used as test subjects in oxygen deprivation experiments at the Institute for Aviation Medicine on Strughold's watch. Despite such revelations, Strughold still has defenders in the military as well as the scientific community, who cite his extraordinary contributions to the American space program.

While most Americans condemn the Nazi scientists who used concentration camp inmates and others as human guinea pigs, the American military went to great lengths to preserve the results of these experiments. Kasich witnessed their effort firsthand.

> I don't know if I told you this, but I remember John [Cashman] taking me to where they were microfilming all of the experiments. Every sheet [of paper] was microfilmed ... he was taking pictures of the document. And I asked him, "How can you do this all day long being in a place where you know there was this mass murder, this torture?" And he said, "Do you realize what they did for humanity?" What the Nazis did for humanity! And there isn't one thing that we learned from their experiments. Not one thing. He [the soldier] thought they had done valuable research, that mankind was going to benefit from their research. It was enough to make you puke. I was ready to grab him.... I couldn't believe my ears when he told me that. And I said, "What experiment do you find most interesting?" He said, "Well, what they would do here, they would get a guy and put him in salt water, freezing salt water and dip him in there until death, near death. Then they'd put him in bed with two women. See how fast he recovered. Then they would put him in bed with one woman to see how fast he recovered...." Now what in heaven's name did that accomplish? Well, then, they would say, "In case the pilot had to parachute into the North Atlantic." There would be no women in the North Atlantic, nor would he [a pilot] survive in the North Atlantic if he landed in the water. He would freeze to death.

The ethics of utilizing knowledge gained through Nazi experiments that were conducted on human subjects is controversial and remains the subject of heated debate. In his paper "The Ethics of Using Medical Data from Nazi Experiments," Baruch C. Cohen observed that many scholars have found multiple references to Nazi experiments in reputable medical journals. Indeed, the writings of some SS doctors have been republished. These references and publications "frequently bear no disclaimer as to how the data was obtained." "The amorphous term 'data' ... seems unattached to the tortured and their pain," he wrote. He observed that

> Holocaust survivor Susan Vogorito found the use of the term "data" a sterile term. She was three-and-a-half when she and her twin sister, Hannah, arrived at Auschwitz. They were housed for an entire year in Mengele's private lab in a wooden cage a yard and a half wide. Without anesthetic, Mengele would repeatedly scrape at the bone tissue of one of her legs. Her sister died from repeated injections to her spinal column. She claims that she is the real data, the living data of Dr. Mengele.

Any analysis that fails to recognize such data as "a blood soaked document" fails to grasp the magnitude of this issue, Cohen concluded. After reviewing the types of Nazi experiments, Cohen gave examples of two scientists who have attempted to make use of knowledge garnered from Rascher's Dachau experiments in hypothermia. Dr. Robert Pozos, director of the hypothermia laboratory at the University of Minnesota School of Medicine at Duluth, included data from Nazi experiments in an article he submitted to the *New England Journal of Medicine*. Pozos rationalized his use of such data by noting that "it could advance my work in that it takes human subjects farther than we're willing." His article was rejected by the journal's editor.

Cohen also cited the work of John Hayward, a professor of biology at Victoria University in Vancouver, Canada. Hayward's research involved the testing of cold water survival suits that are worn by fishermen who operate in Canada's frigid ocean waters. He used Rascher's data to help determine how long such suits would protect the human body. As Cohen pointed out, however, Rascher's test-subjects victims were malnourished and emaciated—hardly the physical counterparts of the well-fed Canadian fishermen, who would be wearing those cold water survival suits. Hayward had no illusions about how Rascher's data had been collected but defended using it. He stated: "I don't want to have to use the Nazi data, but there is no other and will be no other in an ethical world. I've rationalized it a bit. But not to use it would be equally bad. I'm trying to make something constructive out of it. I use it with my guard up but it's useful."

Most scientists who have utilized data garnered from the Nazi experiments on human subjects have employed a similar rationalization. While this knowledge was acquired through morally reprehensible means, they argue, it nonetheless exists and should be utilized to benefit humankind.

They agree with the young soldier who so angered Kasich by asserting that the Nazis had done something for humanity by obtaining this knowledge, so why not make use of it? The United States and other nations had no moral qualms about utilizing Nazi technology in order to advance their development of rockets and jet aircraft. Indeed, the space program of the United States was largely made possible by scientists and engineers who had worked in Nazi Germany.

The question of whether Nazi data should be used remains controversial and sparks heated debate. Cohen concluded his essay by noting that some "have suggested that the use of the data would serve as a lesson to the world, that the victims did not die futilely, and that a post-mortem use of the data would retroactively give 'purpose' to their otherwise meaningless deaths." Cohen counterbalanced this assertion by paraphrasing a letter to the editor of the *New York Times* by Dr. Howard M. Spiro (1924–2012) of the Department of Internal Medicine at Yale. Spiro served as the director of the Yale program for Humanities in Medicine from 1983 until his retirement from the faculty in 1999. His letter, published in the April 19, 1988, edition, succinctly indeed epitomized the essence of the humanities in medicine and deserves to be quoted at length. He wrote:

> No one honors the memory of the victims by "learning" from experiments carried out on them. Instead, we make them our retrospective guinea pigs. Any data obtained in the Nazi concentration camps seems unlikely to be irreplaceable except in their horror.
> Very few experiments are unique. Hans Eppinger, a widely respected professor of medicine in Nazi Vienna, insisted on experiments in the camps that confirmed what had been learned from animal studies. But supposing that we could save a million lives from data that Eppinger ravaged from the bodies of Gypsies. Should we use that data? To do so would put us at risk of retrospectively participating in their torture and murder.
> If expressing revulsion means losing something of value, then we should continue to express our revulsion, particularly if we want to teach our children, and our students, what they should not do. The best argument I've heard for preserving the Nazi data is to keep evidence that those experiments were carried out.
> As long as the data are available, evidence that at least some people did some bad things in Nazi Germany cannot be denied.

In other words, Nazi data indeed should be preserved and utilized—as yet another means to refute the Holocaust deniers. Although the victims of these heinous experiments no longer possess voices, the data that they were tortured and killed to produce speaks volumes.

I remarked that the personnel of the War Crimes Group dealt with horrors that most of us would find overwhelming. He said that a colleague had once told him and several other men, "'It'll take about ten years. After a while, you'll forget it.' Well, you never forget it." Kasich mentioned another colleague who suffered a nervous breakdown. He was "really upset over what happened to these people," he said. "I mean he showed it. And he had a nervous breakdown after he got out, but he was fine while he was working with us."

"When you guys were released from service, were you debriefed or cautioned not to talk about your work?" I asked. Kasich's reply was emphatic.

"No, no, no. Oh, we got the message to keep your mouth shut," he replied.

"So it wasn't necessary to tell you not to talk?"

"No, it wasn't necessary," Kasich said. I asked if he refrained from talking about his work because it was regarded as secret.

"Because if you told the truth, you were a communist at that particular time," he answered. "And that word, if you were branded like that, you were done. You couldn't get work. You couldn't get anything. No one would hire you."

10

Barbie and Bormann
War Criminals

"You've heard of Klaus Barbie?" Bill Kasich asked me. "I wrote a report on him. I thought he had such a funny name." Barbie (1913–1991), a captain in the SS as well as a member of the Gestapo, is known as the "Butcher of Lyon" for the atrocities committed while he served as Gestapo commander in that French city during its German occupation. He indulged his proclivity for sadism by personally torturing prisoners. Simone Lagrange, a thirteen-year-old child at the time, recalled that Barbie was caressing a cat when she was brought to him. She initially assumed that someone who demonstrated such love for a feline couldn't possibly be cruel. Barbie tortured her for eight days. Lise Lesevre, another Barbie victim, was tortured for nine days. He ordered her to strip naked and then almost drowned her in a tub of freezing water. Barbie also struck her with a mace-like instrument that consisted of a spiked ball attached to a chain. The beating broke a vertebrae and left Lesevre disabled for the rest of her life.

Jean Moulin (1899–1943), a high-ranking member of the French Resistance, was Barbie's best-known victim. He refused to give up any information despite being subjected to horrific torture, which included having hot needles inserted under his fingernails. Moulin died while in Nazi custody. Barbie claimed that Moulin committed suicide. More reliable sources maintain that Barbie personally beat Moulin to death. Hitler was delighted by Barbie's campaign against the French Resistance and awarded him the prestigious First Class Iron Cross with Swords in 1943.

Despite writing that report, Kasich was denied the honor of helping to bring this war criminal to justice. Klaus Barbie was never tried by the U.S. Army, since our government viewed him as an asset to be utilized. Unlike the scientists and engineers recruited through Project Paperclip, Barbie couldn't design and build jet aircraft and rockets. His talents were

10. Barbie and Bormann

limited to torture and murder. Nonetheless, Klaus Barbie was recruited by the Allies after the war. He served the British as an anti-communist "expert" and then switched his allegiance to the Americans in 1947. Military intelligence regarded Barbie as a valuable asset and assigned him the U.S. Army's Counter Intelligence Corps (CIC), where he gave his handlers information about ex–Nazis that had been recruited by British and communist cells operating in Europe.

When the French government discovered that Barbie was working for the CIC, it demanded that he be turned over. John J. McCloy, U.S. High Commissioner for Germany, refused. The Assistant Secretary of War during World War II who had been instrumental in persuading FDR to intern Japanese-American citizens as a security precaution, McCloy and the CIC believed that Barbie knew too much about U.S. intelligence operations in Europe.

Krunoslav Draganović (1903–1983) was a Croatian Catholic priest and member of Ustaše, a Croatian fascist organization during World War II when that nation was a satellite state of Nazi Germany. Ustaše was responsible for the murder of about 400,000 Orthodox Christians and Jews during the war. When the Allies triumphed, Draganović established a "ratline" that allowed Nazi war criminals to escape from Europe and begin new lives. The CIC allowed Barbie to escape to Bolivia using Draganović's ratline. Declassified CIA records indicate that Draganović worked for the CIA from 1959 to 1962 and provided the agency with intelligence about Yugoslavia, a communist state that included Croatia within its borders.

Barbie, who lived under the pseudonym Klaus Altmann, thrived in Bolivia and became a lieutenant colonel in the Bolivian Armed Forces. He also drew a covert salary from the West German government, which had recruited him to work for its foreign intelligence agency. Barbie often publicly boasted that he had devised the strategy that enabled CIA-assisted Bolivian troops to locate and kill Cuban revolutionary Che Guevara, who had journeyed to Bolivia in an attempt to overthrow its government.

Serge and Beate Klarsfeld, Nazi hunters with a distinguished record of tracking down fugitive war criminals, identified Barbie as living in Bolivia as early as 1971, but he wasn't extradited to France until 1983. Finally placed on trial in 1987 for crimes against humanity, Barbie was convicted and sentenced to life in prison. He died of leukemia and cancer of the spine and prostate while incarcerated.

Martin Bormann was another Nazi who never stood trial as a war criminal. Kasich recalled,

> Cashman took me to Martin Bormann's house. He had a house in Augsburg. It was a three-storey house. Never entered into [by American military authorities]. It had broken glass on one window basement. It wasn't a basement. I guess the basement was maybe four feet down and that was the first storey. And you could see filing cabinets. It looked like Bormann kept everything. Every piece of paper that he could, he kept. I don't know why they [American military authorities] didn't go in, but I suspect that they wanted to leave it like it was in case he came back to the house. There was surveillance. They were keeping an eye out for him.

Born in Prussia in 1900, Bormann joined the Nazi party in 1927 and the SS ten years later. Bormann served as chief of cabinet in the office of Deputy Führer Rudolph Hess from 1933 to 1941. Bormann's skillful maneuvering allowed him to usurp many of Hess's responsibilities while carefully ingratiating himself to Hitler. Hess's unauthorized flight to Britain in 1941 to seek a negotiated peace with that nation horrified Hitler, who regarded it as a personal betrayal. Hitler abolished the office of deputy führer that same year and created the new post of a party chancellery, to which he appointed Bormann. In terms of power, Bormann was deputy führer in all but name. Bormann's position as Hitler's personal secretary further consolidated, since he was able to control what information reached Hitler as well as limit personal access to him. Hitler even entrusted Bormann with his personal finances, which included royalties from sales of *Mein Kampf* and the use of Hitler's image on German postage stamps.

There was no question of Bormann's guilt as a war criminal. In a memo dated August 19, 1942, Bormann wrote that Slavs possessed no innate right to existence and served only one purpose: to work for Germans. "In so far as we do not need them, they may die. Slav fertility is not desirable," he remarked in the memo. Bormann signed a decree on October 9, 1942, that amounted to a death warrant for all Jews. This decree declared that "the permanent elimination of the Jews from Greater Germany" couldn't be accomplished by forcing them out of the Reich. Instead, elimination could be achieved only "by the use of ruthless force in the special camps of the East." By "special camps," Bormann meant camps that existed solely to murder Jewish men, women and children. Bormann gave Adolf Eichmann and the Gestapo absolute power over Jews by a decree signed on July 1, 1943.

Bormann was at Hitler's side during his final days in the Führerbunker in Berlin, where he witnessed and signed Hitler's last will and testament. He also served as a witness at Hitler's marriage to Eva Braun. Hitler rewarded Bormann for his loyalty by naming him chairman of the

Nazi party. He wanted Bormann to survive and urged him to flee the Führerbunker before the area was overrun by the rapidly approaching Russian army. Hitler and Braun committed suicide on April 30, 1945—Hitler by shooting himself, while Braun took her life with cyanide.

The following morning Bormann was one of a group of four who fled the Führerbunker. The group included SS Dr. Ludwig Stumpfegger, Hitler's personal physician; Artur Axmann, leader of the Hitler Youth; and Hans Baur, Hitler's personal pilot. Baur was captured by Russian troops and imprisoned in the Soviet Union until 1955, when he was turned over to the French and imprisoned for an additional two years. Upon release, Baur sought to capitalize on his association with Hitler by writing an autobiography titled *I Flew with the Mighty*, which was later revised and retitled *Between Heaven and Earth with the Mighty*. Axmann managed to avoid the Russians, adopted a pseudonym and organized a Nazi underground movement. He was arrested in December 1945 by U.S. counterintelligence agents and served three years in prison.

The team of American agents mentioned by Bill Kasich, who kept Bormann's Augsburg home under surveillance, waited in vain. Bormann and Stumpfegger were never apprehended by any Allied government and were widely assumed to have escaped Germany. Bormann was tried *in absentia* at Nuremberg, convicted of war crimes and crimes against humanity and sentenced to death by hanging.

Theories abounded regarding Bormann's fate and whereabouts. Erich Kempka, Hitler's chauffeur, claimed to have seen Bormann killed by a Russian anti-tank shell. Bormann was supposedly sighted in Italy in 1946. Failure to locate him and the lack of a confirmed report of his death fostered the belief that Bormann had escaped Germany and found refuge in a foreign country. There were numerous purported sightings of Bormann during the decades following the war. The general public and even prominent Nazi hunters such as Simon Wiesenthal, who survived incarceration in several Nazi concentration camps, arrived at the consensus that Bormann had reached South America by using the same "ratline" that allowed so many Nazi war criminals to elude justice. Paraguay and Brazil were the nations most frequently cited as Bormann's likely residence.

In 1963, however, a retired postal worker told German police that during the first week of May 1945 Russian troops had forced him to bury two bodies near a railway station at Lehrter. He claimed to have found identification papers on one body that identified the corpse as Stumpfegger. Excavations conducted two years later yielded nothing. On December

7, 1972, however, construction workers uncovered two male skeletons near the spot there the retired postal worker claimed he had been forced to bury two corpses. Shards of glass in their teeth suggested that both men had committed suicide by biting cyanide capsules. Old dental records confirmed the identity of the taller skeleton as Stumpfegger. While Bormann's dental records had been lost years ago, his dental records were reconstructed from memory by Dr. Hugo Blaschke, an ex–Nazi who had been Hitler's personal dentist in addition to performing dental work on Eva Braun, Hermann Göring, Heinrich Himmler and Joseph Goebbels. Bormann's skeleton was preserved by the German government in order to allow additional testing methods of identification to be conducted over the years.

DNA testing in 1998 conclusively proved the skeleton to be the remains of Martin Bormann. His skeleton was cremated and the ashes scattered in the Baltic Sea on August 16, 1999, since authorities feared a grave site could become a shrine for neo-Nazis. That such fears were well-founded is chillingly illustrated by the case of Rudolph Hess, who hanged himself in Spandau Prison in 1987 at age 93. Hess was interred in a cemetery in Wunsiedel, a Bavarian town where his family maintained a holiday home and his parents were interred. His burial site featured an impressive tombstone that bore a German inscription that translates as "I Dared." Hess's grave became a shrine for neo-Nazis, who staged a rally each year on the anniversary of his death. These Third Reich worshipers left elaborate floral wreaths on the grave and gave "Heil, Hitler!" salutes while facing the tombstone. A court order issued in 2005 banning such demonstrations accomplished nothing, so local authorities demanded that Hess's corpse be exhumed and cremated. This was accomplished in 2011, and his ashes were scattered at sea. The beautiful tombstone with its provocative "I Dared" epitaph was blown up and neo-Nazi rallies in Wunsiedel ceased.

11

The Buchenwald Case

BUCHENWALD CONCENTRATION CAMP was founded by the SS on July 19, 1937. Its first inmates previously were incarcerated at the Sachsenberg concentration camp, which was located in Frankenberg. Testimony by inmates affirms that Buchenwald was a hellhole even during its earliest days. Willi Tichauer, in *The Buchenwald Report*, stated that five hundred Jews arrived at the camp on June 13, 1938, and were housed in the so-called "sheep pen," which contained no chairs, table or even beds. Inmates slept on pine branches that were spread across the floor. Those who became thirsty paid one mark for a swallow of water. The meager food rations were stolen by the room attendant, who sold them to the famished prisoners. Toilet facilities consisted of open latrines. Tichauer recalls that some inmates, exhausted from the horrendous work schedule, fell into the latrines while using them and drowned.

An untold number of inmates despaired and chose death by hanging themselves. Others walked into "No Man's Land," which was a five-yard strip of ground in front of the barbed wire. Any inmate who entered that strip was subject to shooting, a penalty that the SS guards were all too willing to enact. The SS further degraded Buchenwald's Jewish inmates by demanding that they contribute what little money they had been allowed to keep to a "fund for the poor." This money went straight into the pockets of the SS.

I asked Kasich about one of the best-known and most despised Nazi war criminals who was prosecuted at Dachau: Ilse Koch. "She was at Buchenwald," he replied. "The commandant of Buchenwald was her husband." They called her the "Bitch of Buchenwald." I asked about her reported propensity for having items such as lamp shades made from the skin of Buchenwald prisoners. Kasich stated:

> She would pick out the ones [prisoners] with tattoos ... walk up and down the [train] platform and pick them out and send them to the gas chamber. Then they

were slaughtered and skinned and she would make lamp shades, gloves and book covers out of the skins. She would give them to people. She had a collection. We had some lampshades in our vaults at Wiesbaden. I saw them.

Buchenwald, liberated by a reconnaissance battalion of the Sixth Army, was the first concentration camp encountered by Allied forces when it still had a large population of inmates: 21,000 men, many of whom appeared to be living skeletons. Margaret Bourke-White documented the living hell that was Buchenwald through her photographs, which were later published in *Life* magazine. Emaciated men lying in their bunks because they're too weak to stand. Countless corpses stacked together like so much firewood. A liberated inmate stands beside a huge pile of human ashes and bones that had been taken from an incinerator. Bourke-White later wrote that she felt that her camera provided some relief by imposing a slight barrier between herself and the horror all around her. The realization that men had committed such atrocities against other men, she remarked, actually made her ashamed to be a human being.

The camp's liberators were so outraged by what they found that they forced residents of nearby Weimar, who claimed to know nothing of the atrocities committed at Buchenwald, to walk through the camp to see its horrors for themselves. Bourke-White photographed them as they lined up waiting their turns to tour Buchenwald. Two men in business suits, one with his arms folded in angry resignation, scowl into the camera.

One of the liberated inmates devoted his life to ensuring that the Holocaust is never forgotten: author and Nobel Peace Prize winner Elie Wiesel. Born in Romania in 1928, Wiesel was fifteen when he and his family were sent to Auschwitz, where his mother and younger sister were murdered. Wiesel and his father were later transferred to Buchenwald, where his father died shortly before the camp's liberation.

The Allies feared that the Nazis would conduct a mass killing of Buchenwald's inmates before the camp could be liberated by the U.S. Army and made at least one attempt to discourage that possibility. Stefan Heymann's testimony in *The Buchenwald Report* reported that airplanes had dropped leaflets that warned the camp's administration and guards against committing atrocities against the inmates and warned that such acts would mean reprisals directed at the civilian population of Thuringia, the German state in which Buchenwald was located. The inmates also learned of the proximity of the Americans when machine gun fire from a plane strafed the camp during a speech by SS Col. Hermann Pister, the camp's commandant.

11. The Buchenwald Case

According to Heymann, the Nazis nonetheless committed atrocities even while the U.S. Army was closing in on the camp. Pister had ordered the evacuation of Ohrdruf, a Buchenwald satellite camp. Nine thousand of this satellite camp's inmates arrived at Buchenwald, where they were sorted into three groups: Germans; foreign Aryans; and Jews. Heymann stated that hundreds of the Ohrdruf inmates had collapsed from exhaustion during the forced march to Buchenwald. They were shot by the SS. A village police officer, who apparently had read one of the leaflets dropped by the airplane, berated one of the murderers by telling him that the villagers would have to pay the price when the Americans arrived and saw these slain inmates.

The Nazis attempted to evacuate the inmates of Buchenwald before the U.S. Army reached the camp, but many of the inmates managed to avoid transport. Others weren't so fortunate. The SS forced 3,105 Jews to march at a double-time pace on the path to Weimar. Heymann reported that forty-seven who couldn't keep pace were shot. David Hackett noted in his introduction to *The Buchenwald Report* that the Nazis tried to cover their bloody tracks as the U.S. Army approached the camp. Inmates incarcerated in the camp jail were murdered during the night of April 10. An inmate orderly was assigned the task of cleaning up the bloodstains. Meat hooks used for hanging bodies in the execution room were removed and their holes filled with cement. A quick coat of white paint was applied to the walls to cover the numerous blood stains. This hasty attempt at a cover-up was botched, however. An American medical officer saw four hooks that hadn't been removed as well as partially filled holes for forty-four more.

Bill Kasich gave me a document from his personal archives titled *An Information Booklet on the Buchenwald Concentration Camp Case, The United States of America v. Josias Prince zu Waldeck, et al., To Be Heard at Camp Dachau, Germany, 11 April 1947*. The booklet is credited as having been prepared by the prosecution staff, which is listed as William D. Denson, chief prosecutor; Robert L. Kunzig of Philadelphia and Solomon Surowitz of New York City, co-prosecutors. The staff members listed include: Stanislaw S. Feldman; Joseph Kirchbaum; Paul Rosenthal; Albert Westerweel; Sarah Goldin; Yolanda E. Keller; Phoebe Sehmann; and Herman Platt.

Robert L. Kunzig merits special mention. A World War II veteran, he embarked upon a successful career in law and politics after his service as a war crimes prosecutor. Kunzig was deputy attorney general of

Pennsylvania from 1948 to 1953 and served as counsel for the controversial House Un-American Activities Committee (HUAC) from 1953 to 1955. In the 1960s, Kunzig worked as an assistant to U.S. Senator Hugh Scott (R-PA) and managed Scott's 1964 senate campaign. President Richard Nixon nominated Kunzig as judge of the United States Court of Claims in 1971, a position that he held until his death in 1982.

Solomon Surowitz also deserves mention. Greene noted that Surowitz tendered his resignation to Denson during the course of the trial. Surowitz explained that he was uncomfortable with the hearsay quality of the prosecution's witnesses. He told Denson that, in his opinion, the witnesses would say anything if it resulted in death sentences for the Germans. Greene, who interviewed Surowitz while researching *Justice at Dachau*, stated that Denson told Surowitz that the prosecution would proceed on the basis of what it had.

Surowitz told Greene during the interview that too often the judges had accepted testimony that would never have been accepted in a court of law. Greene noted that while hearsay evidence is not usually admissible, such testimony was allowed during the war crimes trials if it seemed relevant to a reasonable person. Why was such an exception made? It was regarded as necessary in order to compensate for the fact that most eyewitnesses to these wartime atrocities had been killed.

The information booklet included a stirringly-written "History of the Case." Bill Kasich read part of it aloud to me. He occasionally added a personal comment, some of which are included here.

> On a wooded hill six miles from [the city of] Weimar the site was selected. Near the source of German culture and freedom, the greatest dungeon of democracy was created. This began the infamous career of BUCHENWALD.

Prisoners representing over 30 nations, including Americans, lived, suffered, and died in its confines.

> For almost eight years every type of horror known to man was practised [*sic*] with sadistic pleasure. Whether simple extermination, as in the earlier years, or extermination by "working to death," as later on, the pattern followed was always the same. Break the body; break the spirit; break the heart.
>
> Inmates were given typhus injections in spotted fever experiments; burned alive with phosphorus to try medical remedies; given yellow fever in senseless guinea-pig tests. Thousands were shot to death in "Commando 99": murder in the horse stable. Driven mad, many inmates rushed through the guard chain in the quarry or in the garden and were gleefully shot by the mighty SS. Tattooed inmates disappeared suddenly and reappeared as lampshades, book covers or gloves *(Bill Kasich: "That's Ilse Koch")*. Prisoners were crushed with rocks,

11. The Buchenwald Case

drowned in manure, whipped, castrated, starved, mutilated. Life was torture and torture was life.

Out-commandos were established from the Rhine to the Elbe. Inmates were forced to work in salt-mines, to make munitions for a militant Germany to construct V-1 and V-2 weapons in underground sweatshops *(Bill Kasich: "This is von Braun")*. In the last months of the war, thousands died building a mammoth subterannean [sic] headquarters for the führer at Ohrdruf.

For almost eight years, the Nazis ruled supreme, held to no account—until, on 1 April 1945, their world crashed to ruin: Patton's army liberated Buchenwald Concentration Camp.

A day later, General of the Army Dwight D. Eisenhower visited the camp. White with horror, he summoned his staff and gave the order to call in the press. He then invited a delegation of American Senators and Representatives, British Parliament members and a United nations committee to view the atrocities and report to their peoples. For the first time, the world understood. BUCHENWALD had earned its place in infamy.

For over a year plans for the Buchenwald trial were discussed and correlated. Because of the mistreatment and murder of their citizens, many nations were interested and took part in discussions on the case. It was decided that since Buchenwald had been overrun by the United States Army, resulting in the capture of tons of documents *(Bill Kasich: See, tons of documents)* and thousands of war criminals, it was appropriate that the United States undertake the prosecution.

January, 1947, saw the appointment of the official Prosecution Staff. *William D. Denson*, of Birmingham, Alabama, and New York City, prosecutor of the Dachau, Mauthausen and Flossenbuerg [sic] cases *(Bill Kasich: "I worked on all of these cases")*, was named chief. *Robert L. Kunzig*, Philadelphia attorney, and *Solomon Surowitz* of New York City were made assistants. A loyal group of interrogators, investigators, interpreters and reporters rounded out the staff and made possible, through day and night work, the intense preparation of the case *(Bill Kasich: "It was us at Wiesbaden that did all this preparation")*.

Over six thousand suspects were studied and their personal histories analyzed. Many hundreds of witnesses from virtually every nation in Europe streamed to Dachau, Germany, to assist in any way possible. Finally, thirty-one arch-criminals were selected as representatives of the horror that was BUCHENWALD. The accused were announced to the world; many other would follow in subsequent cases.

On 7 March 1947, at Dachau, the charges were served on thirty men and one woman accused of participating in the common design of operating concentration camp BUCHENWALD. On 11 April 1947, the anniversary of liberation, a crowded courtroom of survivors of the worst torture in centuries would see their former "masters" stand before the bar of justice to answer to the world for their crimes.

The BUCHENWALD case is known to history as *The United States of America v. Josias Prince zu Waldeck et al*. But history will also note all nations, great and small, standing at the side of the prosecutors, fighting intolerance and injustice

... that the world may learn to respect the dignity of the common man, that no Buchenwald may rise again.

As Kasich noted, Ilse Koch indeed had been married to Buchenwald's commandant. After her acquittal by the SS, she settled in Ludwigsburg and lived with relatives until someone recognized her. She was arrested, charged with war crimes and imprisoned at Dachau to await trial. Ilse Koch shared her husband's licentiousness and had numerous affairs with German military personnel during the course of their marriage. Even arrest and imprisonment failed to diminish her libido. One of her lovers, a Buchenwald officer who worked in the prisoner's kitchen at Dachau, ran into Koch. She told him where she was being held, and he dug a tunnel to her quarters. When it was time for Koch to stand trial, she was visibly pregnant. Her condition as well as reports of her collection of items made from the skin of inmates captured public interest. Greene noted that extra rows of wooden theater seats were installed in the courtroom to accommodate the overflow crowd. While most observers dismissed Koch's pregnancy as the result of a hyperactive sex drive, it probably was calculated to elicit sympathy from the court and avoid the death penalty.

Witnesses testified to Koch's sadism, much of it laden with sexual overtones. A former inmate testified that he and another prisoner were working in a ditch when Koch suddenly appeared. She was wearing a short skirt and no underwear. She deliberately straddled the ditch so as to ensure maximum exposure. She asked what they were looking at—and then proceeded to beat them with her riding crop. He also testified that Koch possessed a photo album that had a tattoo on it. He told the court about an inmate had been working without a shirt. The body of the inmate, either French or Belgian, bore numerous tattoos, including one on his chest that featured a sailboat with four masts. Koch noticed his heavily-tattooed body, took down his number and had him called to the gate at evening formation. A half year later, the witness testified that he had been in Buchenwald's pathology department and saw a number of human skins. One of these skins had the sailboat he had seen on the heavily tattooed inmate. When asked by prosecutor William Denson whether he ever saw that skin again, the witness replied that he had seen it on Ilse Koch's photo album. The same witness also stated that he had seen a star tattoo on a pair of gloves owned by Koch.

Inmates who had worked in the pathology department of Buchenwald testified that Koch selected hospitalized prisoners with tattoos to be killed. Prosecution introduced into evidence Exhibit 14—a shrunken head—that one of these inmates identified as that of a Polish prisoner. It was one of two shrunken heads that were shown as attractions to visitors at Buchenwald, according to a witness. U.S. Army Captain Emmanuel Lewis, chief counsel for the defense, attempted to demonstrate during cross-examination that the skins of tattooed inmates had been removed as part of a Nazi medical experiment, rather than to satisfy the whims of Koch. A Dr. Wagner tried to establish a connection between criminals and the tattoos on their bodies, Lewis noted.

The fascination of Wagner and other Buchenwald staff members for human skin was corroborated by Eugen Kogon, a Buchenwald inmate, who escaped shortly before the camp's liberation. Kogon worked with an intelligence team, headed by Second Lieutenant Albert G. Rosenberg, from the Psychological Warfare Division from the Supreme Headquarters of the Allied Forces that had been given the responsibility to document the atrocities perpetrated at Buchenwald. The results of their findings formed the basis for a 400-page typed manuscript titled *Buchenwald Report* that was written by Kogon and included accounts from more than one hundred inmates. Kogon used *Buchenwald Report* as the basis of his landmark book *The Theory and Practice of Hell: The German Concentration Camps and the System Behind Them* (New York: Farrar, Strauss, 1950). *The Buchenwald Report*, translated and edited by David A. Hackett, was published in 1995.

Kogon, who was also a star witness for the prosecution at the Buchenwald trial, noted in his book that Wagner indeed was writing his doctoral dissertation on the subject of criminals and the tattoos they bore, just as Lewis had stated at the trial. According to Kogon, Wagner had the entire camp searched for tattooed inmates and ordered the tattoos photographed. These inmates were later called to the gate by Karl Koch, who personally examined the tattoos and then selected the most elaborate. These prisoners were killed and had their skins removed and chemically treated in Buchenwald's pathology department. Kogon stated the best examples of tattooed skins were kept at Buchenwald and exhibited to SS visitors. Karl Koch had a table lamp made for his home that consisted of human bones that had been stretched over human skin. Kogon also stated that hundreds of tanned human skins were sent to Berlin to comply with orders from SS Col. Dr. Enno Lolling, who had authority over all doctors and medical staff at concentration camps. Lolling escaped prosecution as a war criminal by committing suicide while hospitalized in Flensburg on May 27, 1945.

Lewis placed Dr. Konrad Morgen, the German judge who had

prosecuted Karl Koch, on the stand. Morgen stated that he had searched the Koch house during his investigation of Buchenwald's former commandant. Morgen testified that a thorough search uncovered no lampshades, gloves or photo album made of human skin. While it is tempting to dismiss the testimony of Morgen, who had been a member of the SS, his denial of a skin-bound photo album was later corroborated by a reliable source. In the Author's Note at the conclusion of *Justice at Dachau*, Greene mentioned talking with Barbara Ann Murphy, who worked as a stenographer at the Buchenwald trial. Murphy stated that she had been given Koch's photo album, which a witness had testified was made from human skin, to take to headquarters at Freising. She told Greene that the album was cloth-covered.

While Murphy's sincerity as well as her commitment to the success of the war crimes trials are both certainly beyond dispute, others who deny Ilse Koch's possession of items made from the skin of Buchenwald inmates do so in order to advance an agenda. Holocaust deniers have long sought to discredit accounts of Koch's macabre collections. The deniers claim the products that war crimes prosecutors identified as made from human skin were actually created from animal skin. Scientific analysis, however, affirms that Buchenwald inmates indeed were prized for their skin. A report, dated 5/25/45, sent to the commanding general of the Third U.S. Army and designated "ATTENTION: JUDGE ADVOCATE GENERAL" from the Section of Pathology of the Seventh Medical Laboratory contains the results of an examination of three tanned pieces of skin sent to the lab by Lt. Col. Givin from Buchenwald "with office record designation Case 81-T.J.A." The report's microscopic analysis reads: "The tissue consists of bundles of collagen showing occasional epithelial and sweat glands remnants. Granular black pigment granules are seen between some of the bundles." The report, signed by Chief of Pathology Reuben Cares, concluded that "all three specimens are tattooed human skin."

The U.S. Memorial Holocaust Museum in Washington, D.C., possesses a photograph designated #04885A that it identifies as "View of preserved human organs removed from prisoners during medical experiments conducted in the Buchenwald concentration camp." The photo depicts containers of organs on a small table. The museum notes that "the lender's handwritten caption reads: 'This is part of the laboratory where Ilse Koch tattooed human skins were cured for lampshades.'" The photo is credited "courtesy of Robert Michael Merritt."

11. The Buchenwald Case

While items made from human skin garnered headlines the world over, Greene noted that Denson correctly ascertained that Koch's avid participation in the Buchenwald staff's brutalization and murder of inmates was more likely to result in a conviction. When he placed Koch on the witness stand, she denied any wrongdoing and insisted that she had spent her years at Buchenwald caring for her children. A plethora of witnesses and evidence, however, indicated otherwise. Ilse Koch was found guilty on August 14, 1947, and sentenced to life imprisonment five days later. *U.S. v Josiah, Prince of Waldeck et alia*, the Buchenwald case of which she had been a defendant, resulted in 22 death sentences. Koch's pregnancy ensured that she wouldn't join the condemned.

Koch again made headlines on September 16, 1948, when U.S. Army General Lucius Clay, in his capacity as Military Governor of Germany, commuted her sentence to four years in prison. An article published in the September 24, 1948, edition of the *New York Times* quoted Clay as saying, "There was no convincing evidence that she selected inmates for extermination in order to secure tattooed skin or that she possessed any articles made of human skin." The American press was virtually unanimous in its criticism of Clay's decision. In a letter that was reprinted in newspapers across the nation, Denson denounced Clay's commutation of Koch's sentence as a mockery of justice. The public agreed with Denson to such an extent that a U.S. Senate subcommittee, chaired by Senator Homer Ferguson (R-MI), investigated the matter in order to determine whether sufficient grounds existed for Clay's decision.

Clay's commutation of Koch's sentence was hardly an isolated anomaly. The U.S. Army had established five boards of review charged with examining the sentences meted out by our courts. The United States and Soviet Union were now locked in the Cold Water, and Washington wanted to ensure that Federal Republic of Germany, which would be created in 1949 from the American, British and French occupation zones, would be a dependable ally.

Accordingly, the Truman administration pressured these review boards to show leniency. In *Justice at Dachau*, Greene cited a commutation that almost pales Koch's into insignificance by comparison. Heinrich Himmler created the *Einsatzgruppen* (translated as "task forces" or "deployment groups") in 1939 and placed them under the command of Richard Heydrich as a special unit with the SS. The *Einsatzgruppen* functioned as mobile killing teams that killed, primarily by shooting, groups that had been marked for extermination by the Nazis: Polish intellectuals;

gypsies; Soviet political commissars; partisans; and Jews. Historian Raul Hilberg estimated that the *Einsatzgruppen* killed over two million people during the course of World War II, including 1.3 million Jews.

Fourteen of twenty-one *Einsatzgruppen* leaders placed on trial had been sentenced to death by an American tribunal. Greene noted that only four were hanged. The responsibility for such leniency rested primarily with the review boards rather than Clay. According to Greene, Clay was overwhelmed by the number of cases awaiting review and tended to approve almost all of the boards' recommendations. Death sentences of Nazi war criminals were reduced from 426 to 298. Clay advised the review committees to remain silent about these commutations. Newspaper and magazine articles, photographs and newsreels had left American citizens well acquainted with Nazi atrocities.

Clay knew that most Americans strongly supported the trials of war criminals and would be angered to learn that so many commutations were being granted in an attempt to gain the support of West Germany. He was right. The senate subcommittee mirrored the outrage felt by the public when it denounced the military's effort to conceal the fact that Koch's sentence had been so significantly reduced. The committee also castigated the commutation itself. Koch had been a willing participant—a "volunteer," as Senator Ferguson put it in his final report—and her actions deserved only utter contempt. The commutation of her sentence and the attempt to conceal it from the public, he concluded, constituted a blemish on democratic justice and must not be repeated.

Clay's commutation of Koch's sentence allowed her to escape American justice but not the consequences of her actions at Buchenwald. She was tried by a West German court and convicted in 1949 for incitement to murder, incitement to attempt murder and incitement to commit great bodily harm. Sentenced to life imprisonment on January 15, 1951, Koch appealed to have the sentence overturned. Her appeal was denied. She submitted several petitions for a pardon to the Bavarian Ministry of Justice, all of which were denied.

Koch was all but forgotten when the child she had conceived while a prisoner sought her out. Born in 1947, Uwe Kohler (his mother's maiden name) was taken from her at birth. When he learned that Ilse Koch was his mother, Uwe began visiting her in prison. The two were reported to have forged a strong bond. Uwe arrived at the prison for a visit on September 1, 1967, only to be informed that his mother had committed suicide in her cell by hanging herself with bed sheets. Uwe Kohler always denied his mother's guilt and maintained that she was the victim of "treachery." Koch's supporters frequently portrayed her as a victim. Greene observed that Alfred Seidel, her attorney, submitted many requests to the Ministry of Justice for a pardon, including one that suggested his client was the victim of an extensive lobbying effort conducted by American Jews.

12

The Nazi Underground in Post-War Germany

I WAS A LITTLE SURPRISED when Kasich mentioned that he and the other young men of the War Crimes Group were occasionally able to escape their responsibilities by engaging in the Great American Pastime. "We were playing baseball," he recalled. "I was pitching for the War Crimes Group. We were called the Jury Boys. We won the Division, the second half of the Division."

There were other diversions for American troops in post-war Germany. "But John [Cashman] took chances," Kasich noted. "I don't know how he got out of there alive." I asked him what kind of chances Cashman took.

> Well, he would pick up girls and so on and so forth. And spend the night. And then he would come back. Which I would never have done. I never did do it because I thought too much of my body to cheapen myself. Because a lot of them [American military personnel] got syphilis and other diseases. When I was there, there were diseases all over the place. In fact, we had a little park and in that park they had a sign: "84 cases of VD were contracted in this park." And warning the guys there were too many diseases. You could see diseases on the women's feet. They had sores and everything.

"German women?" I asked. Bill replied, "Yeah. German women."

Kasich wasn't exaggerating the level of sexual promiscuity in post-war Germany. In *The Nuremberg Legacy: How the Nazi War Crimes Trials Changed the Course of History*, Norbert Ehrenfreund observed that the sexual revolution associated with the 1960s was already occurring in the Germany of the late 1940s. Many American military personnel as well as civilians working for the military lived with or had affairs with German women. Ehrenfreund attributed these relationships to the simple attraction that existed between the hundreds of thousands of American men

12. The Nazi Underground in Post-War Germany 157

in Germany, who lacked women, and German women, who had lost their husbands and boyfriends during the war.

While there is a great deal of truth in this explanation, there were also grim economic factors in play as well. Joseph Persico, in his *Nuremberg: Infamy on Trial*, noted that Tech Sergeant Hal Burson conducted some field work in post-war Germany by patronizing bars. Burson, whose broadcasts were aired daily over the Armed Forces Radio Network and heard by GIs in virtually every post in Germany, had been sent to Nuremberg to cover the trials. He visited the city's bars in an effort to acquaint himself with Germans and learn how they were coping in the post-war era.

German men, Burson concluded, suffered from psychological emasculation. There were few employment opportunities available to them and many depended on their women for financial support. German women found it easier to land jobs with their nation's Allied conquerors. They also had the option of becoming their mistresses. Their husbands and boyfriends had little recourse except to turn a blind eye to these financial hardship–induced sexual liaisons.

There was an active Nazi underground in post-war Germany. I asked Kasich if some of these amorous women could have initiated relationships with American military personnel—particularly members of the 7708 War crimes Group—for the purpose of being murdered.

> Yeah. Well, this is what I was afraid of. In fact, this laundry man ... came in at Christmas and he said, "Why don't you come over for Christmas? We don't have much, but we'd like to invite you because you've been so good to us." And I looked at John [Cash] and John shook his head no. Of course John took chances but, with this one, he felt as if we were being set up. The guy could have been legitimate. Maybe he appreciated what we did but we said, "No, thank you."

Kasich told the following story to give an idea of how easily information about members of the War Crimes Group passed to Germans.

> We were in Augsburg ... as we were coming back [from a brief excursion], this beautiful blonde girl—this was, I don't know if this was November or December—was on a bike. Beautiful girl, in shorts, and I usually was in the middle and the other two [John Cashman and Don Baghetto] were on the side of me. And she said, "Bill!" And I turned around and looked at her and walked to her bike and I got hold of the handle bars and I looked her square in the eyes and I said, "How do you know my name?" She said, "I just did." And I asked her, "What do you want?" And she said, "Is my sister Ilse working?" And I said, "Yes."

Evidently, Ilse had found employment with the U.S. Army in one capacity or another. Kasich had no idea who Ilse was or whether she was

Playing baseball gave these men a chance to unwind (courtesy Bill Kasich).

working. He replied "yes" merely to get rid of the woman. Still, Kasich found it disconcerting that a woman he had never seen before knew his name and recognized him by sight.

> But it scared me. And they [members of the Nazi underground] usually used the beautiful girls to entice the guys. But not being horny, I stayed clear of all of them because I didn't want to become diseased or a casualty. You learned to sleep hearing everything. You could hear a pin drop and you slept that way. And you were skeptical. We had to go [out] in fours. And if a man came for you, [or] even if a woman was walking towards you, you had to be on guard because you didn't know as he came by, [he] would drop a knife in his hands and you would get it in the stomach. And before you knew what was happening, he was gone.

I said that it was a dangerous time to be young. Kasich replied, "Yes." He then told me why.

General Hellmuth Reymann, appointed by Hitler to serve as commander of the German forces in the fast-approaching battle for Berlin, had ordered every bridge in Berlin to be prepared for demolition. At the time, Albert Speer recalled in his memoir, Reymann was subordinate to General Gotthard Heinrici and, at a meeting held at Heinrici's headquarters on April 15, 1945, Speer, who realized that the war was indeed lost, attempted to talk Reymann out of it by pointing out that the destruction of every bridge in Berlin would destroy the industrial life of Berlin for the

12. The Nazi Underground in Post-War Germany

foreseeable future. The impasse was resolved when Heinrici issued orders that bridges would be destroyed only during the course of important military actions. Heinrici also ordered that explosives be removed from the vital arteries of Berlin's railroads and highways.

The next day Speer and Lt. Col. Manfred von Poser drove to the woods of Schorfheide, which he described as Göring's "animal paradise," where Speer drafted a statement that he hoped would lead to an end to the war with Germany left more or less intact. He called for soldiers and civilians alike to prevent the demolition of bridges, factories and railroads as well as the release of all political prisoners—including Jews—to the Allies. Speer urged the surrender of cities and villages without a fight and the prohibition of "Werewolf" activity, a term that will be defined in a moment. He then had von Poser take a note written in pencil to the general manager of the Berlin Electricity Works to make certain that the supply of electrical current to the most powerful radio station in Germany would continue until it was taken by the Allies in order to ensure that this declaration was broadcast. Speer noted that this station, located in Königs Wusterhausen, regularly broadcast Werewolf messages. This declaration, Speer stated, was supposed to be the station's final broadcast.

This landmark broadcast, however, was never made. Heinrici, who

From left: John Cashman, Bill Kasich and Donald Boggetto of the 7708 War Crimes Group (courtesy Bill Kasich).

supported Speer's decision to issue such a statement, thought that the Russians would overrun the station before Speer finished the broadcast. He advised Speer to record his speech on a phonograph record that could be played at the station before it was captured by the Russians. In the chaos of Nazi Germany's death throes, however, no recording equipment could be located. With Speer's speech undelivered, a ban on Werewolf activity never went into effect.

Richard and Clara Winston, the translators of Speer's *Inside the Third Reich*, felt obligated to include a translators' note to help readers make sense of his use of the word "Werewolf." Rather than creatures from a horror movie, these Werewolves were guerrillas who were supposed to comprise a last-ditch resistance to the Allies who had entered Germany. The Winstons noted that the Allies indeed took this threat seriously but no resistance appeared. They conclude that the Werewolves were just another lie put forth by Joseph Goebbels' propaganda machine. Bill Kasich begs to differ.

The September 18, 2000, article in *The Telegraph* that introduced me to the War Crimes Group quoted Kasich as saying: "We had to constantly watch for German assassins who wanted to kill us. We lost four U.S. agents who were picking up war criminals for trial."

While addressing the high school students at the veterans' reunion, Kasich remarked that members of the War Crimes Group were on a hit list of German assassins that he called "Werewolves," who comprised a Nazi underground that existed in the shambles of the Third Reich. He told the students: "We had to be on guard or the assassins would kill us. They would capture you and cut open your stomach."

A year later, while addressing a class of high school students, Kasich again stressed the dangers associated with working with the War Crimes Group. "We had to be constantly on the lookout for Nazi assassins who wanted to kill us," he was quoted as telling the students. "Four of our agents were killed hunting down war criminals who murdered Jews and U.S. soldiers in prison camps."

During my first interview with Kasich, I asked about these murderers when he mentioned, "We [the War Crimes Group] were losing them [field agents assigned to locate and apprehend accused war criminals]. If they [Werewolves] caught them [field agents], they'd cut out your stomach. They were their [Germans who still supported the Third Reich] assassins."

I had no familiarity with Nazi werewolves at the time and asked whether they worked for a central organization, or were they freelancers. Kasich replied:

12. The Nazi Underground in Post-War Germany

They were assassins, or terrorists as we'd call them today. And they were good at it. They were perfectionists, and you had to be on the lookout all the time because you didn't know where they were going to strike. And when I was there I was told there were also women that belonged to the Werewolves. Four agents were killed at one time. It was in 1946, around July sometime. Reports were coming in every once and a while that so-and-so got killed.

Kasich noted that, except when transporting prisoners, members of the War Crimes Group were ordinarily unarmed.

We couldn't carry guns. You couldn't defend yourself. The only time I carried a gun, I think it was three times when I went to deliver prisoners to Dachau. And we were given guns. I was given a .45 [a Colt Model 1911A1 .45 semi-automatic pistol, the standard U.S. military sidearm at the time], and twice I was told to take the clip out of it and put it in my pocket, right in front of Otto Scorzeny's outfit. Of course we had Thompson sub-machine guns in front [of Skorzeny's men].

I wanted to return to the four men killed by Werewolves and asked what they were doing at the time of their murders. "They were picking up prisoners," Kasich replied. Were all four men killed at once? "All at once—by Werewolves." Kasich then shared this:

They knew where we were. In our office there were four Nazis that we turned in. Truman signed a decree that we could hire ex–Nazis for the military government and there were four in our office. A fellow by the name of Otto used to talk to me all the time. He wanted me to know what happened on the Eastern Front. He didn't think these things were being told to us.

Otto evidently had a lively interest in the Eastern front. In another interview, Kasich recalled Otto saying with considerable disgust, "The Schweinhund sucked us into Russia." Kasich said that he had no idea to whom Otto was referring.

I saw him [Otto] one day. We were going for lunch. I left my camera in [the office]. I went back for it because I had one camera that was stolen from me. He was going through Frank's [Frank Morgan] papers on his desk. What he didn't know was that what I had on my desk was the same thing that Morgan had. Morgan as the head of it. But it would circulate through about six or eight of us, the same document, to make sure that we didn't leave anything out. What one man forgot, the other one would pick up.

The clear implication, of course, is that "Otto" was gathering intelligence for a Nazi underground. I brought up Otto during our second interview in order to obtain more details about this incident. "I don't know what happened to him," Kasich said. "They took him away. He never did show up." He thought Otto might have been imprisoned by the U.S. military. I said that Otto was obviously interested in those papers.

> Yes. He made a mistake. If he went through my papers, nothing would have been said. I would have thought he was straightening them out. But he went through Morgan's. And Morgan didn't have any more papers than I did because it [any particular paper] went around in a circle.

I asked about American military personnel who were killed. Kasich's introduction to the precariousness of life in post-war Germany occurred early. He arrived by train at Wiesbaden, where he was picked up by a driver.

> So he took me to the barracks. Now, it wasn't a barracks. It was a three-storey house. I forgot [the name of] the street. It was off Wilhelm Strasse, and I was there with twenty others. I think it was a little bigger place than this [the book shop, where the interview was being conducted], a little wider, but it was bunk to bunk then. All of us stayed there about two to three days. It stunk in there, people passing gas and everything. I said, "My God! I've got to get out of here!" So not knowing anything, without being told anything, there was an empty building or apartment house to the north of us, right next door, that wasn't being used. So three of us who were in the prosecution section said, "Well, let's go over there and see if it's open." So we don't want the east side and this is all blocked off. You could get some rooms in front so we'll see what's on the other end, which was a mistake. But we thought we were safe.

Kasich soon discovered just how wrong they were.

"Well, this was at dusk and we worked 'til about five-thirty and we went to dinner and by the time we got back we went to our billets," Kasich said. He and the other men suddenly heard noises from the room next door.

> So I hollered out, "What's going on in there?" And this other guy said, "Well, he's probably drunk." I said, "How the hell do you know he's drunk?" See ... you don't stumble like that and he was going around the room. We didn't hear anything. We didn't get a reply [to the question "What's going on in there?"]. So I said, "Let's get out of here." I hollered out, "Get your guns and let's get out of here. Call the MP's." So we went outside and hollered out, "Get the MP's! Get the MP's!"

I asked Kasich whether he and his fellow soldiers indeed were armed.

> No, we weren't armed. We weren't allowed to carry guns at all. We couldn't even defend ourselves. I guess they thought you'd get drunk and kill a fellow soldier if you had a disagreement.... So it was late. We were waiting for the MP's, and we went back to our apartment and I said, "We need a hammer and some nails." They [his roommates] said, "What the hell are you talking about, Kasich? What's going on?" So I said, "I don't know." So I got a hammer and got some nails and nailed the door up at the top and at the bottom. I said, "That son of a bitch comes in, he's

going to have a fight on his hands." So we're laying there and someone tried to get in, wiggling the door. I said, "Okay, guys, get your guns out, point them at that door and if that son of a bitch comes in, let him have it." Of course, which was a lie. We were bluffing. You had to bluff because when I walked out [in the town streets], I always had my shirt out like I have here [in my book shop during the interview] and I'd put my hand in here because I didn't know who was coming down the street, even with four of us. He [an unknown assailant] could pull out a knife ... stick you in the stomach and in a crowd he could disappear before they [American military personnel] even knew what was happening.

Kasich discussed this incident in another interview and went into more detail about its aftermath.

We just waited and waited. Then, the next morning, they [the MP's] said they had got him. At the office, I was asked to help clean out his room and by the time we got there, the Grave Registration was in there. They [the Werewolves] had cut out his stomach and thrown his intestines all over the room.... I went out and got nails and nailed our doors shut. About two days after that, we were moved for a little security but still you couldn't carry a gun.

I asked if this man was one of the four killed by Werewolves that he had mentioned in *The Telegraph* article. "No, this was separate," Kasich replied. "You can't put everything in a newspaper article." How many American military personnel would you estimate were killed by the Nazi underground? "I'd say eight to fifteen, to my knowledge," he answered. Were these Americans killed for their work in bringing Nazi war criminals to justice?

Oh, yeah.... When we went out, we were always told that if you were in a jeep to put the windshield up. What they would do—they had wireless, they had walkie-talkies—they would put up piano wire and if the windshield was down and there was no protection or something to cut the wire, off comes your head.

I remarked that danger existed, even though the war was over. "Oh, yes. There was a war going on after the war," Kasich replied. "It was minor, but from the Danube they would fish out an average of two [American military personnel] per week."

I asked who killed these men. "Nazi agents." I showed Kasich that section of Charles Whiting's 1972 work *Hitler's Werewolves: The Story of the Nazi Resistance Movement, 1944–1945*, in which the author claimed that Werewolf activity ended with the surrender of Nazi Germany. Kasich quickly replied, "No, no, no, no, no. That is not right. No." He maintained that World War II was followed by yet another conflict that pitted American military personnel against militant Nazis, which he described as "a little war going on after the war." A bit later during that same interview,

Kasich again turned his attention to Whiting's claim and said, "No, that's not right."

During our only interview, Ralph Schulz also touched upon the Nazi underground and the danger it posed to American military personnel. "We went to a circus one day to be guards," he told me, "and they told us then there was a group that was being organized. A pro–Nazi group of Germans and we should be on the lookout for them trying to do something dramatic at that circus."

Although nothing happened at the circus, Schulz stated, "They [members of the pro–Nazi group] were there." He didn't recall the Nazi underground being referred to as Werewolves and confided, "I never felt in danger." Schulz told me—and he was being only semi-facetious—that he felt somewhat endangered by young soldiers who were just arriving in Germany and "couldn't control themselves." He recalled a young GI who was serving on guard duty and somehow managed to shoot himself in the foot with a .45.

Schulz agreed with Kasich, however, that members of the Nazi underground in post-war Germany preyed on Americans and other Allied military personnel. "The young Germans who had been educated by the Nazis were just then attaining their majority," he said. "They were the most dangerous, they told us." He recalled hearing about a GI who had been murdered at Nuremberg. I asked whether this GI had met his death at the hands of the Nazi underground. "Easily, easily," Schulz replied. He stated that Nazi operatives often employed a highly-recognizable method when committing murder: garroting. "That was a sign that it had been a neo–Nazi group."

Members of the War Crimes Group and other Allied personnel in post-war Germany were under no illusion that surrender by Karl Dönitz, Hitler's successor, meant an end to all hostilities. As it became obvious the war in Europe was drawing to a close, many Americans speculated whether die-hard Nazis would attempt to carry on the struggle. In an article titled "Hitler's Final V Weapon," Major Erwin Lessner, a popular author of that era, offered a possible scenario. "V Weapon" refers to the deadly V-2 rockets that Nazi Germany launched against Allied nations late in the war. Lessner wrote that

> Information from inside Germany reaches the outer world only in small and incoherent bits to be put together with the help of logic, experience and guesswork. All the signs indicate that the Germans are preparing for intensive guerrilla warfare. Piecing the fragments together, this is how it is likely to work out:

12. The Nazi Underground in Post-War Germany

Someday—the exact date is anybody's guess—the Wehrmacht's resistance will suddenly come to an end, without a formal surrender or even a request for an armistice. The Allied armies, rapidly advancing through Germany, will find only a few German soldiers, apparently on their way home. The civilian population will be sullen and uncommunicative—as it already is in the border regions—but there will be hardly any hostility.

Then, all of a sudden, a guerrilla blitz will strike. On the German guerrilla D-Day, hundreds of raiding parties will strike Allied communications, stores, resting troops and ground installations, trying to inflict as much damage and as many casualties as possible. The raiders will hit and run with lightning speed before the occupying troops can recover from the initial shock. The first blow will be followed by rapid attacks at many points, designed to disrupt defensive measures.

The German guerrillas will be tough, well-trained and well-equipped youngsters. Each man will carry a light automatic weapon, and each platoon will be supplied with heavy machine guns, small mine throwers and a light anti-aircraft cannon. They will ride light motorcycles with a 15-cubic-inch two-cycle engine, while the larger weapons will be carried on heavier motorcycles of the well-known BMW model.

Lessner warned that these motorcycle-riding Nazi guerrillas "could become a major headache" for the Allied forces "for some weeks, perhaps for a couple of months, but no longer." He predicted they would fail because they lacked the spirit of the anti–Nazi underground that had existed in German-occupied nations during the war. Lessner also speculated that these guerrillas "would be organized by highly antagonistic groups, pursuing different objectives and essentially eager to betray one another."

Lessner's portrayal of marauding Nazi motorcycle gangs armed with automatic weapons now seems like a storyline from a particularly bad B-movie. Still, it seemed reasonable to most Americans that over a decade of Nazi indoctrination had rendered the German people incapable of passively accepting surrender to their enemies. Even with the Wehrmacht defeated, fanatical civilians would surely launch a last-ditch effort against Allied military personnel that attempted to occupy Germany.

The term werewolf (in German: *werwolf*) was taken from *Der Wehrwolf*, a 1910 novel by Hermann Löns. Harm Wulf, the novel's protagonist, is a peasant living in Lower Saxony during the Thirty Years War (1618–1648) whose family is killed by enemy soldiers. Wulf organizes his neighbors into a band of guerrillas that pursue, harass and kill these soldiers. Although a work of fiction, the historical parallel was so striking that Himmler chose it as the name of this Nazi guerrilla force.

Scholars have pointed out, however, that the Nazis had overlooked a rather important detail. *Werwolf* is derived from the Old High German word *Wer* (man) and wolf. In mythology it refers to a lycanthrope—a human who physically becomes a wolf. The character created by Löns is nothing of the kind, of course. Löns invented the word *Wehrwolf* from the German *Wehren* (to defend) and wulf (wolf), the protagonist's name.

Löns, an ardent outdoorsman and conservationist, wrote novels, poems and songs that celebrated rural life in Germany. He volunteered for service in the Imperial German Army in 1914 at age 48 and was killed in combat just three weeks after enlisting. His works—particularly *Der Wehrwolf*—continued to sell well, even after his death. Although Löns died six years before the founding of the Nazi party, German right-wing extremists found much to admire in his work. Löns's idealization of the robust German peasantry who enjoyed an almost mystical bond with their land blended well with Nazi *Blut und Boder* (Blood and Soil) ideology, which glorified country life and rural hardiness.

Nazi propagandists told Germans that their nation had been victimized by Jews, an alien people that exploited the Fatherland and would ultimately destroy it if left unchecked. Identifying the marauding soldiers who murdered the family of Harm Wulf in seventeenth-century Germany with twentieth-century Jews allowed Nazi ideologues to co-opt *Der Wehrwolf*. Like Harm Wulf and the other peasant sons of the soil, contemporary Germans were urged to avenge the harm done to their kinsfolk by an enemy who had invaded their Fatherland. The success of the Nazi party in promoting the reinterpretation of *Der Wehrwolf* is underscored by the novel's sales figures: by 1945, 865,000 copies had been sold in Germany. In the autumn of 1944, the Nazi Party published a "special edition" of *Der Wehrwolf* for Germans who were to be trained as guerrilla fighters. A year later, when the Third Reich was in its death throes, several German newspapers serialized the novel in order to inspire and provide hope to their readers. By this time, the Fatherland was being invaded by enemy armies bent on its destruction. Like Harm Wulf, the modern Werewolf was expected to take up arms to defend the very soil that gave him life. Twentieth-century werewolves included both genders. Perry Biddiscombe's *The Last Nazis: SS Werewolf Guerrilla Resistance in Europe 1944–1947* includes a photo of a matronly-looking German woman receiving instruction from a German soldier in the use of a *Panzerfaust*, a single-shot anti-tank weapon. Biddiscombe notes that the Werewolf movement included a women's component.

Despite the experiences of the War Crimes Group in post-war

Germany, Werewolves were not originally intended to be civilians operating as guerrillas, who harassed and killed enemy troops that occupied the Reich. It was regarded as treason in Nazi Germany to regard even the possibility of defeat. In the late summer of 1944, as the Americans and British began pushing east while Soviet forces continued their drive west, Himmler initiated Operation Werewolf. These units, consisting of uniformed German soldiers who had been given special training in guerrilla warfare, would battle the enemy in German-conquered territories that had been retaken by the Allies. As conceived by Himmler, there was to be nothing "last-ditch" about Operation Werewolf. The territory in which they operated would eventually be retaken by the Wehrmacht. It was no coincidence that Himmler chose to call these behind-the-lines fighters Werewolves. Biddescombe states that Himmler told his SS section chiefs at a conference held in the autumn of 1944 that he drew the name from Löns's novel.

Himmler chose Hans-Adolf Prützmann to serve as the national coordinator of Operation Werewolf. A member of the Nazi party since 1929 who joined the SS a year later, Prützmann had served as the SS police commander in German-occupied Ukraine. His background in guerrilla warfare included organizing ethnic Germans as well as Ukrainian nationalists into combat units that fought Soviet partisans and the Red Army. Prützmann and his staff set up headquarters in a camouflaged train code-named Krista.

Werewolves received their training at Hitler Youth combat training camps, Wehrmacht sapper schools and even some public schools. Biddescombe notes that Canadian troops discovered dummy hand grenades in a classroom along with wall posters demonstrating the proper technique for slipping a grenade into enemy jeeps. Other German schools offered more advance training such as demolition and sabotage instruction.

Karl Siebel, a Nazi who had been attached to the Werewolf movement, consulted with SS experts in guerrilla and counter-guerrilla tactics to produce an eighty-page illustrated booklet titled *Werewolf: Tips for Ranger Units* that served as a Werewolf training textbook. Written in simple, straightforward language, the booklet is a basic instruction manual in committing sabotage and making booby traps. A section of this manual teaches Werewolves how to notch trees so that they fall to block roads. Another section confirms Bill Kasich's statement concerning piano wire strung across roads as a Werewolf booby trap. An illustration that accompanies the text shows a piano wire—designated a "decapitation wire"—stretched across a road. The wire has been wrapped around a tree on each side of the road and then anchored by pegs hammered into the ground.

According to Biddiscombe, hundreds of decapitation wires were laid in Occupied Germany. Although no decapitations were reported, several Allied troops and even German civilians were injured. Military personnel learned to neutralize the threat by welding vertical iron bars to the bumpers or grills of their vehicles, which broke these wires. Although Biddiscombe reported that most Allied injuries from decapitation wires occurred during the period 1945–1946, he noted that a German driver was injured in May of 1949 when he struck a wire that had been intended for French military personnel. Decapitation wires were still very much in use when Kasich served in the War Crimes Group.

Determining which killings and acts of sabotage were actually committed by Werewolves can be challenging. Military historians long attributed the death of Major Tom Poston, liaison officer to Field Marshal Bernard Montgomery, to Werewolves. In his *Hitler's Werewolves: The Story of the Nazi Resistance Movement 1944–1945*, Whiting noted that Poston had a reputation for recklessness and often took back roads that hadn't been cleared and secured. On April 21, 1945—just two weeks before Germany's surrender—Poston took such a German road and was ambushed by assailants identified by Whiting as a band of fanatical German boys. These boys had hidden in a ditch in what Whiting construed as an example of Werewolf training and sprang into action with the approach of Poston's jeep. Whiting's account has Poston driving his jeep directly at the boys in a typically daredevil ploy. He was struck by a bullet, however, and his jeep skidded into a ditch where, bleeding to death, the 25-year-old officer fired his revolver until it was empty. In *Monty's Greatest Victory: The Drive for the Baltic April–May 1945*, however, Whiting wrote that Poston was ambushed by German troops rather than Werewolf guerrillas.

Werewolves were not above claiming credit for acts in which they had played no role whatsoever. For example, Werewolf Radio declared that its operatives had killed U.S. Army Major General Maurice Rose on March 30, 1945. Rose met his combat death when his motorized military column, which included a tank as well as an armored car, was attacked by German tanks in a rural area south of the city of Padersborn. He was shot by a German soldier with a machine pistol, who had emerged from one of the attacking tanks. Rose reached for his service pistol in a desperate effort to fight back, even when his death was certain. Before he could remove his pistol from its holster, however, he was struck by several bullets, including one to the head.

The Werewolves probably claimed responsibility for Rose's death for the sake of sheer propaganda. He was the highest-ranking American military officer to be killed in the European Theater during World War II. Rose was also the highest-ranking Jew in the U.S. Army. Both his father and grandfather had been Polish rabbis.

Other murders were unquestionably the work of Werewolves. Fritz Lotto, the son of a Lutheran clergyman, attended a Werewolf training program in late 1944, where he was instructed that it was allowable to intimidate the civilian population in Allied-occupied territory as well as to assassinate Germans likely to collaborate with the Allies when the *Wehrmacht* pulled out. Biddiscombe believes that two mayors were murdered in Westphalia by Werewolves under Lotto's command.

Mayors seen as collaborators were frequently targeted by these guerrillas. When Aachen fell to the U.S. Army, Franz Oppenhoff was selected to be the city's first mayor under American rule. Aachen's population had stood at about 160,000 before the American occupation. Most of its residents, along with its government officials and municipal records, were evacuated east of the Rhine to keep them out of Allied hands. Ironically, the U.S. Army after taking the city also evacuated thousands of its remaining citizens to internment camps for screening. Oppenhoff, an attorney and conservative Catholic, was appointed mayor of a city that by now had only a few hundred inhabitants, most of whom had been assigned by the army to clean up the rubble of battle.

Even among such a greatly reduced population, the Nazi underground was able to maintain a strong presence in Aachen. But as Biddescombe noted, these diehards lacked the capability to assassinate Oppenhoff. Himmler and Goebbels were outraged that the Americans had installed a non–Nazi mayor and both reportedly demanded the collaborator's murder. According to Biddescombe, Himmler personally signed the decree that demanded Oppenhoff's murder. Herbert Wenzel, a Werewolf, assembled a five-member hit team comprised that included a woman: Ilse Hirsh. A fanatical Nazi, Hirsh was a veteran of the League of German Girls, the girls' branch of the Hitler Youth. In Aachen she had served in the Work, Faith and Beauty Society, which was a Nazi organization for German females between the ages of 17 and 21. Since the German evacuation of her city, she had been supervising Work, Faith and Beauty Society members tasked with digging field fortifications. Other team members included Josef Leitgeb, a Waffen-SS radio operator and second-in-command of the team, and Erich Morgenschweiss of the Hitler Youth. Both men had received Werewolf training from Wenzel. Two other men, former border guards who were familiar with the area and served as guides, rounded out the team.

The operation was code-named *Karnival* (Carnival), which could have referred to the goal of conducting the assassination during the pre-Lenten season or the level of enjoyment that the killing of a collaborator was supposed to give to the German people. Biddescombe reports that by February of 1945, Hitler himself was following the mission's development.

The Karnival hit squad parachuted into the Netherlands on March 19 from a captured American B-17. Armed with pistols for their mission, they shot to death a Dutch border guard who demanded to see their papers. Hirsh became separated from the others during this incident and made her way into Aachen alone. When she reunited with other team members in the city, she informed them that she had learned where Oppenhoff lived. The American-appointed mayor was shot to death on March 25 by Leitgeb. He and two other members of the hit squad had gained access to the mayor by dressing in *Luftwaffe* coveralls and pretending to be German fliers who had been shot down and needed supplies. Leitgeb was killed by a land mine a few days later during the outfit's return to German-controlled territory.

Biddescombe wrote that the Werewolf movement never enjoyed the support of a majority of the German people. The military regarded the very notion that Werewolves could accomplish what the *Wehrmacht* could not— the defeat of the Allied armies—as patently ridiculous. Civilians feared that Werewolf acts of sabotage and assassination would lead to reprisals by the Allies. While Albert Speer's recorded appeal for an end to the Werewolf movement was never broadcast over German radio, another demand for the termination of Werewolf activities was indeed broadcast just a few days after Speer's recording. Admiral Karl Dönitz, who had succeeded Hitler as Germany's head of state, made a speech broadcast by German radio on May 6, 1945, in which he asked all Germans to refrain from participation in underground organizations, including the Werewolf movement. The next day Dönitz ordered military commander Alfred Jodl to act as his representative by signing the German instruments of surrender at Rheims, France.

Many historians date Dönitz's speech as the formal end of the Werewolf movement. Captured by the Allies, Prützmann committed suicide on May 21, 1945, depriving the Werewolves of their titular leader. Neither Dönitz's speech nor Prützmann's death deterred the most fanatical Nazis from continuing to engage in underground activities. True believers continued to engage in their campaign of sabotage and assassination, as both Kasich and Schulz confirmed in their interviews.

13

Walter Kirkland

Family Man

MASSACHUSETTS RESIDENT PAUL DOWD "almost fell out of my chair," as he put it in a 2021 e-mail to me when he read *Unsung Heroes of the Dachau Trials*. Bill Kasich gave me the photo that appears in Chapter 3, "Report of the Deputy Judge Advocate for War Crimes," which depicts four young members of the War Crimes Group at work in their office. Dowd told me that he and his family were certain that one of the young men was Walter C. Kirkland, his late father-in-law. Kirkland "was only a kid then, 18–19 years old," Dowd noted.

He assured me the "photograph has made the entire family circuit" and "everyone is in agreement that whoever took that photograph did in fact capture Walter at his work station." According to Kirkland's discharge papers, which Dowd shared with me, he had been a clerk-typist. He wished that his father-in-law "were alive today" because "I'm certain he would have enjoyed the small notoriety attached to seeing his Army unit portrayed in your fine book."

I put Dowd in touch with Bill Kasich, who assured him that he remembered his father-in-law. Kasich told Dowd that Kirkland had been a member of the "Jury Boys," which was the War Crimes Group's baseball team. He sent Dowd a photo of the team in which Kirkland is clearly visible.

Kirkland never had a chance to read *Unsung Heroes of the Dachau Trials*. He died in 2010, nine years before the book's publication. My first thought was regret that I hadn't interviewed him so that I could have included his recollections in my book. Further dialogue with Dowd convinced me that there had been no lost opportunity, however. His father-in-law had little desire to share his experiences while serving with the War Crimes Group.

In an e-mail, Dowd wrote that "Papa didn't talk much about his time in uniform. He did tell me he was part of the WCU [War Crimes Unit] but never got into any specifics. The most demonstrative Walter became in my presence was saying something like 'I saw all those bastards up close,'" a reference to the defendants awaiting their trials. "Everything else concerning the WCU was 'broad strokes.' Looking back, clearly he did not want to talk nor think about those times."

In another e-mail, Dowd told me his father-in-law had attended some of the war crimes trials. "He gave me a ticket—like a carnival ticket—that allowed admittance to one of the trials," Dowd wrote. "I later donated it to the USS *Salem* museum in nearby Quincy, Mass."

7708 War Crimes Group member Walter Kirkland (courtesy Paul Dowd).

When Kirkland shared memories of his army days, "it was mostly of the funnier things such as being a northerner taking basic training in the deep south; being 'that guy' who dropped the live hand grenade in the pit during practice; and being demoted from sergeant to corporal in Germany on the same day he was promoted because the inspecting officer pulled a loose thread off of his newly sewn sergeant chevrons," Dowd stated.

In addition to providing Dowd with that photo of the baseball team, Kasich acquainted him with the work of the War Crimes Group. It helped him understand just why his father-in-law was so reluctant to discuss the subject. Members of the 7708 War Crimes Group "surely witnessed the fresh aftermath of more horror in the performance of their duties than any person should have to see in a hundred life-times," Dowd concluded.

"Walter was a wonderful man, kind and generous, with a fierce love of God, country and family," Dowd assured me. Walter Kirkland's love for his family surely reinforced his desire to spare them explicit knowledge of the horrors perpetrated by Nazi Germany.

14

Otto Ludwig Stein
Refugee and Interpreter

On February 2, 2023, Deborah Stein contacted me. Otto Ludwig Stein, her late father, was a German-born Jew whose family escaped from Europe and arrived in the United States on New Year's Day of 1940. Stein became an American citizen when he enlisted in the army in 1944 and served as an interpreter for the War Crimes Group after the war. He died in 2014 when I was still writing the first edition, so his recollections weren't included. However, Deborah Stein provided the transcript of an interview in which Stein discussed his work with the group.

Stein was born in Augsburg in 1925, and his parents "were both teachers and educators in the large sense." The family moved to Berlin when Stein was six. His parents "took over a large home for feeble-minded children and adults which was run by the Jewish community." The Steins remained in Berlin until they ultimately left Germany.

Although the family was impacted by the Nuremberg Laws, which were passed in 1935, Stein's father was a world war veteran so "we had certain privileges." He recalled that some German Jews clung to the belief that "things wouldn't get any worse and if you were a real patriot you will survive." He specifically cited a group of German Jews "who called themselves—I don't know exactly how to put it—'Germans of the Jewish Confession,' sort of trying to imply that they really were German first. It didn't make any difference in the long run."

An article titled "Uyghurs and Germans of Mosaic Confession" by Jewish Advocacy for Uyghurs, posted on Medium in 2020, made much the same point. "Jewish secularism in pre–Holocaust Germany was characterized by many people who considered themselves 'Germans of Mosaic Confession'" (*Deutschen mosaischen Konfession* or גרמנים בני דת משה,) who stressed that the German components of their identity were equal to or even greater than the Jewish components," the article noted. "As we know today, no Jew was ever able to become 'German enough' to be spared."

Stein stated that he might well have been the only Jewish student at his gymnasium, which in Germany is a high-ranking secondary school. "And I was treated pretty well," he recalled. Stein spoke warmly about his homeroom teacher who "was a very staunch Nazi but he was not an anti–Semite." When students took weekend trips and stayed at Hitler Youth hostels, this teacher "insisted that I come along, which was against the law ... he insisted that as long as I was a member of the class, I was going to be part of it. And when things got a little bit more nasty, and when my father went to talk to the teacher about it, then for a while things got really straightened out, and the kids held open doors for me, which they hadn't done before. It wasn't a hundred percent kind of thing."

Stein concluded this segment of the interview with the astonishing assertion, "There were honest-to-goodness Nazis who did not buy antisemitism." He then added, "But in the end, it simply didn't work." He recalled, "Somewhere along the line, I don't remember the exact time ... things became much tougher in the gymnasium and ultimately it became by law that I had to go to a Jewish school."

Stein was then asked when his family began to consider leaving Germany. "I don't think we did much before ... November 9." He was referring to *Kristallnacht*, "the Night of Broken Glass," which occurred on November 9–10, 1938. Encouraged by the Nazi party, thugs vandalized Jewish homes and businesses in addition to attacking Jewish residents. "Broken glass" refers to the numerous windows that were shattered during those pogroms, which occurred throughout Germany as well as German-occupied Austria and the Sudetenland. Stein recalled a policeman showing up at their house that night. "We asked him what was going on, why he was there and he said, 'Don't worry about it. Go to bed.' And then we found out the next day that in fact it was *Kristallnacht*. In another institution that was for the deaf children in that same suburb, the director had been taken to Sachsenhausen," which was a concentration camp located at Oranienburg. It was in operation from 1936 until the end of the war.

The Stein family left Germany with meager resources. "You were only allowed to take ten marks out. The rest of the money had to stay behind. Everything had to stay behind except bare household goods." The Steins made their way to the Netherlands and then journeyed to the United States. He became an American citizen when he enlisted in the U.S. Army in 1944 after completing high school. "I went back [to Europe] with the infantry. We were replacements for the Battle of the Bulge. We moved up through Luxembourg, this side of the Rhine." Stein worked as an interpreter. He was then assigned to "a war crimes investigation team in Reginsburg [sic]." Regensburg is a city in eastern Bavaria. Stein was transferred to Augsburg, where the War Crimes Group was headquartered at the time.

Stein talked about the fate of Allied aircraft personnel who were shot down over Germany. "Munich had a heavy concentration of anti-aircraft [guns]," he noted. "Farmers would catch them with pitchforks and stuff like that." When 7708 investigators entered a village and inquired about downed airmen, however, residents would deny any knowledge of survivors. "You would go the priest—this was all Catholic territory—and the priest would say, 'My people would never do evil.'"

When the investigators would then go to the graveyard, however, "there would be an unmarked mound." Digging into that mound revealed corpses wearing flight jackets that contained holes. "Christianity didn't extend to the enemy," Stein stated.

"I was just a tech-sergeant, so I was basically just interpreting," he noted. But interpreters such as Stein were vital to the legal proceedings because the officers didn't know German. "So we did basically all the work. We not only did the interviewing, we then ultimately did the translations, and the officers just signed their names." Stein's life settled into a routine. "During the week we'd be down in Dachau interviewing all these guys, and on the weekends we could go home."

Stein said that "some of our officers were assigned as defenders" while others "on the war crimes team were prosecutors." Defending the accused wasn't easy but "we tried to make a reasonable defense for these bad eggs." He then added, "Most of them were pretty bad eggs."

Stein told the interviewer that he didn't recall most of the defendants' names after so many years. However, "one of them I remember very well ... a professor at the University of Munich by the name of Klaus Schilling [misspelled as "Schulling" in the interview transcript], a very old, distinguished looking gentleman, who had spent all of his life studying malaria. And he thought he was very close to the solution." But Schilling was confronted by what Stein facetiously called "a minor problem." The "final tests would have to be done on humans."

Born in Munich July 5, 1871, Schilling was appointed director of the Tropical Medicine division at the Robert Koch Institute in 1905. Upon his retirement from the institute in 1936. Schilling moved to Italy where he was allowed to use inmates of psychiatric hospitals as test subjects for immunization experiments. Italy had invaded Ethiopia the previous year and its fascist government feared troops would contract malaria.

When SS chief Heinrich Himmler learned of Schilling's work, he suggested that the professor go to Dachau and use inmates as human guinea pigs. Stein recalled Schilling defending his work by arguing that millions in Africa were suffering from malaria, and that by sacrificing these Dachau inmates, "he would really save a large part of the world [from] this dreaded disease. The fact that these emaciated people ... weren't volunteers didn't enter into the game at all."

Schilling was by no means abandoned by his family and friends. "As his witnesses, his family and his neighbors came, and they all attested to the fact that he was a good father, and he was such a nice guy, and gentle. His minister came and said he was a good, kind man, a church-going type." A colleague of Schilling from the university also maintained that he "was an honest, serious type who had never done any evil."

Just as this colleague was exiting the witness chair, however, a prosecutor described by Stein as "a young brash lieutenant" who was "really obnoxious as far as I was concerned" asked a question that destroyed Schilling's defense. "Professor," he asked, "would you do the same?" After thinking for a moment, the professor replied no. "And that hung Mr. Schilling," Stein stated.

The United States Holocaust Memorial Museum notes that Schilling attempted to vindicate himself in an address to the court that included this statement:

Schilling at his trial (United States Holocaust Memorial Museum, National Archives and Records Administration, College Park).

On the gallows. A still from a film recording Schilling's execution (United States Holocaust Memorial Museum, National Archives & Records Administration).

> I have worked out this great labor. It would be really a terrible loss if I could not finish this work. I don't ask you as a court, I ask you personally to do what you can; to do what you can to help me that I may finish this report. I need only a table and a chair and a typewriter. It would be an enormous help for science, for my colleagues, and a good part to rehabilitate myself.

He then broke down and cried.

Schilling was executed by hanging at Landsberg Prison on May 28, 1946. According to Horace Hansen in *Witness to Barbarism*, Schilling's last words were "I am not guilty. Please get it over with."

When asked how in his opinion the Dachau trials differed from the much better-known Nuremberg trials, Stein replied, "Here we had real criminals. They were caught. There was no question that those guys did it. We had witnesses." Stein believed that "the Nuremberg trials dealt more with principles than individual misdeeds."

Returning to the United States after the war, Stein attended the University of Minnesota on the GI Bill. He earned a doctorate in botany. "He completed a post-doctoral fellowship at Brookhaven National laboratory, participating in some of the early studies on the effect of radiation on plant life," according to his obituary in the June 18, 2014, edition of the *Daily Hampshire Gazette*. Stein joined the botany department at the University of Montana at Missoula and then came to the University of Massachusetts at Amherst, where he taught until his retirement in 1990. His papers are housed at that university's library.

15

John Henry Pohlman

War Crimes Attorney from the Gateway City

BORN IN ST. LOUIS ON AUGUST 2, 1917, John Henry Pohlman graduated from Soldan High School in that city. His family lived at Washington Place in the Central West End. He graduated in 1939 from Mississippi College in Clinton, Mississippi, where he "gained the school's 'special distinction award' for high academic achievement," according to the *St. Louis Globe-Democrat*. His father, John Harry Pohlman, was an attorney and young Pohlman followed in his footsteps by attending Yale Law School, where he served on the staff of the *Yale Law Review*. During his final year of law school, he attempted to enlist in the U.S. Navy but was rejected because of his poor eyesight. He received his degree in 1942.

According to the "Historical Note" that accompanies the John Henry Pohlman Papers that are housed in the archives of the State Historical Society of Missouri, Pohlman "enlisted as a private in the Army around May or June [of 1942]." Upon passing the Missouri Bar exam, he began working in his father's law office. He "was called into military service on September 3, 1942," completed basic training and was promoted to corporal on December 10.

"Between December 17, 1942, and March 17, 1943," the Historical Note states,

> Pohlman completed officer training at Fort Benning, Georgia, and was commissioned as a Second Lieutenant. From March to September, he was stationed at Camp Crowder, Missouri, where he was platoon leader of Company C, 57th Battalion, 12th Regiment. He additionally performed the duties of Trial Judge Advocate and engaged in the prosecution of courts martial cases. He earned a promotion to First Lieutenant on March 17, and then remained stationed primarily at Camp Fannin, Texas, from September 1943 to October 1944.

15. John Henry Pohlman

Pohlman shipped out to Europe in November 1944 as the regimental personnel officer with Company I, 2nd Infantry Regiment, 5th Infantry Division. As a member of General George Patton's Third Army, he participated in the Lorraine Campaign, the Allied invasion of German-occupied eastern France and western Germany. "After the Germans' Ardennes Counteroffensive at the Battle of the Bulge in December and January, Pohlman spent most of the winter in Luxembourg. He additionally served as trial judge advocate for General and Special Courts Martials in March of 1945."

Following Germany's surrender, Pohlman served with the 2nd Infantry as an internal staff officer, then as a liaison officer and finally as a regimental personnel officer. He also served as a law member of a General Court, where he was promoted to captain. On November 8, 1946, Pohlman was temporarily discharged from the Army and returned to St. Louis where he resumed his law practice. However, he had requested that the army recall him to active service because he very much wanted to participate in the war crimes trials. "Then on January 30, 1947," the Historical Note states, "Pohlman's request to be recalled into the Army was fulfilled, and he began working as a 1st Lieutenant Legal Officer with the 7708 War Crimes Group."

In a letter from Dachau to his father dated April 21, 1947, Pohlman mentioned an upcoming case, which would be his first as a member of the

7708 War Crimes Group attorney John Henry Pohlman (courtesy State Historical Society of Missouri).

War Crimes Group. "I spend the week-end here as I have a series of cases to get ready for trial" and "have the defense in one case coming up Thursday." This case, the trial of Eugen Hermann Noky, took place on April 24, 1947, at Dachau and is of interest primarily because it was the only case in which Pohlman served as a defense attorney rather than a prosecutor. Noky was a 43-year-old technical sergeant in the Waffen SS who had worked as a "motor car painter" in civilian life. Pohlman wrote his father that the case "was given me just so that I would have one opportunity to defend a case." He had no illusions about securing a not-guilty verdict. "There really isn't much I can do for the man as he shot four Russians in a concentration camp hospital when the Russians," by which he meant the advancing Soviet army, "were about to overrun the place."

Pohlman knew his defense options were limited. "All he can do is plead superior orders," he confided to his father, "but he won't get too far with that." Nonetheless, he saw a slight glimmer of hope for Noky. "However as he was actually in the army and was given a direct order to do the shootings, I might be able to get him off with a light sentence, but I don't count on it." The prosecutor, Pohlman noted, "has a pretty good case."

Noky was indeed found guilty and sentenced to hang. Pohlman filed an appeal for review on May 1. The facts of the case are succinctly stated in the Review and Recommendations document issued by the Deputy Judge Advocate's Office and dated August 4, 1947. Noky, a German national, stood accused of two violations of the "Laws and Usages of War." Specifically, Noky "at or in the vicinity of Peggau, Austria, in or about April 1945" did "wrongfully encourage, aid, abet and participate in the killing of non–German nationals who were inmates at the Peggau concentration camp, who were then in the custody of the then German Reich." Peggau was a satellite camp—the document refers to it as an "outcamp"—of the Mauthausen concentration camp.

The document's "Summary of Evidence" section states, "With the advance of the Russian armies in Austria in the spring of 1945, an evacuation of prisoners from Camp Peggau ... was undertaken during 2–3 April 1945." This evacuation was no isolated incident. Concentration camp guards typically evacuated prisoners when Allied forces closed in. About 33,000 inmates of Sachsenhausen were evacuated during the night of April 21–22, 1945. In his work *Night,* Elie Wiesel described the death march from Buna to Gleiwitz in which he was forced to participate. The following order as stated in Summary of Evidence was typical of such a forced evacuation. "As an incident of this operation, orders were issued that all inmates who were unfit for transport were to be shot."

15. John Henry Pohlman

As a loyal member of the Waffen SS, Noky indeed killed four non–German nationals in response to the order given to him by *Obersturmfuhrer* Miroff. Using his "Austrian service pistol," Noky shot them in the neck "from a distance of only a few centimeters." However, he also killed a fifth inmate "without any instruction from his superior." The first four "presumably Russian" inmates were selected from the infirmary patients "as being incapable of walking or unfit for transport." It was uncertain whether Noky, a superior officer or the infirmary capo made the death selections. "No objection was made by Noky to the performance of this task," it was noted. The former motor car painter soon killed again. "Subsequent to these killings, Noky entered the infirmary and killed an inmate referred to as "the chief idiot in the camp." He murdered this inmate in response to "pleas of the capos," who regarded the man as annoying.

In his defense, Noky admitted killing the first four inmates but denied selecting them for death and insisted that he was merely carrying out the orders of his superior officer. The Review and Recommendation document indeed states that Miroff admitted telling Nory to kill those four inmates. However, the document states that "no effort was made to show, as to the fifth killing, that the accused had received a specific direction to kill this victim." Furthermore, Noky's "own testimony indicates he did not consider any general orders as requiring the killing" and "the superior was not present."

The Questions of Law section of this document specifically addresses the "superior orders" defense. Noky "sought to justify his action by offering evidence to show that he was acting in compliance with 'superior orders.' Compliance with superior orders does not constitute a defense to the charge of having committed a war crime." A number of judicial precedents are cited to corroborate this assertion, the first of which is a case having its genesis in the American Civil War: the trial of Henry Wirz.

Born as Hartmann Heinrich Wirz in Switzerland 1822, Wirz immigrated to the United States and joined the Confederate army when the Civil War broke out. He gained notoriety as the commander of Camp Sumter Military Prison at Andersonville, Georgia. Conditions inside the prison were horrendous. Food rations were consistently inadequate, while the prison guards refused to allow concerned local residents to give gifts of food to the malnourished men. A small creek choked with filth was their only water supply. Disease was rampant, especially scurvy and dysentery. At least 13,000 prisoners of war died while incarcerated.

Wirz was arrested at Andersonville on May 7, 1865, and tried for conspiracy and murder by a military tribunal in Washington, D.C., from August 23 to October 18. "One of the great paradoxes of the Wirz Trial is that both prosecution and the defense sought to prove that Wirz was following orders," according to the article about Wirz that is posted on the web site of Andersonville National Historic Site. "The prosecutors hoped to convict higher ranking Confederate officials and Wirz hoped to absolve himself by passing responsibility up the chain of command." He was convicted, sentenced to death and hanged on November 10, 1865.

Wirz is regarded as a martyr by neo–Confederates and other Old South aficionados. The Tennessee Division of the Sons of Confederate Veterans posted an article on its web site titled "The Trial of Major Henry Wirz: A National Disgrace." Captain Glen LaForce, the author of this article, correctly noted that "in 1908, the United Daughters of the Confederacy erected a monument to Wirz in the town of Andersonville, where a memorial service for Wirz is still held annually. In 1977, the Sons of Confederate Veterans named Wirz the 'martyr of the Confederacy' at their national convention, and in 1981 that same organization awarded Wirz their Confederate Medal of Honor."

In addition to Pohlman's May 1, 1947, petition for review, no less than five persons filed petitions for clemency that month as well, including Noky's wife, brother and brother-in-law. Nonetheless, the Deputy Judge Advocate's Office ruled that "the findings of guilty are warranted by the evidence. The sentence is not excessive" and recommended "the findings and sentence be approved."

"In all other cases," the Historical Note states,

Hermann Eugen Noky (courtesy State Historical Society of Missouri).

"Pohlman worked on the prosecution, either as assistant or chief prosecutor. In total, Pohlman served as assistant prosecutor in 10 war crimes cases, and as chief prosecutor in 15 cases. As chief prosecutor, Pohlman brought cases against 25 accused, 9 of whom were sentenced to death."

Pohlman's April 21, 1947, letter to his father isn't entirely concerned with legal matters, however. "I went to the opera in Munich Saturday night and Sunday morning and heard Beethoven's 'Fidelio' and Puccini's 'Tosca.' They were both very well done. The music in 'Fidelio' was particularly good, but was more symphonic than operatic." It's not clear from Pohlman's letter where he witnessed these performances. The Munich Opera House, more properly known as the National Theater, was destroyed by Allied aircraft bombing during World War II.

"I hope that Bill [Pohlman's younger brother] came out OK on his college entrance exams," he wrote, "but I know that they must have been very stiff." After a few more comments about Bill, Pohlman shared an experience that offers insight into life in post-war Munich. "I was offered a pure-bred dachshund pup (with registered papers) for a carton of cigarettes and may get him in a few weeks. They have dog food for sale in the Munich PX so I could feed the dog pretty well without resorting to scraps as most people seem to do around here. A lot of the dogs are sick a good part of the time for that reason." Pohlman didn't seem to realize that residents of post-war Germany found it challenging to feed themselves and lacked funds to purchase dog food. Pohlman sent his father some souvenirs: "American script to show you what it looks like." He noted the script ran in denominations from five cents to $10. "They may not be exchanged with Germans, but are good in army establishments, money orders, travellers [sic] checks, etc." During this period, many Germans used cigarettes as a currency substitute.

The Historical Note states that "one of his [Pohlman's] first major trials as a prosecutor was that of Heinrich Trixl, held May 9, 1947. Heinrich Trixl (b. 1910), a Waffen SS private, was the prisoner detail leader a Dachau subcamp." The Review and Recommendations document, issued by the Deputy Judge Advocate's Office and dated June 25, 1947, affirms that Trixl stood accused of two charges of violating the laws and usages of war. The particulars of the first charge state that Trixl while at Dachau "between about 1 January 1942 and about 29 April 1945," did

> willfully, deliberately, and wrongfully encourage, aid, abet and participate in the subjection of civilian nationals of nations then at war with the then German Reich to cruelties and mistreatment, including killings, beatings, tortures,

starvation, abuses and indignities, the exact names and numbers of such civilian nationals being unknown but aggravating many thousands who were then and there in the custody of the German Reich in exercise of belligerent control.

The second charge cited Trizl for committing such "cruelties and mistreatment" against "members of the armed forces of nations then at war with the then German Reich, who were then and there surrendered and unarmed prisoners of war in the custody of the then Germany Reich ... the exact names and numbers of such prisoners of war being unknown, but aggravating many hundreds."

Trixl was an Austrian who had been an unspecified "merchant" in civilian life. While the Historical Note states that Trixl was a private, the Review and Recommendations lists his rank as SS technical sergeant. He served as a "prisoner detail leader" who was "assigned to training guards at Kaufering No. 11," which was a Dachau subcamp. Trixl began this assignment in November of 1944. He became a concentration camp guard after wounds made him unfit for combat duty.

The defendant was accused of beating prisoners "frequently and severely." Trixl sometimes used a rifle "but more often ... a heavy club." He beat a Greek prisoner so severely that he died four days later. A Czech prisoner died two days after a beating delivered by Trixl.

In his defense, Trixl conceded that he "occasionally delivered a box on the ear to prisoners in order to punish them for wrongful conduct" but denied beating them with a club. He insisted that he neither carried nor even owned a club. Furthermore, Trixl claimed that the concentration camp guards under his commanded had been specifically instructed not to strike prisoners.

Trixl was found guilty and sentenced to thirty years' imprisonment. In its review of the case, the Deputy Judge Advocate's Office ruled that the evidence was sufficient to sustain the court's guilty verdict and the 30-year sentence wasn't excessive.

Pohlman was an amateur photographer. In a May 31 letter to his father, he wrote about finishing "the one reel of film with the pictures of the Jewish crematories on it while I was at Berchtesgaden and also another that I took down there." While at Berchtesgaden, he "went up the mountain to Hitler's Eagle's Nest which is quite impressive. The last 300 yards you go up in an elevator to a so-called 'Teahaus' (tea house) which is perched right on top of a mountain."

Commissioned to be built by Martin Bormann in the summer of 1937 and financed by the Nazi party, Eagle's Nest was completed in 13 months. It was used exclusively for party and government functions. It came through the war relatively unscathed by Allied bomber raids. Other buildings, however, were not so fortunate. "Hitler's house and the other houses and hotels for guests are below and were all bombed out," Pohlman wrote. By "Hitler's house," he probably meant the living quarters reserved for Hitler when he came to the site. Hitler visited Eagle's Nest at least 14 times. Pohlman also mentioned visiting Salzburg, Austria, to view a castle once owned by King Ludwig II of Bavaria.

He then shared news of his pending cases. "I have a case to try on Monday that should be very short, and then another set for Wednesday that may keep me in court for four or five days. I expect a bit of trouble on the latter one which is another flyer case as the accused has worked up some kind of alibi." However, Pohlman wrote that he believed would "be able to break it down."

Pohlman wrote a letter to his mother the next day. His first thoughts were of home and family. "I am glad that Bill is taking good care of my car," he wrote, "and hope that it is useful to him this summer and that he has a good time with it." He then assumed the role of older brother. "But caution him to be careful with it and watch the oil (as it uses about a quart every 200 miles) and have it well greased. I think it should be sold before it starts to get cold in the fall, since it is quite old."

He told his mother that "if it was over here I could probably get about $1500 [more than $20,000 in 2023 dollars] for it as cars are at a premium, but it would not be worth the time and expense to get it to New York." After offering additional advice regarding the proper care for his car and expressing approval for the news that Bill had a new girlfriend, Pohlman returned to the war crimes trials.

"A lot of the people here do not realize the general importance of what is being done in the war crimes trials." By "a lot of the people here," it is uncertain to whom Pohlman is referring. Members of the 7708 War Crimes Group certainly realized their "general importance." Perhaps he meant the non-war crimes American military personnel or the German people themselves. "Historically," Pohlman told his mother, "I think they will be recognized as one of the high points of the occupation of Germany, as they are establishing a whole new concept of law that to a great extent never existed before."

In Pohlman's opinion, the "high points of the occupation" were too few. The war crimes trials "is one of the few good points of the occupation, as in general the occupation is being very poorly handled, with immature soldiers and inexperienced officers trying to run a country of 80 million people. Also they have too many German born people here who are more interested in taking care of their friends and relatives than in following army and government policy which in general is well meant."

Pohlman was correct in noting that the occupation of Germany was fraught with difficulties. According to the article "Occupying Germany and Japan" by Kristen D. Burton on the web site of New Orleans' National World War II Museum, "Many US service members did not receive training for interacting with citizens." The article quotes an American soldier who observed, "You were not exposed to civilians [during combat], suddenly you got to feed them, you have to keep some discipline, you got to have laws, and that's what the military government does."

Pohlman's comment that many Germans were "more interested in taking care of their friends and relatives than in following army and government policy" might have been directed at the black market that thrived in post-war Germany. The residents of the former Reich endured constant deprivation.

German resentment toward American military personnel "only grew as it became clear the Americans had an abundance of resources at their disposal in comparison to the Germany people," Burton stated. "With more rations than either the British or French, the Americans enjoyed luxuries the Germans lacked." Burton quoted an unnamed "British political advisor in Germany" who made the grim observation, "the Americans have built up against them a strong feeling of resentment, if not hate, and of contempt among nearly all classes of the German population."

A July 5 letter to his father provides an introduction to another case prosecuted by Pohlman.

> I haven't had much time to write lately as I have been kept quite busy. I started my flyer case last week with the Belgian locals, only to have it turn out during the trial that another murder had been committed in addition to the one charged. After a long talk with the court, and over objection of defense counsel, I got a general continuance pending further investigation on the spot in Belgium. The defense counsel and I were going to fly to Brussels but couldn't get a special plane in time and so Claudio Delitala (the St. Louis lawyer) was ordered by the court to go in our place. We furnished him with interrogatories and I gave him a list of witnesses to try to bring back to Dachau. One has arrived and has implicated another person who I am going to try to join with the original accused. Delitala is due back tomorrow and we will probably continue the trial the end of the week.

Claudio Delitala indeed was a "St. Louis lawyer." The 1940 census gives his address as 445 DeBaliviere. Born in Italy in 1894, Delitala became a naturalized American citizen in 1918. He served in the U.S. Army from 1918 to 1919. According to the *Biographic Register of the Department of State*, Delitala earned a law degree from Creighton University in 1919 and then went into private practice.

Pohlman's reference to "flyer case" and "Belgian locals" suggests Pohlman was referring to *U.S. vs. Gustav Karl Wilhelm Ruester*. The defendant was a railroad official who was accused of shooting a downed American flyer who was in the act of surrendering. The incident occurred in the Belgian city of Mons. Ruester was convicted and sentenced to death. When the case was reviewed, however, the findings and sentence were disapproved because of "insufficiency of evidence."

He then mentioned the upcoming trial of Otto Skorzeny.

> There is a case starting soon that will be rather interesting and which I intend to get some pictures of. It concerns the SS General Skorzeny who rescued Mussolini from prison after the Italian coup d'etat and who attempted to capture Eisenhower in Luxembourg during the Ardennes campaign. Col. Rosenfelt is prosecuting and Col. Durst defending. Skorzeny was also head of the German equivalent of the OSS and trained all the German spies. There is quite a bit of sentiment in his favor as he is not known to have committed any atrocities and was a very good soldier for the Germans. It will be a hard case to try.

His information was faulty. Skorzeny served in the Waffen SS as a *Obersturmbannführer* (lieutenant colonel). He never attained the rank of general. The "German equivalent of the OSS" was the Abwehr and it was never headed by Skorzeny, nor had he "trained all the German spies."

The Abwehr was founded in 1921, well before the Nazi era. Wilhelm Canaris served as the Abhwehr chief from 1935 to 1944. The SS regarded the Abwehr as a rival and constantly worked to undermine its credibility. Canaris' bluntness regarding the failure of the Russian campaign branded him a defeatist. Hitler signed a decree on February 18, 1944, that abolished the Abwehr. Its duties were taken over by the Reich Main Security Office. Deemed a traitor to the Reich, Canaris was hanged at Flossenbürg concentration camp on April 9, 1945. Among the prisoners hanged with Canaris was the theologian Dietrich Bonhoeffer. Their dangling corpses were left to rot.

In Chapter 7, Bill Kasich quoted John Cashman's interview with Skorzeny, which casts doubts on any plan to kidnap Eisenhower. Pohlman's admission that "there is quite a bit of sentiment in his favor" is revealing in light of Skorzeny's acquittal. Yes, Skorzeny indeed "was a very good soldier for the Germans." But as Kasich noted, Otto Skorzeny possessed "a murderous skill" and "his purpose in life was to kill."

In an August 11 letter to his father, Pohlman mentioned recent and upcoming trips. "Salzburg was very nice, and I may go back again this coming weekend but I am not sure about that," he wrote. "I will probably go down to Venice, Italy the weekend of the 1st of September and meet some friends who are from Vienna who will join me there." The tone of the letter abruptly shifts as Pohlman returned to his trial work. "Friday I finished my flyer case involving one Hans Heitkamp and got a sentence of life imprisonment. I thought that was rather good as my only witness was Karl Drossler who did the actual killing." Drossler had been tried earlier, found guilty and sentenced to death.

The trial of Hans Heitkamp took place August 7–8, 1947, and indeed resulted in a conviction. The Review and Recommendations issued by the Deputy Judge Advocate's Office states that

> On about 20 March 1945, an American pilot made a forced landing near the village of Quirnbach, Germany and was taken into custody by a Gestapo agent named Figl. The flier was escorted to the offices of the headquarters of the Gestapo. The Gestapo chief, with threats, ordered the Gestapo agent, Master Sergeant Drossler, to take this flier into the woods and shoot him. The accused, a technical sergeant, on orders from the Gestapo chief, accompanied Drossler to the woods. The flier was shot and killed by Drossler, who admitted the shooting, asserting that he did it due to the pressure of and pursuant to the command of the accused. He testified that the accused was an SS officer candidate and therefore his superior.

Drossler, mentioned by Pohlman as his "only witness," is indeed identified by the Deputy Judge Advocate's Office as having been convicted in the case of *United States v. Drossler* and "sentenced to death in the previous case for his participation in the incident." The Gestapo chief gave Drossler "a machine pistol"—probably a 9mm-caliber MP40—to kill the flyer. This chief then ordered Heitkamp to accompany Drossler, presumably to make certain his order was carried out.

Upon reaching the woods, Heitkamp "checked a spot on the map which he was carrying as to where the flyer was to be killed." Drossler testified that he "begged the accused to speak to the Gestapo chief so that he would not have to kill the flier, but the accused said the order had to carried out." Heitkamp, who was armed with a pistol, "stood behind Drossler and gave the order to shoot, which he, Drossler, then and there did with the machine pistol." When Drossler returned to the village, he was in possession of the flier's jacket as well as his lighter and a package of Camel cigarettes, which he passed around.

Drossler stated that there was an attempt to cover up the flier's murder. When "he returned to the Gestapo headquarters and reported the killing to the Gestapo chief, on the order of the Gestapo chief, he made a false written report that the flyer had been shot while attempting to escape." The next morning, Drossler took two men with him to the woods to bury the murdered flier. He told the men, "You don't need to be shocked. This man has been bombing deliberately villages and cities, perhaps even your own relatives." A hole was dug and the flier buried. When one of the men asked Drossler if he could build a cross over the flier's grave, Drossler replied, "If we dared to talk about anything we had seen in the woods, the same thing would happen to us." Two or three weeks later, one of the men who helped to bury the flier brought American soldiers to the grave and helped to exhume the body.

In his defense, Heitkamp denied that he was an SS officer candidate and had designated the spot where the flier was to be killed. He even disputed Drossler's testimony that the Gestapo chief had given him a machine pistol. Drossler, he insisted, had returned from patrol while the flier was in the Gestapo chief's office. He had his machine pistol with him, "and in view of the fact he was so equipped, the Gestapo chief ordered him to shoot the flier on the outskirts of the village." Heitkamp maintained that Drossler "was the senior and in charge and was the responsible person."

The Sufficiency of Evidence section of the review states:

> While the real purpose of the accused's accompanying Drossler to the scene of the shooting is not too apparent, the Court might well have concluded that he went to supervise or to assure effect execution of the Gestapo chief's order and that the presence of the accused as a watchman created a degree of immediate compulsion, which caused Drossler to carry out the order of the Gestapo chief. While the testimony of the accused and Drossler contradict each other on some points, on the whole they corroborate each other, though each attempts to place the guilt on the other. With regard to the evidence offered in support of the superior orders, the accused was not ordered to shoot or to direct the shooting of the flier in the presence of his superior and was not under immediate compulsion.

The guilty verdict was upheld and the sentence judged not excessive. In its Review and Recommendations, the Deputy Judge Advocate's Office again cited the Wirz case as comprising a precedent that "compliance with superior orders does not constitute a defense to the charge of having committed a war crime."

According to the Historical Note, "The last war crime case prosecuted by the 7708 War Crimes Group was the trial against Heinrich Rixen, held on December 3 and 4, 1947," and Pohlman served as the chief prosecutor. According to the Review and Recommendations document dated January 29, 1948, on November 26, 1944, a Canadian flyer parachuted to the ground near Springe, Germany. Rixen, a member of the German army who was a convalescent patient at a military hospital in Springe, shot and killed this flier while escorting him to the hospital. Rixen claimed he killed the young Canadian in self-defense.

The flier was discovered leaning against a tree by a witness armed with "a Mannlincher [*sic*] hunting rifle, calibre 5.6 [mm]," which was loaded with dum-dum rounds. This witness "testified that the effect of such bullets was to make an aperture of the same size as the bullet where it entered an object, but to make an opening approximately the size of a man's hand when the bullet passed through an object." A 5.6mm bullet is better known to Americans as a .22-caliber round. The Hague Convention of 1899 prohibited the use of dum-dum rounds in warfare, which was a point not lost on the prosecution.

The Mannlicher (not "Mannlincher," as it is spelled in the document) was a bolt-action rifle. The fact that the murder weapon took a 5.6mm round indicates that it was the Mannlicher–Schönauer model. Manufactured in the old Austro-Hungarian Empire, these rifles were purchased in large numbers by the Greek army in 1903. Although never adopted by a major power, a few Mannlicher–Schönauer rifles saw service with Austro-Hungarian troops during World War I. A civilian version of the Mannlicher–Schönauer was also marketed in 1903.

Heinrich Rixen (courtesy State Historical Society of Missouri).

15. John Henry Pohlman

Rixen requested the witness give him the hunting rifle so he could guard the flier. The chief physician at the hospital "was riding in a coach toward the hospital and saw the accused armed with a rifle going the same direction on foot behind the flyer who was walking with the aid of two large sticks which he used in the manner of a skier." Upon arriving at the hospital, this physician told a sergeant that a prisoner would soon arrive. When Rixen arrived, however, he was alone. When the physician asked about the flier, Rixen replied that he had threatened him so he shot him. Clearly shocked, the physician told Rixen, "But one doesn't do such things. One doesn't shoot right away." Rixen, according to the document, "replied to the effect that the flyer had threatened him and where the accused came from such flyers were always shooting at women and children and would frequently be lynched."

The flier's body was found in a ditch. He had been shot in the back of his head. The Canadian was buried in a local cemetery the next day.

The Sufficiency of Evidence section of the document dismisses Rixen's plea of self-defense as "based solely on his self-serving testimony and statements. The evidence that the bullet entered the back of the flyer's head definitely contradicted the claim of the accused that he shot the flyer in self-defense." Both the conviction as well as the sentence—death by hanging—were upheld.

The Questions of Law section addresses the issue of jurisdiction. The defense challenged the jurisdiction of the court on the grounds that the crime had been committed in the British Zone of Occupied Germany. "War criminals, brigands, and pirates are the common enemies of all mankind," the document states, "and all nations have an equal interest in their apprehension and punishment for their violations of international law."

When the Dachau trials were concluded, Pohlman was transferred to Munich, where he reviewed war crimes trials. Then, according to the Historical Note, "he was reassigned to the Joint Affairs Section of the Munich Military Post and served as a legal officer giving general legal advice to army personnel on marriage, divorce, income tax, wills, power of attorney and other matters." In April the Office of the Military Government (OMG) transferred him to the German Courts Branch.

"In May, the administrators formally requested that Pohlman take up civilian employment as Judge for the Judge Advocate Section, Munich Courts Branch, Legal Division, OMGUS, stating that his services were 'urgently needed' due to his legal experience working as an Army officer within the military government." He was relieved from active duty in the army on July 8, 1948.

Pohlman's new duties allowed him adequate space time to attend the law school at the University of Munich to pursue a doctorate in international law. This graduate of Yale Law School surely recognized that enrolling at such a prestigious institution of higher learning would enhance his career. Founded in 1472 and formally known as Ludwig Maximillian University, the school had incurred heavy damage during World War II. According to the university's web site, 70 percent of its buildings were in ruins and one-third of its library holdings had been destroyed. The years of Nazism had compromised its faculty's scholarly credibility. "About eighty percent of its academic staff were rated as politically suspect and were dismissed," the web site states. Nonetheless, the OMG allowed the university to reopen on July 23, 1946.

In a letter dated February 10, 1949, Pohlman informed his parents that he was engaged to Elizabeth "Betsy" Rogers of Eutaw, Alabama. A fellow Yale Law School graduate, Rogers had worked for the military government in the Legal Advice Branch since 1947. She and Pohlman met in 1948.

They never married, however. Pohlman was fatally injured in a car crash in Bolzano, Italy, and died on February 22, 1949. His death received extensive coverage by the St. Louis media. In an interview following his son's death, John Harry Pohlman told a reporter that much of his son's efforts in post-war Europe "were devoted to planning and obtaining passage of legislation to break up the large scale smuggling of commodities intended for the black market," according to an article in the *St. Louis Post-Dispatch*. "In this he worked extensively with French and Italian authorities, as well as the Bavarians."

John Henry Pohlman is buried in Saint Peter's Cemetery in Saint Louis County. His papers were donated to the State Historical Society of Missouri by William Pohlman in 2021.

16

The Struggle Continues

TOWARD THE END OF OUR SINGLE INTERVIEW, Ralph Schulz talked about Col. Eichmann's attempt to persuade him to remain in the army and attend Officer Candidate School. Even if he left the army, Eichmann had told Schulz, he'd probably grow discouraged with civilian life and would want to return to the army—and he'd be most welcome. But Schulz told me that he had "no impulse" to return to the army. "I didn't feel like it was my thing," he said. "I wanted to go back to school."

I had stated at one point that the members of the War Crimes Group were terribly young to be given such a heavy responsibility. Schulz replied that I was "right that we were too young for what we were asked to do by a lot of people" and these young men "grew up pretty quickly." I asked what was his most memorable experience while serving with the War Crimes Group. Schulz replied that the "wake-up call" from Col. Eichmann regarding the importance of their work had certainly made quite an impression on him. After a moment of reflection, however, he said that seeing the mass graves and crematory at Dachau had impacted him much more than Eichmann's words. Schulz again stressed that he had seen the camp before it had been "cleaned up" and noted that he had been required to sleep at the site when assigned to temporary duty.

> We played on a golf course. We took trips. We played ball.... We did things that relieved us. But when you get back to the point where you say, What do I remember from it, those aren't the things you remember. What you remember are looking at that evidence about atrocities.

"We had so much physical evidence that has since been denied," he told me. "I hate to see it die," Schulz said. I asked if "it" meant knowledge of the war crimes he and his fellow veterans had investigated. "Yes," he replied. "That experience. Because that means we'll have to do it again sometime. I hope they don't have to face the kind of thing we did because it's so discouraging (regarding) human nature."

Schulz would find it encouraging to know that the struggle against Holocaust denial continues. While a fanatical fringe will always insist that the Holocaust never occurred, scholars and other citizens of the global community will never allow such a vile lie to achieve general acceptance. I didn't remind Schulz of the genocides that have occurred since he and those other young Americans sacrificed their youth and innocence to apprehend and convict war criminals. When I conducted these interviews, I was familiar only with the genocides in Cambodia in the 1970s and Rwanda in the 1990s. I later found Genocide Watch, a web site that listed all genocides that have occurred in the world since 1945. The list ran over ten pages. Schulz was right. The knowledge that so many genocides have been perpetrated since the war crimes trials that followed World War II indeed makes one discouraged regarding human nature.

Epilogue

Bill Kasich and Ralph Shultz are quoted extensively in this work, since they contributed the greatest amount of material. Thanks to Kasich, I was able to connect with other veterans of the U.S. Army 7708 War Crimes Group. The information they provided me, however, was brief and fragmentary. Some consisted of one or two word-answers. Other veterans, however, provided responses that merited inclusion.

The lengthiest contribution I received through the U.S. Mail came from Everett "Tex" Wieting, who sent me a mini-autobiography that he had handwritten on sheets of lined paper. Born in a two-room sharecropper's house near Marlin, Texas, in 1927, Wieting served as manager of the War Crimes Group's Files and Message Center. This was an important division of the group since the responsibilities of what Wieting called "the records section" included "the complete filing and maintenance of all War Crimes Group material." The records section was also responsible for "the preparation and distribution of all official WCG reports, including pre-trial, trial, and post-trial minutes of all judicial activity."

Wieting wrote that Wiesbaden "was basically a resort town" and the literal meaning of its name is "bath in the meadows." Late in the war, he noted, Wiesbaden had incurred considerable damage from British air raids. Wieting thought that these bombing missions were "a deliberate act of revenge for the bombing of civilians in England by Germany." While other members of the War Crimes Group unwound by playing baseball, Wieting and Joe Brinko, his best friend in the group, "played table tennis at the Red Cross Club almost every night." He also wrote that the "War Crimes Group had their own private club, The Flamingo, which usually had talented entertainment. In post-war Germany, show business acts would basically perform for lodging."

While in Wiesbaden, the War Crimes Group was located in a building that previously had been a bank. Members of the group used the bank's copying machine, which Wieting described as "an antiquated diesel-driven affair that resembled a truck." He "basically devised a special filing system" to facilitate the location of requested material, "but the most integral part of it was usually my memory." Wieting had the greatest respect for Col. Clio Straight. We "had a very special relationship without regard to the difference in rank." Straight "never let military protocol get in the way of doing his job" and "I doubt whether he knew me as anyone but 'Tex.'"

Wieting recalled German prisoners of war being put to work when it came time to move the group's massive files. "When we moved from Wiesbaden to Augsburg we sealed the files but German POWs did the lifting and the U.S. Constabulary guarded the rail cars during shipment." Wieting's duties afforded him the opportunity to witness history. "One benefit of having regular courier runs was that I could travel the thirty miles to Dachau most afternoons to observe the Buchenwald trial. I remember Ilse Koch as being a carbon copy of 'Gravel Gertie' of *Dick Tracy* fame."

One of Wieting's most intriguing missions occurred on December 31, 1946, when he "was given a very important official document (sealed) that had to be delivered to the I.G. Farben Complex in Frankfurt" on "the morning of January 2, 1947." I.G. Farben was the German chemical company that manufactured Zyklon B, the poisonous gas used to kill Jews during the Holocaust. The "very important official document" that he delivered almost certainly was related to the war crimes trial of the company's board of directors, which was held in 1947.

Lowell Robinette wrote that he "entered the army as a draftee in November, 1945" and "after basic training was assigned to the 7708th War Crimes Group in April, 1946." His rank was Tech 5 and he worked as a clerk "to maintain/file records of German prisoners in our custody and attempt to associate these prisoners with our 'wanted' list." He wrote that his most memorable experience was taking "a German SS prisoner to Dachau from our Wiesbaden office for internment."

Robert Gottschalk e-mailed me that he enlisted in the army on October 30, 1945. "My mother had to sign for me," he noted, "as I was not yet 18 years of age." He underwent basic training at Fort Sill, Oklahoma, where he met Lowell Robinette. "We were assigned together from the time we finished Basic Training to our Discharge 15 months later." He and Robinette "rode box cars across France and arrived at Erlangen, Germany for assignment." Upon arriving in Wiesbaden, Gottschalk "was given choices of area of service."

I could have gone out in the field as an interrogator of witnesses, but chose to work in the office. I was assigned to the Processing Department. It consisted of taking the statements sent in by the interrogators and summarizing the facts and cross-indexing with 3 × 5 cards, the time, place, kind of incident, names of accused, witnesses and victims so that upon review, cases could be built on these happenings.

One of the questions I posed in the survey that I snail-mailed to these veterans asked how they were affected by their service with the 7708 War Crimes Group. "Reading about the incidents caused me to realize how many innocent people are harmed in any armed conflict." His experiences with the group made him almost "a Peacenik, except when threatened." Rather than making him a cynic, "My experience in Service has strengthened my faith."

Serving with the group wasn't drudgery, according to Gottschalk. "We really only worked 8 hours a day, 5 days a week and had the rest of the time to sight-see." During his two leaves, both of which lasted two weeks, he traveled to Paris, London, Rome and Switzerland. Gottschalk concluded his reply by noting that his time with the War Crimes Group "was educational and mind forming."

Fretwell G. Crider took the time to respond to my query with a letter dated April 29, 2003, despite the ordeal he was undergoing. "I was diagnosed as having lymphoma (cancer)" and "am being treated for same with chemotherapy which has its ups and downs—i.e., good days and bad days. On this, one of my good days, let me try to answer your inquiry although I seem to have mislaid your questionnaire." He then described his duties.

> I served as an Administrative NCO (T/4) with the Processing Section War Crimes Group in Wiesbaden, Germany for seven months. I performed duties as a processor for depositions, correspondence, and investigation reports received from different sources, and analyzed all of this material to segregate the pertinent facts relating to war crimes under various categories. I then summarized this information on to work sheets to be used by the prosecution staff. I maintained a card system consisting of cross references between scenes of crime, name of accused, witnesses, and victims, in addition to case locator files with summary of cases.

Crider concluded his missive by again apologizing "for this inordinate delay in answering your letter. I hope the circumstances will make amends for me."

George Kumm was also experiencing health problems when I was researching this book. After receiving my questionnaire in the mail, he called me on March 10, 2003, to explain that he is legally blind. I interviewed him over the phone and repeated his answers into my ancient (even in 2003) handheld cassette-tape recorder.

Before entering the army in 1945, Kumm was in charge of displays placed in the windows of a department store. He was supposed to undergo eighteen weeks of basic training but they took him out of it after just eleven weeks and put him in an office because he knew how to type. Kumm was sent to France and then Belgium before going to Wiesbaden. When I asked Kumm his rank, he replied that he was a sergeant "for five minutes." A sergeant wanted to put him in the regular army. Kumm told the sergeant what he thought of the regular army and his promotion "was pretty much over."

Kumm worked in the personnel section of the 7708 War Crimes Group. His duties included bringing in witnesses and suspects and then interviewing them. Kumm told me that his most memorable experience was attending the trials. He "saw everyone" at the trials and told me he felt an intense hatred for the defendants.

I asked Kumm to describe his most dangerous experience while serving with the War Crimes Group. He had been warned not to go anywhere alone in Germany "because they would get you in an alley and cut you up." Nonetheless, he once hitchhiked alone to Wiesbaden so he wouldn't be declared AWOL. Kumm was picked up by a German driving an army truck. He arrived at Wiesbaden in one piece. Kumm wasn't familiar with Paperclip. When asked how his time with the War Crimes Group had changed his life, Kumm replied, "I grew up a little faster than I might normally have."

Robert W. DeCoursey sent me a handwritten letter dated June 1, 2001, with a July 29, 2001, addendum. He "was a student at Yale in August 1945 when the draft loomed" and decided to enlist in the army "because they promised Europe, not Asia." Europe appealed to DeCoursey for reasons that decidedly set him apart from the other veterans I interviewed. "My parents had travelled often in Europe, taking students at the school where they taught on bike tours of France, the Low Countries and Germany," he wrote, "so I was very interested in a chance to go where they had played tourist. Also I spoke pretty good French."

It took DeCoursey nine months to complete basic training due to an injury incurred playing basketball. He joined the War Crimes Group at Wiesbaden. He noted that the group had a liaison unit in the French zone "and maybe I went to WCG because of my good French." While it indeed would have made sense to assign DeCoursey to the French unit, he wrote that "in the Army, such a rational result is seldom achieved." After he had been in Wiesbaden for several weeks, "I was in fact assigned to the British Zone liaison and team and I spent all of my WCG time in the British Zone."

The British and French had competed for DeCoursey. "I was once told that the French Zone Major and the British Lt. Colonel both asked for me and the Colonel pulled his rank." DeCoursey believed that his fluency in French "and maybe some assumption that a Yale sophomore might have some brains" made him appealing to the British.

DeCoursey was a "buck private" through November 1946. "By February 1948," he wrote, "I had been promoted 3 times and was a sergeant." The British Zone headquarters was located in Bad Oeynhausen. DeCoursey described his duties. "From time to time our lawyers in Wiesbaden/Dachau would need to bring a German resident in the British Zone to the U.S. Zone, either to testify as a witness or, very rarely, to be tried as a criminal." DeCoursey "would pick up the body desired and drive him or her to Paderborn, the nearest substantial town in the U.S. Zone." Someone from the War Crimes Group would meet DeCoursey there and take the witness or war criminal "the rest of the way." Since he wasn't stationed with the War Crimes Group, DeCoursey "usually had no idea what case my witness was involved in."

None of the men and women transported by DeCoursey attempted to escape. "They were usually cold, wet, scared witless and without any papers if they escaped," he wrote, "so they never did either escape or try." DeCoursey was familiar with the campaign to recruit Nazi scientists and engineers, but "To the best my knowledge, none of those I drove ended up in Paperclip."

Only one veteran of the 7708 War Crimes Group had second thoughts after providing me with his recollections. The man in question returned the release form unsigned and said that he didn't want his memories exploited. I accepted his decision with regret. A particular incident he described in his original letter was very moving indeed.

Bibliography

"Agreement for the Prosecution and Punishment of the Major War Criminals of the European Axis, and Charter of the International Military Tribunal." International Committee of the Red Cross. Accessed August 21, 2014. https://ihl-databases.icrc.org/ihl/INTRO/350?OpenDocument.

Anderson, Duncan, John Primlott, and R.M. Connaughton. *The Battle of Manila*. London: Bloomsbury, 1995.

Appendix: Documents Concerning Ilse Koch. Jewish Virtual Library. Accessed August 11, 2014. https://www.jewishvirtuallibrary.org/appendix-ilse-koch.

Associated Press. "Money for Nazis Angers White House." *St. Louis Post-Dispatch*, October 21, 2014.

Biddiscombe, Perry. *The Last Nazis: SS Nazi Werewolf Resistance in Europe 1944–1945*. London: Tempus, 2000.

Bourke-White, Margaret. *Dear Fatherland: A Report on the Collapse of Hitler's Thousand Years*. New York: Simon & Schuster, 1946.

Boyne, Walter J. "Project Paperclip." *Air Force Magazine: Online Journal of the Air Force Association*, June 2007. Accessed June 19, 2014. http://www.airforcemag.com/MagazineArchive/Pages/2007/June%202007/0607paperclip.aspx.

Buchanan, Patrick J. "Pat Buchanan's Response to Norman Podhoretz's Op-Ed." November 5, 1999. Patrick J. Buchanan Official Website. Accessed July 21, 2014.

Burton, Kristen D. "Occupying Germany and Japan." October 21, 2020, National World War II Museum. Accessed July 15, 2021. https://www.nationalww2museum.org/war/articles/united-states-occupying-germany-and-japan#:~:text=A%20British%20political%20advisor%20in,little%20to%20ease%20these%20tensions.

"Captain Henry Wirz." Andersonville National Historic Site. Accessed July 7, 2023. https://www.nps.gov/ande/learn/historyculture/captain_henry_wirz.htm.

Cogon, Eugene. *The Theory and Practice of Hell: The German Concentration Camps and the System Behind Them*. New York: Strauss, 1950.

Cohen, Baruch C. "The Ethics of Using Medical Data from Nazi Experiments." Jewish Virtual Library. Accessed November 18, 2014. https://www.jewishvirtuallibrary.org/the-ethics-of-using-medical-data-from-nazi-experiments.

Criminals Before the Nuremberg Military Tribunals. Washington, D.C.: U.S. Govt. Printing Office, 1949–1953, Vol. I, Jewish Virtual Library. Accessed June 27, 2014. https://www.jewishvirtuallibrary.org/charter-of-the-international-military-tribunal.

Crutchley, Peter. "How Did Hitler's Scar-Faced Henchman Become an Irish Farmer?" BBC Digital & Learning, December 30, 2014. Accessed July 18, 2015. https://www.bbc.com/news/uk-northern-ireland-30571335.

Davidson, Tom. "Army Veteran Domitrovich Is Last Living Survivor of WWII Massacre at Malmédy." *Ellwood City Ledger*, January 24, 2017.

Bibliography

Deputy Judge Advocate's Office. Review and Recommendations, *United States v. Eugen Hermann Nory*, August 4, 1947. Accessed July 3, 2023. www.jewishvirtuallibrary.org/jsource/Holocaust/dachautrial/20.pdf.

Deputy Judge Advocate's Office. Review and Recommendations, *United States v. Hans Heitkamp*, September 25, 1947. Accessed July 18, 2023. www.jewishvirtuallibrary.org/jsource/Holocaust/dachautrial/fs37.pdf.

Deputy Judge Advocate's Office. Review and Recommendations, *United States v. Heinrich Trixl*, June 25, 1947. Accessed July 9, 2023. https://www.jewishvirtuallibrary.org/jsource/Holocaust/dachautrial/d81.pdf.

Deputy Judge Advocate's Office, 7708 War Crimes Group, European Command. *United States v. Kurt Andrae et al. Review and Recommendations of the Deputy Judge Advocate for War Crimes*. April 15, 1948. Jewish Virtual Library. Accessed August 30, 2014. https://www.jewishvirtuallibrary.org/jsource/Holocaust/dachautrial/n6.pdf.

"Dr. Klaus Karl Schilling testifies at the trial of former camp personnel and prisoners from Dachau." United States Holocaust Memorial Museum. Accessed May 30, 2023. collections.ushmm.org/search/catalog/pa1069345.

Dougherty, Kevin. "Memorial Honors AF Victims of WWII Mob." *Stars and Stripes International Edition*. August 25, 2004. Accessed July 23, 2014. https://www.stripes.com/news/memorial-honors-victims-of-wwii-mob-1.23576.

Dunphy, John J. "Bringing war criminals to justice." *The* [Alton, IL] *Telegraph*, May 15, 2021.

———. "Immigrant became an interpreter for War Crimes Group." *The* [Alton, IL] *Telegraph*, May 20–21, 2023. Reprinted in "A Jewish Refugee Who Served as an Interpreter for the U.S. Army 7708 War Crimes Group." *Medium*, May 31, 2023.

———. "War Crimes Group Veteran Shielded His Family." *The* [Alton, IL] *Telegraph*, June 10–11, 2023. Reprinted on *Medium*, June 16, 2023.

Ehrenfreund, Norbert. *The Nuremberg Legacy: How the Nazi War Crimes Trials Changed the Course of History*. New York: Palgrave Macmillan, 2007.

Eliach, Yaffa, and Brana Gurewitsch, eds. *The Liberators*. Brooklyn: Center for Holocaust Studies Documentation and Research, 1981.

Elsworth, Catherine. "I Gave Goring [sic] His Poison Pill, Says American." *Telegraph*, February 8, 2005.

Foley, Charles. *Commando Extraordinary*. New York: G.P. Putnam's Sons, 1955.

Gilmore, Glenda Elizabeth. *Defying Dixie: The Radical Roots of Civil Rights, 1919–1950*. New York: W.W. Norton & Company, 2008.

Goldstein, Richard. "William R. Perl Is Dead at 92; Built Sealift Rescue of Jews." *New York Times*, December 29, 1998.

Greene, Joshua M. *Justice at Dachau: The Trials of an American Prosecutor*. New York: Broadway Books, 2004.

Hansen, Horace. *Witness to Barbarism*. St. Paul: Thousand Pinetree Press, 2003.

Hiscocks, R.D., J.L. Orr, and J.J. Green. *Report on Visit to Luftfahrtforschungsanstalt Herman Göring, Volkenrode, Brunswick*. Accessed June 23, 2014.

"History of Sorts: Dr. Klaus Schilling." dirkdeklein.net/2017/03/08/dr-klaus-schilling. Accessed May 29, 2023.

Holocaust Education and Archive Research Team. *Klaus Barbie: The Butcher of Lyon*. Accessed July 26, 2014. http://www.holocaustresearchproject.org/nazioccupation/barbie.html.

Hunt, Linda. *Secret Agenda: The United States Government, Nazi Scientists, and Project Paperclip, 1945 to 1990*. New York: St. Martin's Press, 1991.

Interrogation Records Prepared for War Crimes Proceedings at Nuremberg 1945–1947. National Archives Trust Fund Board; National Archives and Records Service. Washington, 1984.

"An Interview with Dr. Otto Stein." Conducted by Henry Grodzins. Transcript provided to the author by Deborah Stein.

Jacobsen, Annie. *Operation Paperclip: The Secret Intelligence Program That Brought Nazi Scientists to America*. New York: Little, Brown, 2014.
Janssen Militaria. "Dr. Leonardo Conti." Accessed June 19, 2015. http://www.janssen-militaria.com/Biography_Leonardo_Conti.html.
"John Henry Pohlman Dies in Italy of Auto Injuries." *St. Louis Globe-Democrat*, February 27, 1949.
"John Henry Pohlman Fatally Hurt in Italy." *St. Louis Post-Dispatch*, February 27, 1949.
John Henry Pohlman Papers: Historical Note, State Historical Society of Missouri. Accessed June 30, 2023. files.shsmo.org/manuscripts/saint-louis/S0282.pdf.
Karacs, Imre. "DNA Test Closes the Book on Mystery of Martin Bormann." *Independent*, May 4, 1998. Accessed August 14, 2014. https://www.independent.co.uk/news/dna-test-closes-book-on-mystery-of-martin-bormann-1161449.html.
LaForce, Glen. "The Trail of Major Henry Wirz: A National Disgrace." Accessed July 3, 2023. https://www.tennesseescv.org/uploads/1/3/6/5/136584498/the_trial_of_major_henry_wirz-_a_national_disgrace.pdf.
Lagnoldo, Lucette. "A Scientist's Nazi Past Haunts Prestigious Space Prize." *Wall Street Journal*, December 1, 2012.
Lee, Martin A. *The Beast Reawakens*. New York: Little, Brown, 1997.
Lessner, Major Erwin. "Hitler's Final V Weapon." *Collier's Weekly*, January 27, 1945.
Lindbergh, Anne Morrow. *The Wave of the Future: A Confession of Faith*. New York: Harcourt, Brace and Company, 1940.
Lindbergh, Charles A. "Des Moines Speech." *The American Experience*. Accessed June 22, 2014.
Lipstadt, Deborah. *Denying the Holocaust: The Growing Assault on Truth and Memory*. New York: The Free Press, 1993.
Loewy, Erwin, and Hydropress, Inc. Documents. Lehigh University. Accessed July 2, 2014. https://www.lehigh.edu/library/speccoll/loewy.html.
Ludwig Maximilian University at Munich. "Reconstruction and Expansion after the Second World War." Accessed July 30, 2023. https://www.lmu.de/en/about-lmu/lmu-at-a-glance/history/contexts/reconstruction-and-expansion-after-the-second-world-war/index.html.
Maclean, French L. "John C. Woods." *The Fifth Field*. Accessed February 23, 2015. http://thefifthfield.com/biographical-sketches/john-c-woods/.
"Malmédy Massacre Investigation." Report of Subcommittee of the Committee on Armed Forces, United States Senate.
"Memorandum from Deputy Theater Judge Advocate to Co. Straight, Col. Jaworksi, September 12, 1945." Dachau Trials. Jewish Virtual Library. Accessed July 14, 2014.
Meyer, Eliah. *Objective List of German and Austrian Scientists (1,600 "Scientists")*. Joint Intelligence Objectives Agency. January 2, 1947.
Milton, Sybil. "Photographs of the Warsaw Ghetto." Museum of Tolerance Online. Accessed July 11, 2014.
Muszynski, Wojciech Jerzy. "The Polish Guard Companies of the U.S. Army After World War II." *The Polish Review* 56, no. 4 (2011).
"Nazi Euthanasia Program: Persecution of the Mentally and Physically Disabled." Jewish Virtual Library. Accessed December 24, 2014. https://www.jewishvirtuallibrary.org/nazi-persecution-of-the-mentally-and-physically-disabled.
"Nazi War Crimes Trials: Hadamar Trial, October 8–15, 1945." Jewish Virtual Library. Accessed December 30, 2014. https://www.jewishvirtuallibrary.org/hadamar-trial-october-1945.
Nizkor Project. "Mel Mermelstein." Accessed July 17, 2014.
Opening of CIA Records Under Nazi War Crimes Disclosure Act. Nazi War Crimes and Imperial Japanese Government Records Intra-Agency Working Group. Accessed July 25, 2014.

Bibliography

"Organization of Former SS Members (ODESSA)." *Jewish Virtual Library*. Accessed August 17, 2015. https://www.jewishvirtuallibrary.org/organization-of-former-ss-members-odessa.

Ove, Torsten. "Obituary: Charles F. Appman/Survivor of Malmédy Massacre During World War II." *Pittsburgh Post-Gazette*, August 30, 2013.

Palash, Ghosh. "The Irish Nationalist and the Nazi: When Eamon De Valera Paid His Respects to Adolf Hitler." *International Business Times*, September 10, 2013. Accessed July 20, 2015. https://www.ibtimes.com/irish-nationalist-nazi-when-eamon-de-valera-paid-his-respects-adolf-hitler-1403768.

Parker, Danny S. *Fatal Crossroads*. Philadelphia: Da Capo Press, 2012.

Persico, Joseph E. *Nuremberg: Infamy on Trial*. New York: Viking, 1994.

Pool, Bob. "Former GI Claims Role in Goering's Death." *Los Angeles Times*, February 7, 2005.

Rare Historical Photos. Henry Ford receiving the Grand Cross of the German Eagle from Nazi officials, 1938. Accessed August 6, 2023. https://rarehistoricalphotos.com/henry-ford-grand-cross-1938/.

Rashke, Richard. "America's Secret Government Program to Hire Nazi War Criminals." *Daily Beast*, August 2, 2013. Accessed June 20, 2014. https://www.thedailybeast.com/americas-secret-government-program-to-hire-nazi-war-criminals.

Raviv, Dan, and Yossi Melman. "The Strange Case of a Nazi Who Became an Israeli Hitman." *Haaretz*, March 27, 2016.

Records of United States Army War Crimes Trials; United States of America v. Otto Skorzeny et al. Accessed June 1, 2015.

Reel, A. Frank. *The Case of General Yamashita*. Chicago: University of Chicago Press, 1949.

Reidel, Durwood. "The U.S. War Crimes Tribunals at the Former Dachau Concentration Camp: Lessons for Today?" *Berkeley Journal of International Law* 24, no. 2 (2006).

"Review of the Staff Judge Advocate: *United States v. Joseph Hartgen et alia*." August 23, 1945. Accessed July 24, 2014.

Roosevelt, Franklin D. "Statement of the Plan to Try Nazi War Criminals." The American Presidency Project. Accessed August 23, 2014. http://www.presidency.ucsb.edu/ws/index.php?pid=16174.

Rubin, Barry. *Modern Dictators*. New York: McGraw-Hill, 1987.

Schulz, Ralph. "Eyewitness Accounts: The Nashville Holocaust Memorial." Accessed January 9, 2017. http://www.nashvilleholocaustmemorial.org/eyewitnessaccounts.html.

Skorzeny, Otto. *Otto Skorzeny: My Commando Operations. The Memoirs of Hitler's Most Daring Commando*. Translated by David Johnston. Atglen, PA: Schiffer Military History, 1976.

———. *Skoreny's Secret Missions: Memoirs of the Most Dangerous Man in Europe*. Translated by Jacques LeClerecq. New York: E.P. Dutton, 1950. This book was later republished in a different translation by Greenhill Press under the titles *Skoreny's Special Missions: The Memoirs of 'The Most Dangerous Man in Europe* and *Skorzeny's Special Missions: The Autobiography of Hitler's Commando Ace*.

Smith, David. "Barbie 'Boasted of Hunting Down Che.'" *Guardian*, December 22, 2007. Accessed July 25, 2014. https://www.theguardian.com/uk/2007/dec/23/world.secondworldwar.

Sparks, Felix L. "Dachau at Its Liberation." 157th Infantry Association. June 15, 1989. Accessed September 15, 2014.

Speer, Albert. *Inside the Third Reich*. New York: Macmillan, 1970.

Spiro, Howard M. "Let Nazi Medical Data Remind Us of Evil." *New York Times*, April 19, 1988.

Tanaka, Yuri. "Last Words of the Tiger of Malaya, General Tomoyuki Yamashita." *Asia-Pacific Journal: Japan Focus*, September 22, 2005. Accessed January 24, 2015. https://apjjf.org/-Yuki-Tanaka/1753/article.html.

Taylor, Tetford. *The Anatomy of the Nuremberg Trials: A Personal Memoir*. New York: Alfred A. Knopf, 1992.

———. *The Buchenwald Report*. Translated and edited by David Hackett. Boulder: Westview Press, 1995.

———. *Nuremberg and Vietnam: An American Tragedy*. Chicago: Quadrangle Books/Random House, 1970.

United States Army Investigation and Trial Records of War Criminals. *United States of America v. Andrae et al.* (and Related Cases), April 27, 1945–June 11, 1958. National Archives Microfilm Publications. Pamphlet Describing M1079.

United States Supreme Court. Application of Yamashita, 327 U.S. 1 (1946).

United States v. Gustav Karl Wilhelm Ruester. Accessed July 19, 2023. www.jewishvirtuallibrary.org/case-no-6-155-us-vs-gustav-karl-wilhelm-ruester.

United States v. Heinrich Rixen. ICC Legal Tools Database, legal-tools.org/doc/f02918/pdf/. Accessed August 8, 2023.

Utley, Freda. *The High Cost of Vengeance*. Chicago: Henry Regnery Company, 1949.

Van Gelder, Lawrence. "Otto Skorzeny, Nazi Commando, Dead; Rescued Mussolini from Italian Peak." *New York Times*, July 8, 1985.

Wallace, Max. *The American Axis: Henry Ford, Charles Lindbergh and the Rise of the Third Reich.* New York: St. Martin's Press, 2003.

"War Crimes Branch Completes Historical Work in Wiesbaden." *Wiesbaden Post*, November 7, 1946.

Watts, Roderick H. "Wehrwolf or Werwolf? Literature, Legend or Lexical Error into Nazi Propaganda?" *The Modern Language Review* 87, no. 4 (1992).

Weingartner, James J. *Americans, Germans and War Crimes Justice: Law, Memory and the Good War*. Santa Barbara, CA: ABC-CLIO, 2011.

———. *Crossroads of Death: The Story of the Malmédy Massacre and Trial*. Berkeley: University of California Press, 1979.

"Wernher von Braun Biography." International Space Hall of Fame at the New Mexico Museum of Space History. Accessed July 7, 2014. http://www.nmspacemuseum.org/halloffame/detail.php?id=29.

Whiting, Charles. *Hitler's Werewolves: The Story of the Nazi Resistance Movement, 1944–1945.* New York: Stein and Day, 1972.

———. *Massacre at Malmédy*. New York: Stein and Day, 1972.

———. *Monty's Greatest Victory: The Drive for the Baltic April–May 1945*. London: Leo Cooper, 2002.

Wiesel, Elie. *The Night Trilogy*. New York: Hill and Wang, 1985.

"Wilhelm Canaris." Jewish Virtual Library. Accessed July 18, 2023. www.jewishvirtuallibrary.org/wilhelm-canaris.

Yakstis, Ande. "Former Soldier Relates Hunt for War Criminals." *Telegraph* (Alton, IL), March 3, 2001.

———. "War Crimes Soldiers Speak." *Telegraph* (Alton, IL), September 22, 2000.

———. "War Crimes Vets Holding Reunion." *Telegraph* (Alton, IL), September 18, 2000.

———. "Witnesses to Horrors of Holocaust Reunite." *Telegraph* (Alton, IL), September 21, 2000.

Yamashita v. Styer, Commanding General, U.S. Armed Forces, Western Pacific. No. 61; Misc. and No. 672. Argued Jan. 7–8, 1946. Decided Feb. 4, 1946. Accessed January 23, 2015.

Young, Robert L. "Operation Lusty." *Air Force Magazine: Online Journal of the Air Force Association*, January 2005. Accessed June 20, 2014.

Zeller, Tom Jr. "The Nuremberg Hangings—Not So Smooth Either." *New York Times News Blog*, January 17, 2007. Accessed February 23, 2015. https://thelede.blogs.nytimes.com/2007/01/17/the-nuremburg-hangings-not-so-smooth-either/.

Index

Aachen 169–170
Abraham, Bruce 6
Acheson, Dean 118–119
Anti-Defamation League 2, 9–10
Appman, Charles 73–74
Arafat, Yasser 106
Arnold, H.H. 118

Barbie, Klaus 140–141
Boggetto, Donald 159
Bonhoeffer, Dietrich 22
Bormann, Martin 46, 141–144
Bose, Subhash Chandra 107–108
Bourke-White, Margaret 146
Brandon, Lewis 9–11
Braun, Wernher von 126–130
Brinko, Joe 197
Buchanan, Patrick 131
Burton, Ellis 132

Cashman, John 60–61, 94–95, 97, 142, 159
Charlemagne Division 47
Clay, Lucius 153–154
Clifford, Clark 119
Conti, Leonardo 98
Crider, Fretwell G. 199

Dachau 1–2, 6–7, 13, 15–16, 18–26, 33, 70, 145, 177, 185, 188
Dachau liberation reprisals 24–27
DeCoursey, Robert W. 200–201
Denson, William 2, 16, 148, 150
Detmers, Heinz 13–15
Dietrich, Josef 73
Domitrovich, Stephen 74–75
Dönitz, Karl 63, 164, 170
Draganović, Krunoslav 141
Dubno Massacre 55, 58–59
Durst, Robert 99

Eichmann, Adolph 83
Eichmann, Otto W. 70–71, 99–100, 195
Eisenhower, Dwight 93–94, 117–118
Everett, Willis 84

Ford, Henry 120–121
Franco, Francisco 104–105

Gardner, Andrew G. 70, 99–100
Genghis Khan and His Legacy 76
Goebbels, Joseph 114, 169
Göring, Hermann 6, 54–55, 57–58
Gottschalk, Robert 198–199
Guevara, Che 141

Halow, Joseph 2, 9–16
Harris, Whitney 59
Heitkamp, Hans 190–191
Hess, Rudolph 77, 142, 144
Himmler, Heinrich 76, 135, 167, 169
Hitler, Adolf 77, 127, 142–144, 166, 170
Holocaust denial 2, 9, 71, 195–196
homosexuals in Nazi Germany 22–23
Horthy, Miklós 91

I.G. Farben 198
Innocent at Dachau 2, 7, 12–16, 80, 83
Institute for Historical Review 2, 7–8

Jaworski, Leon 112, 114
Jodl, Alfred 62–64
Josias, Prince zu Waldeck 11–12

Kármán, Theodore von 118
Kasich, Bill 5–6, 29, 33, 45, 53–56, 58–62, 73, 80–81, 89, 93–98, 102, 112, 116, 128, 132–133, 136, 139–140, 144, 145, 147–148, 156–161, 162–164, 171–172, 189, 197
Kennan, George 119

Index

Kirkland, Walter 171–173
Koch, Ilse 11, 145, 150, 152–155, 198
Koch, Karl 11–12
Kramer, Dr. Walter 11–12
Kristallnacht 120, 175
Kumm, George 199–200
Kunzig, Robert L. 147–148

Landsberg Prison 14, 178
Lindbergh, Anne Morrow 120
Lindbergh, Charles 120
Lipstadt, Deborah 9–10
Loewy, Erwin 124–125
Löns, Hermann 166

Malmedy Massacre 5–6, 73–89
McCarthy, Joseph R. 85
Mermelstein, Mel 10
Mossad 108–110
Moulin, Jean 140
Mussolini, Benito 90

Nasser, Gamal 105
Nehlson, Hermann 124 125
Niemöller, Martin 22
Noky, Eugen Hermann 182–184
Nuremberg Trials 3, 44, 178

ODESSA 96–97

Patin, Albert 123–125
Peiper, Jochen 73, 76, 89
Perl, William 83–84
Perón, Juan 105, 112
Pétain, Phillippe 48–49
Pohlman, John Henry 180–194
Polish Guard 69, 97
Poullada, Leon 130
Project Paperclip 116–139, 201
Putt, Donald 116–117, 121–123, 125, 132

Quisling, Vidkung 47–48

Rascher, Sigmund 134–137
Reuster, Gustav Karl Wilhelm 189

Rickhey, Georg 123–126, 129–131
Rixen, Heinrich 191–193
Robinette, Lowell 198
Roden, Leroy van 84–85
Roosevelt, Franklin D. 18–19
Rosenfelt, A.H. 100, 102
Rudolph, Arthur 131–132

Salmon, Emil 122–123
Schilling, Klaus 176–179
Schulz, Ralph 6–7, 55, 65–73, 115, 164, 195–197
Simon Wiesenthal Center 10
Skorzeny, Otto 90–111, 189
Smith, Myron 6, 66
Southern Poverty Law Center 2, 7, 9
Speer, Albert 126–128, 158, 160, 170
Stein, Otto Ludwig 174–179
Stivers, Herbert Lee 57–58
Straight, Clio 20, 29–30, 31–32, 34–35, 37–39, 42–47, 49–52, 55, 84, 88, 198
Strughold, Hubertus 136
Surowitz, Solomon 147–148

Taylor, Telford 18–19, 58, 128
Trixl, Heinrich 185–186
Truman, Harry 118–119

U.S. v. Andrae et alia 130
United States v. Klein et alia 35–37
United States v. Stroop et alia 37–38
Utley, Frieda 82–83

Valera, Eamon de 106–107

Weingartner, James J. 84, 88
werewolves 159–161, 163–171
Der Wehrwolf 166
Whiting, Charles 89, 163–164, 168
Wiesel, Elie 146, 182
Wieting, Everett 197–198
Wirz, Henry 183–184
Woods, John C. 56–57

Yamashita, Tomoyuki 39–42

www.ingramcontent.com/pod-product-compliance
Lightning Source LLC
Chambersburg PA
CBHW032043300426
44117CB00009B/1175